# JOACHIM MURAT

JOACHIM MURAT, AFTERWARDS KING OF NAPLES
FROM THE PAINTING BY GÉRARD AT VERSAILLES

# MARSHAL MURAT

## King of Naples

BY

A.H. ATTERIDGE

WITH PLANS AND ILLUSTRATIONS

The Naval & Military Press Ltd

*Published by*

**The Naval & Military Press Ltd**
Unit 5 Riverside
Bellbrook Industrial Estate
Uckfield, East Sussex
TN22 1QQ England

Tel: +44 (0) 1825 749494
www.naval-military-press.com

*In reprinting in facsimile from the original, any imperfections are inevitably reproduced and the quality may fall short of modern type and cartographic standards.*

# CONTENTS

## CHAPTER I
### FIRST YEARS (1767-1795)

The Murats—Joachim's youth at La Bastide, Cahors and Toulouse—enlists in the cavalry—the Revolution—the Fête of the Federation—flight of the King—a love affair—the Constitutional Guard—promoted Lieutenant—aide-de-camp to d'Urre—Mion Bastit—treason of Dumouriez—Murat promoted Captain—service with Landrieux's 'poacher-hussars'—war services—quarrel with Landrieux—Thermidor—Murat a while in prison—rejoins regiment in Paris—helps Bonaparte on the day of Vendémiaire—promoted Colonel . . . . . . . . 1

## CHAPTER II
### THE CAMPAIGN OF ITALY (1796-1798)

Murat chef-de-brigade and aide-de-camp to Bonaparte in Italy—goes to Paris with dispatches—rejoins army as Général de Brigade—Valeggio and Mantua—mission to Genoa—capture of Leghorn—taken prisoner at Brescia—with Masséna in the Tyrol—relations with Bonaparte—Rivoli—fall of Mantua—march into Venetia—meets Caroline Bonaparte—mission to the Valtellina—with Bonaparte at Rastatt—Roman expedition . . . . 21

## CHAPTER III
### EGYPT AND SYRIA (1798-1799)

Attached to the 'Army of the East'—Malta—landing in Egypt—Rosetta—a narrow escape—battle of the Pyramids—Murat Governor of Kelioub—action at Damanhour—Syrian expedition—battle before Gaza—Acre—Murat in northern Palestine—relief of Safed—siege of Acre raised—retreat to Egypt—battle of Aboukir—Murat wounded and promoted to General of Division—sudden return to France with Bonaparte . . . . . 38

## CHAPTER IV
### BRUMAIRE—MARRIAGE TO CAROLINE BONAPARTE—MARENGO (1799-1800)

Murat's share in *coup d'état* of Brumaire—leads attack on the Five Hundred—message to Caroline—death of Pierre Murat—Murat married—commander of cavalry of the 'Army of Reserve'—projects for the Italian campaign—passage of the Alps—action at Galliate—entry into Milan—fall of Genoa—Marengo—Murat returns to Paris with Bonaparte . . . . . . . . 52

vi        JOACHIM MURAT

## CHAPTER V
### THE 'ARMY OF OBSERVATION'—COMMAND IN ITALY (1800-1801)

Letters to La Bastide—the camp of Beauvais—command at Dijon—Murat at Geneva and Milan—serves in Italy under General Brune—march into central Italy—affairs of Naples—Ancona occupied—birth of Achille Murat—Murat as a diplomatist—the Neapolitan treaty—Murat at Rome—returns to Florence—affairs of Egypt—Murat and Caroline—inauguration of the new 'Kingdom of Etruria'—conquest of Elba—Murat appointed Commander-in-Chief of the 'Army of Italy' with headquarters at Milan . . . . . . . . . . . . 67

## CHAPTER VI
### MURAT COMMANDER-IN-CHIEF AT MILAN (1801-1803)

Reports on the affairs of the Cisalpine Republic—a new Constitution—Caroline at Milan—Peace of Amiens—Murat's fortune—revisits Paris—marriage of Louis Bonaparte and religious marriage of Murat and Caroline—return to Milan—the Constitution proclaimed—mysterious visit to Paris—Rome and Naples—birth of a daughter—Murat provides for his nephews and nieces—quarrels with Vice-President Melzi—troubles with Italian Liberals—Bonaparte insists on reconciliation with Melzi—birth of Lucien Murat—outbreak of war—quarrel with St. Cyr . . 86

## CHAPTER VII
### MURAT MILITARY GOVERNOR OF PARIS (1803-1805)

Murat summoned to Paris—the elections—visit to La Bastide and Cahors—elected to the Assembly—Military Governor of Paris—affair of the Duc d'Enghien—coming of the Empire—Murat Marshal, Imperial Prince and Grand Admiral—the Élysée given to Caroline—the Coronation—projects against England—impending war with Austria—reconnaissance of south Germany—Murat Grand-Master of the Cavalry and Lieutenant-General of the Emperor—General Belliard—Murat at Strasburg—march into Germany—a forecast . . . . . . . . 101

## CHAPTER VIII
### THE CAMPAIGN OF ULM AND AUSTERLITZ (1805)

Murat screens the great turning movement round Ulm—passage of the Danube—Wertingen—dispute with Ney—Murat's mistakes—Haslach and Elchingen—Mack trapped at Ulm—pursuit of the Archduke Ferdinand—advance into Austria—Murat occupies Vienna—seizes the Danube bridge by a trick—Höllabrun and Austerlitz—death of Murat's mother . . . 119

# CONTENTS

## CHAPTER IX

### MURAT GRAND DUKE OF BERG—THE JENA CAMPAIGN (1806)

Remodelling of Germany—the Grand Duchy of Berg—Murat's entry into his capital—quarrel with Blücher over the possession of Essen and Werden—Napoleon preserves the peace—affair of the fortress of Wesel—Agar, Count of Mosbourg—Murat in Paris—Caroline helps him to obtain enlargement of his duchy—war with Prussia—Murat again commands the cavalry—Jena and Auerstadt . . . . . . . . . . . 138

## CHAPTER X

### THE PURSUIT AFTER JENA—WARSAW—THE EYLAU CAMPAIGN (1806-1807)

Erfurt—the dash for Berlin—surrender of Spandau—battle of Prenzlau—surrender of Hohenlohe's army—Lasalle takes Stettin—Napoleon's congratulations—pursuit of Blücher and Weimar—they surrender at Ratkau—results of the pursuit—Murat sent to Warsaw—hopes of the Polish crown—Poniatowski and the sword of Bathori—fighting on the Narev—campaign in East Prussia—Eylau—the great cavalry charge—informal truce and winter quarters . . . . . . . . . . 149

## CHAPTER XI

### HEILSBERG, FRIEDLAND AND TILSIT—THE SPANISH ADVENTURE (1807-1808)

Reorganization of the cavalry—battle of Heilsberg—pursuit after Friedland—Murat receives Russian request for an armistice—Tilsit—Murat disappointed in his hopes for Poland—returns to Paris with Napoleon—Caroline's court at the Elysée—current gossip about her conduct—marriage of Antoinette Murat—a link with the Franco-German war—increase of territory of Berg—Murat's plans suddenly changed by a mission to Spain—his instructions—hurried departure for Bayonne . . . . . 165

## CHAPTER XII

### MURAT LIEUTENANT-GENERAL OF THE EMPEROR IN SPAIN (1808)

Occupation of the northern fortresses of Spain—Murat at Vittoria and Burgos—first signs of trouble—optimism of Napoleon—Murat ordered to occupy Madrid—revolt at Aranjuez—Murat acts as arbiter between rival parties—arranges for future of Spain to be at Napoleon's disposal—suppresses rising of 2 May—expects the crown of Spain—suddenly hears Joseph is to have it—offered choice of Portugal or Naples—accepts crown of Naples—illness and disappointment . . . . . . 176

## CHAPTER XIII

### JOACHIM NAPOLEON, KING OF NAPLES (1808-1812)

Visit to Paris—entry into Naples—difficulties and disappointments—expedition to Capri—Napoleon's ill-humour—continual friction between him and Murat—Caroline's position—war of 1809—Anglo-Sicilian expedition against Naples—divorce of Josephine—Murat at the family council at Paris—failure of Murat's Sicilian expedition—Napoleon's displeasure—growing alienation of Murat—projects for making himself independent of Napoleon—birth of the 'King of Rome'—temporary reconciliation and renewed friction—Caroline intervenes—war with Russia—Murat to command cavalry of the Grand Army . . . . . . . 198

## CHAPTER XIV

### THE CAMPAIGN OF RUSSIA (1812)

Murat's conduct as a cavalry leader—failure at Wilna—scene with Montbrun—heavy losses in horses—was Murat to blame?—advance to Smolensk—quarrels of Murat and Davoût—Cossack tactics—Borodino—Murat enters Moscow—touch with the enemy lost—Moscow on fire—Russians reappear south of the city—Murat defeated at Winkowo—the retreat—terrible losses of the cavalry—Napoleon suddenly starts for Paris, leaving Murat in command of the Grand Army . . . . . . . 222

## CHAPTER XV

### MURAT LEAVES THE ARMY—RETURN TO NAPLES—QUARREL WITH NAPOLEON—OVERTURES TO THE ALLIES—GOES TO DRESDEN (1812-1813)

Retirement across the Niemen—Berthier's warning letters to Napoleon—Murat's outburst against the Emperor—defection of the Prussians—further retirement—Murat hands the command over to Eugène and starts for Naples—anger of Napoleon—Murat at Caserta—negotiations with Austria—and England—armistice in Germany—Murat's perplexities—ultimatum from the French ambassador at Naples—Caroline appeals to Napoleon—he summons Murat to Dresden . . . . . . . 239

## CHAPTER XVI

### THE LEIPZIG CAMPAIGN—MURAT ABANDONS THE FALLING EMPIRE—TREATY WITH AUSTRIA—HESITATING PART IN THE ITALIAN CAMPAIGN (1813-1814)

Temporary reconciliation with Napoleon—brilliant part in the victory of Dresden—Leipzig—return to Italy—relations with Italian patriots—negotiations with Austria—Fouché intervenes

# CONTENTS

—Neapolitan army goes north—Austria forces a decision—Treaty of Naples makes Murat her ally—he joins his army—correspondence with Eugène—strange overtures to Napoleon—fighting at Rubiera and Reggio—fall of Paris—end of the Italian campaign . . . . . . . . . 256

## CHAPTER XVII

MURAT RAISES THE STANDARD AGAINST AUSTRIA—DEFEAT AND DISASTER—MURAT A FUGITIVE DURING THE HUNDRED DAYS—THE TRAGEDY OF PIZZO (1814-1815)

Murat's anxieties about his position at Naples—projects for heading an Italian movement—Napoleon escapes from Elba—Murat declares war against Austria—disastrous campaign—flight from Naples—reaches Cannes—Napoleon refuses to see him—news of Waterloo—the 'White Terror'—Murat a fugitive—reaches Corsica—adventures there—project of a raid on Calabria—offer of an asylum in Austria—Murat's expedition sails from Ajaccio—gives up his project and decides to go to Trieste—sudden change of plans—landing at Pizzo and call to arms—Murat a prisoner—the court-martial—last letter to his family—Murat and Canon Masdea—the execution . . . . . . 276

## APPENDIX

NOTE ON SOME SOURCES AND AUTHORITIES FOR THE LIFE OF JOACHIM MURAT . . . . . 298

INDEX . . . . . . . . . . . 301

# LIST OF ILLUSTRATIONS

JOACHIM MURAT, AFTERWARDS KING OF NAPLES . . *Frontispiece*
    From the painting by GÉRARD at Versailles

                                                                                              FACING PAGE

CAROLINE BONAPARTE, ABOUT THE TIME OF HER MARRIAGE . 56
    From a lithograph by DELPECH

MURAT IN COURT COSTUME—AS GRAND DUKE OF BERG . 144
    After the painting by GÉRARD

MURAT WITH NAPOLEON AT THE BATTLE OF EYLAU . 162
    From the painting by BARON GROS in the Louvre, Paris

MARIE CAROLINE, QUEEN OF NAPLES . . . . . 208
    From an engraving by MARIE ANNE BOURLIER

THE RETREAT FROM MOSCOW . . . . . . 232
    From the painting by MEISSONIER in the Louvre, Paris
        (Photograph by W. A. MANSELL)

JOACHIM MURAT, KING OF NAPLES . . . . . 272
    From a lithograph by SCHUBERT (Collection, A. RISCHGITZ)

# LIST OF PLANS

THE CAMPAIGN OF ULM, 1805 . . . . . . 120

MURAT'S PURSUIT OF KUTUSOFF AND SEIZURE OF
    VIENNA . . . . . . . . . . 129

MURAT'S PURSUIT OF THE PRUSSIAN ARMY AFTER
    JENA AND AUERSTAD . . . . . . . 150

# JOACHIM MURAT

## CHAPTER I

### FIRST YEARS

### 1767-1795

CAHORS is a quaint old-world city of Guienne. One might call it a country town were it not for its twelfth-century cathedral, which gives a claim to higher rank. Its steep, narrow streets climb the hill round which the river Lot loops in a close curve forming in old days the moat for its ramparts. The ruined aqueduct is a monument of still older times when it was a Roman colony. There are vineyards on the hillsides around, and the wine trade helps to keep the place busy; and there are malodorous tanneries in the outskirts and the smoking chimneys of potteries.

The people of the city and the district, of which it is the local capital, belong to the race of the Gascon borderland —Frenchmen, but with a difference. There is the fire of the south in their blood and their brains, and a temperament that helps to wild adventure, bold speculation, imagination that may take the turn either of boastfulness or romancing. There is a strain of the mysterious Basque race in these quick-witted, nervous men of the Dordogne and the Lot and Garonne, perhaps, too, a tinge of non-European blood from the time of the Moorish conquest. This local temperament must not be left out of account in telling the strange story of a man who was born in this country of Cahors a little more than twenty years before the great Revolution gave quick-witted, daring men wonderful opportunities—the son of a country innkeeper, who fought his way to a kingdom.

A few miles north of Cahors, on a bare, almost treeless, plateau, stands the village of La Bastide. It is now known as Bastide Murat; it used to be La Bastide Fortonière, or La Bastide en Quercy. Here, when Louis Quinze was King of France, Pierre Murat and his wife, Jeanne Loubières, kept the village inn and posting-house. A prosperous man was Pierre Murat, for, besides the profits of his hostelry, he was intendant or agent for the Talleyrands, who were the great landowners of the district. He belonged to the better class of small country folk, though in the registry of his marriage he is described as a 'travailleur.' Pierre's father, in the marriage contract, dated 10 January, 1746, gives him half his property, which shows that if he was a 'worker' it was on lands held by his people. His wife, Jeanne Loubières, brought him as her dowry forty-two livres (that is francs, not pounds sterling), some household stuff in the way of sheets and linen, some pewter for the table, a sheep and its lamb, and a *coffre*, the oaken chest that contained the trousseau the French girl of the country then as now made with her own needle. At the inn of La Bastide there were five children of the marriage, two sons and three daughters, senior to Joachim Murat.[1] He was born on 25 March, 1767, and baptized next day in the parish church of La Bastide. He was given the name of Joachim in honour of his godfather, Joachim Vidieu.[2]

In the days of the Terror an attempt was made to bring Murat under the law of the 'suspects' by proving that he was an aristocrat by birth. It was then that he procured

---

[1] There were twelve children in all, but six had died in infancy.
[2] The record in the church register of La Bastide gives the Murats a second surname which does not appear in the contract and registry of Pierre's marriage. The record made by the curé runs thus:—

'L'an mil sept cent soixante et sept, et le vingt et cinquième jour du mois de mars, est né dans la présente paroisse Joachim Murat-Jordy, fils légitime de Pierre Murat-Jordy et de Jeanne Loubières, de la présente paroisse, et a été baptisé le vingt et six du dit mois dans l'église de la présente paroisse, par moy soussigné. Parrain a été Joachim Vidieu, de la présente paroisse, marraine Jeanne Albrespit, cousine germaine du baptisé, de la présente paroisse.'

# FIRST YEARS

from the authorities of La Bastide copies of his father's contract of marriage and his own registration of baptism, and was better pleased to see that old Pierre had been officially described as a 'travailleur' than if he had posed as a landed proprietor even on the smallest scale.

Joachim Murat was a younger son. The law of equal division of property was still in the future, and it was intended that his eldest brother André should inherit the inn of La Bastide and the little farm. The army, the navy, the civil service, were all careers in which there was a poor prospect for the son of a commoner, and still more for a country-bred commoner's son. The nobles and the wealthy townsfolk were the only people who could look for certain promotion and safely prosperous careers in the service of the State in any of its branches. Probably this was why it was decided that Joachim should be educated for the Church. There the patronage of the Talleyrands would be useful to him. They were helpful from the outset. It was, thanks to their protection that, when he was ten years old he was given a *bourse* or scholarship at the college of Cahors, where he was to make his classical studies in preparation for the seminary.

We have no record of Joachim's schoolboy years at Cahors under the shadow of the cathedral, or of the holidays at La Bastide. We only know that he did sufficiently well to be sent on from the college to the archi-episcopal seminary of Toulouse, where the future hussar was one of a community of young students *en soutane*, busy with philosophical and theological studies, and having his place on Sundays and feasts in the surpliced choir of the cathedral.

He had not yet taken the irrevocable step of receiving Orders as a sub-deacon, and was still free to choose another career, when his twentieth birthday was approaching. There was no vocation for a priestly life, but instead a longing for adventure and vigorous action. In February 1787 there came a crisis of which we have no details. We only know that on the 23rd of the month, without consulting his people at La Bastide, he took a step that disappointed all their hopes and plans. He suddenly left the seminary. A cavalry regiment, the Chasseurs à Cheval de Champagne,[1] had halted that day at Toulouse, on a route march, changing its place of garrison from Auch to Carcassonne. To one of the sergeants of Captain Neil's company there came a would-be recruit, clean-shaved, and, so far as this went, unsoldierly looking, but a strong-limbed fellow five feet six and a half inches high, with black hair and dark eyes, a loud voice and a swaggering manner—Joachim Murat of La Bastide. Next day he marched out of Toulouse as Private Murat in the service of King Louis XVI, having exchanged the *soutane* for a green uniform with white facings. It was only two years to wait until 1789 would make all things possible, even for a private of Chasseurs in a provincial garrison.

From Carcassonne the regiment was sent to Schlestadt in Alsace, where it was stationed when the year of the Revolution came. By that time Joachim Murat, thanks to the good education he had received at Cahors and at the seminary of Toulouse, had won rapid promotion. In the two years since he joined the Chasseurs he had passed through the grades of corporal and sergeant, and was now *maréchal des logis* (quarter-master-sergeant) in his regiment. In the summer of 1789, when all France was ringing with the news that the Bastille had fallen, he obtained a prolonged leave of absence, and, for the first time since his enlistment, revisited the inn of La Bastide.

The leave of absence was lengthened out from month to month, for Maréchal des Logis Murat had work to do at Cahors and elsewhere in the neighbourhood. National Guards were being enrolled and drilled, and the young soldier's services were useful to unmilitary municipals. He had thrown himself heart and soul into the new order of things, with good reason, for the privileges that kept all the upper rungs of the military ladder barred to such as he and open only to nobles and roturiers had been swept away. In the spring of 1790 came the summons to the Departments to send detachments of the new National Guard to Paris.

---

[1] Later known as the 12th Chasseurs à Cheval.

# FIRST YEARS

The citizen soldiers were to muster in their tens of thousands for the Feast of the Federation of all France pledged to the defence of the new constitutional monarchy. King Louis was to swear allegiance to it at an altar erected in the Champ de Mars, and surrounded by the armed delegates of all France, on 14 July—the anniversary of the great day of the Bastille.

Murat was sent to Paris by the Department of Lot, of which Cahors is the capital. He was in charge of the detachments of Federal National Guards from the canton of Montfaucon, the district round La Bastide. He was a unit in the great gathering of 200,000 men that was marshalled around the 'altar of the fatherland' in the Champ de Mars. He saw King Louis take the oath to the Constitution, amid the plaudits of the multitude, while cannon roared out a salute that was echoed by batteries on the hilltops round Paris, and taken up by answering cannon from town to town till it thundered from the forts of Toulon by the Mediterranean, from the ramparts of Grenoble among the Alps, and Schlestadt in the Rhineland; from Calais on the Channel, and Brest and Rochefort on the Atlantic. France was noisily rejoicing in the coming of the new Golden Age, in happy ignorance of the days of darkness that were so near. That loud, far-sounding salute had an immediate consequence, which to many seemed an evil omen. It brought down from cloudy skies a deluge of rain, marring sadly the religious ceremony, of which the central figure at the improvised altar was Murat's patron of his college days, Talleyrand de Périgord, Bishop of Autun—soon to cast the crozier aside and begin a new career of revolutionary politics and crooked diplomacy.

Murat lingered on in Paris for months after the celebration. At first it was a holiday time, with much patriotic feasting of the Provincial Federates by their Paris friends and comrades. After this period of holiday-making, Murat seems to have stayed on in Paris for the practical reason that he was too short of funds to pay his way home. The Departmental authorities had not been prompt in remitting the allowance for expenses promised to their delegate. At last, with the new year of 1791, came a peremptory notice from the War Office that his long leave was at an end, and he must forthwith rejoin the Chasseurs à Cheval at Schlestadt.

He wrote on 4 January, 1791 a petition to the ' Administration of the Department of the Lot,' setting forth that, having been sent in the previous July to Paris with the ' national troops of the canton of Montfaucon,' ' he had been obliged to incur expenses that were much more considerable than had been anticipated, inasmuch as the stay of the Federate troops at Paris had been prolonged by circumstances that could not have been foreseen, as is shown by the accompanying certificates from the Paris municipality.' He reminds the officials that the Department was, by the decree of the National Assembly, bound to provide all necessary funds for the delegates, but he had so far received nothing, and Paris was an expensive place, on account of the great concourse of people that had been drawn thither. He had exhausted his private resources, and asked for a payment on account, at the very least—all the more because he was under orders to proceed to Schlestadt.

The administration remitted a hundred livres, a disappointingly small sum, and Joachim Murat bade temporary farewell to Paris, and returned to garrison duty with the regiment in the dull frontier fortress between Vosges and Rhine.

In the beginning of June there were strange movements of troops in the eastern districts of France. The Marquis de Bouillé was concentrating a little army at the frontier fortress of Montmédy, and stringing out detachments of cavalry in towns and villages along the road to Paris. There was talk of an important convoy of treasure soon to be moved eastwards from the capital. A detachment of the Chasseurs à Cheval was ordered from Schlestadt to Montmédy as part of these mysterious arrangements. Murat did not go with it

No treasure convoy came along the elaborately guarded Paris road, but, instead, the lumbering travelling carriage, conveying the fugitive royalties of France—stopped at last by insurgent country folk who made King Louis and Queen Marie Antoinette their prisoners at Varennes, while the locally detailed escort that should have carried them off to Bouillé's headquarters at Montmédy slept and blundered or lost their way.

When the news came to Schlestadt that the King and Queen had tried to escape across the frontier and had been conveyed back to Paris, there was anxious questioning in the regiment as to the fate of the detachment sent off to Montmédy by that royalist plotter, De Bouillé, now himself in flight from France, and there was a patriotic eagerness to assure all Frenchmen that the regiment knew nothing of the conspiracy to steal away the King. The colonel of the Chasseurs, Monsieur d'Urre de Molans, aristocrat though he was, had decided that his lot must be thrown in with the new Constitutional order of things. He accepted the proposal that a deputation should be sent to Montmédy to see how the detachment there was faring, and arrange for their rejoining the regiment. The adjutant of the Chasseurs and Maréchal des Logis Murat were chosen for this important mission.

Murat gave an account of it in a letter to his elder brother Pierre, dated from Toul on 5 July, 1791. He was very busy, he said, and living in the midst of general excitement, but he snatched a moment to write to ' the best of brothers, whom he would always love.' He asked him to assure his father and mother that they need have no anxiety about him. He was working hard for promotion, and would soon be made quartermaster.

'I have just come from Montmédy' [he continued], 'three leagues from Varennes, where the King was arrested. I was deputed by my comrade to go to Montmédy to obtain information as to the position of other comrades of mine who were sent there on detachment. Montmédy was to have received the King, and our regiment was to have guarded him. I saw the apartments prepared for him there. I send you two speeches that we delivered. I made one, and our adjutant the other.'

These orations were meant to assure the people of Toul that the Chasseurs were sound ' patriots ' who had no idea that they were being used to protect the King's flight. He ended his letter with good wishes to all his relations and friends, and especially for the Bastit family, small proprietors in his native village, where the head of the family was the local notary. There is a special mention of Mion Bastit, the daughter of the house, in terms that indicate that during Murat's stay at La Bastide there had been some love-making. 'Remember me to good old Bastit,' he says, ' and I beg you to give me news of the charming Mion. Do not forget this.' Then there is a quaintly worded request that Pierre would, on his behalf, ' embrace the municipality.' Pierre was a member of it, and had apparently spoken of resigning his position. Murat in a postscript begs him not to do so, and takes occasion to refer once more to his speech, of which he was obviously proud :—

'Do not send in your resignation, and do not forget that your brother would die rather than cease to be a patriot, or be false to the sentiments of patriotism expressed in the speech which he had the honour to deliver in presence of the municipality of Toul, having been deputed by his comrades to give them proof that we had no knowledge of the doings at Montmédy.'

Here already we see signs of the boastful spirit that ran through so much of his after life, the Gascon spirit of swagger, display, and self-assertion.

On 8 February, 1792 Murat was chosen as one of the mounted detachment of the new Constitutional Guard assigned by the Legislative Assembly to the King, nominally a royal guard of honour, really a precaution against a renewal of the attempt at evasion. The officers and soldiers of the Guard were nominated by the Departments to which they belonged. Among Murat's comrades was Jean Baptiste Bessières, another future marshal of France, but then a lately enlisted private in a cavalry regiment. Bessières came from Preissac in Murat's Department of the Lot, and was thus almost a neighbour. In a later official document

# FIRST YEARS 9

he is spoken of as his cousin, though it is doubtful if there was any real relationship.

Murat's service in the Constitutional Guard was of the briefest. He joined on 8 February and resigned his position on 4 March. The immediate occasion was a sentence of confinement in the *salle de police*, ordered for having been absent from a roll call. He preferred to leave the Guard rather than undergo this slight punishment. But he at once wrote to the Departmental Council of the Lot to explain that the real reason for his resignation was not this trifling incident, but the fact that he had found himself 'among reactionary influences,' and had been directly tempted by some of his officers to leave France and take serivce with the army of the *Emigrés*, then being organised at Coblenz. He said that among others the lieutenant-colonel of the Guard, Descours, had offered him forty louis d'or as bounty and travelling expenses if he would accept the proposal. The Departmental authorities passed on the complaint to the Legislative Assembly, and Murat's testimony was quoted by the Deputy Bazire, when he denounced the Guard as a hotbed of royalism, and demanded and obtained its disbandment.

Murat returned to his old regiment, now known as the 12th Chasseurs à Cheval, with the reputation of an incorruptible patriot. He was promoted to the rank of sub-lieutenant on 15 October, and to that of lieutenant a fortnight later on the 31st.

In November he was back in Paris again for a short time, making some purchases for his colonel and for the regiment. Since 10 August the King was a prisoner in the Temple. Since the early summer France had been at war with Austria and her allies. The country had been invaded, and in September Valmy had been won and the Republic proclaimed. A letter of Murat's from Paris to his brother Pierre is dated with a mixture of new and old styles, '19 novembre 1792, l'an I$^{er}$ de la République.' He tells Pierre of his mission to the capital. Good luck has come his way with the advent of the Republic. 'Now that despotism has expired everything looks bright for me.' He is arranging with 'General' Santerre to get a horse for his own use. Santerre was one of the great men of the moment. The brewer of the Faubourg St. Antoine had been general of the National Guard since the attack on the Tuileries on 10 August. Then he writes of his hopes and prospects :—

'I have presented a memoir to the Minister [of War] ; a general is to get me his reply, and this general is himself going soon to be the Minister. If this happens, my lot will be a very fortunate one. I am a lieutenant, and if my colonel is made a general, about which there is no doubt, I am to be his aide-de-camp and a captain. At my age, and with my courage and military talents, I may go still further. God grant that I may not be disappointed in my expectations.'

No lack of self-confidence and self-assertion here. As for his 'military talents,' he had had as yet no opportunity of displaying them on a more trying field than the parade ground.

If Murat had already been in action there cannot be a doubt that in this letter home there would have been some allusion to the fact. He was not the man to hide even one ray of light under a bushel. It is likely that so far he had been engaged in depot and administrative work, for which his previous occupation in the quartermaster's department of his regiment fitted him. The Chasseurs à Cheval had been attached to the army of the north under Dumouriez in Flanders, and Jemappes had been fought and won, but Murat does not boast of any share in his comrade's laurels, so it is fairly certain that he had not yet seen his first field of battle.[1]

When Murat wrote this letter to his favourite brother,

---

[1] M. Frederick Masson (*Napoléon et sa Famille*, i. 309), after mentioning Murat's promotion to lieutenant, adds that he owed this rapid advance to his colonel, D'Urre de Molans, who having been promoted brigadier general took him with him as his aide-de-camp. And he goes on to say :—
'On peut penser que Murat avait fait la première campagne de l'Armée du Nord avec son régiment, qui, officiellement, à assisté au combat de Grandpré, au siége de Landrecies, à la bataille de Jemappes et au combat de Saint-Trond, mais on ne sait rien d'autre que son rapide avancement sur la part qu'il a pu prendre à ces faits de guerre.'
Jemappes was fought on 6 November, 1792. On the 19th Murat was

# FIRST YEARS

Pierre had been dead and buried in the churchyard of La Bastide for more than a month. He died on 8 October, leaving three children, and a widow who expected soon to give birth to a fourth. When he learned the news, Joachim undertook to provide for the education of his nephews and nieces, and kept his promise faithfully.[1]

D'Urre de Molans did not get his promotion and the command of a cavalry brigade till the beginning of the next year, and then chose Murat as his aide-de-camp, but the expected promotion to the rank of captain did not come till some months later. Between November 1792 and the middle of February 1793 Dumouriez had overrun Belgium, but even in this campaign Murat appears not to have had any experiences of active service in touch with the enemy. The Chasseurs were kept on the French border in Artois on garrison and line of communication duties. Events were now moving fast. The King was executed in January, and the Committee of Public Safety created the same day. A few days later its terrible auxiliary, the Revolutionary Tribunal, came into existence, and the guillotine began to work permanently. Nation after nation joined the coalition, till Europe was in arms against the Republic, and Carnot, at the Paris War Office, called for a levy of 300,000 men to defend the country.

There are extant two letters of Murat, both written from Paris on 25 February, 1793, showing that he was again employed on a mission to the Government by his chiefs. One of the letters is a communication to the municipality of La Bastide, written in the oratorical style Murat sometimes adopted at this period, when half France was taking theatri-

writing this long letter home, telling of his work in Paris. Is it possible that if he was fresh from a victory in Flanders, he would be absolutely silent about it? His war services in 1792 are clearly the outcome of his biographer's idea that 'he must have been there.' As we see from Murat's letter, D'Urre de Molans did not get his promotion to the rank of general till later, and Murat was still only hoping to be his aide-de-camp.

[1] The eldest son, Jean Adrien Murat (born 1785), was killed while serving on board Admiral Dumanoir's flagship, the *Formidable*, in the action off Cape Ortegal, 4 November, 1805, in which Strachan took the four ships that had escaped with Dumanoir from Trafalgar. The youngest child, Antoinette Murat, was made a princess by Napoleon, and married (4 February, 1808) Prince Charles of Hohenzollern-Sigmaringen.

cal poses and holding forth in semi-classical language on the glories of the Republic and the duties of patriotism in its defence. It was meant to encourage the young men of La Bastide to hasten to the frontiers. There was an allusion to attempts of malicious persons to make out that he was an aristocrat. But he said proudly, ' I think I am well enough known for my zeal and patriotism to be beyond all doubt.'

The other letter was to his eldest brother, André, the quiet, plodding, home-loving man, who always refused to leave La Bastide, and even when his brother was a king was content to be *maire* of his village. André had lately lost his wife. His brother advises him not to marry again, and promises to do what he can to help in supporting their parents. He had apparently not yet given up the idea of himself taking a wife from La Bastide, but had ceased to be keen on the old love affair, for alluding to some news conveyed in a letter of André's he writes :—

' You say that Mion Bastit has been annoyed with me. I am not surprised at it. I thought they were all against me, like the set of aristocrats they all are. . . . I have written to Mion Bastit. What after all are her intentions ? I know nothing of them. Tell her to reply to me at once, for I expect I shall have to leave Paris in ten days for Holland. I have been appointed aide-de-camp to a general ; I have a horse that has cost me sixty louis, and I have to buy another. They are very dear.'

He tells André that at Paris there had been some talk of his being elected a deputy to the Convention. ' I have not much talent,' he says (with unusual modesty), ' but with my good intentions and my courage, I would do more than many of those who are there.' He suggests that his brother should advise any of the local young men, who join the new levy of 300,000 to come to him at Arras, ' at any rate they will then serve as mounted soldiers.' He has already had the brother of the ' Constitutional ' curé of La Bastide promoted as quartermaster-sergeant in his company. He returns to the subject of Mion Bastit, with an inquiry as to whether she is flirting with the young men at La Bastide. It is a rambling letter, hurriedly written. At the end there is news of the war. He had supper with General Dampierre at Valenciennes on the 15th, before he came on to Paris. The enemy is everywhere defeated. The camp of Famars has been taken and Tournay evacuated by the allies. But Murat talks of these victories as one who has only heard of them.

The letter to Mion Bastit led to nothing. A couple of lines in a letter to André, dated nearly a month later (22 April), shows that he is angry at her neglect of him. ' Mion has not replied to me. Let her arrange things as she pleases. I laugh at it all.' The bit of romance thus flickers out of Murat's life, and Mion's name presently disappears from his correspondence. An inquiry in a letter home a few months later is the last reference to her. It looks like a piece of mere reminiscent curiosity as to what she has been doing. ' Dites-moi ce que fait Mion Bastit.' If he had married the village girl he would have closed the way to a throne.[1]

Murat made only a brief stay in Paris and was soon again on the northern frontier, and acting as aide-de-camp to General d'Urre. In March Dumouriez was in full retreat before the Austrians. On the 18th they defeated him at Neerwinden. Custine had failed on the Rhine. A Spanish army was in the Pyrenees. An English army would soon be across the Channel to help the Austrians in the north. There was a semi-panic in Paris in which all the extreme elements came to the front. The Revolutionary Tribunal was given new powers. Revolutionary Committees were ordered to be formed in every city and town to hunt out the disloyal and encourage the ' patriots ' to volunteer for the defence of the ' Fatherland in danger.'

Dumouriez, now unsuccessful and in slow dogged retreat, had long been suspected of slackness in his zeal for the Revolution. He had a prince on his staff, young Philippe Egalité, one day to reign as Louis Philippe, and he had

---

[1] François Bastit, Mion's brother, was elected to the corps législatif, under the Consulate, thanks largely to Murat's influence. He was his life-long friend.

spoken strongly of the execution of the King as a piece of folly. To Dumouriez's headquarters on 2 April came the Minister of War, Bournouville, with four delegates of the Convention, inviting the general to go to Paris with them and explain his conduct at the bar of the Assembly. Dumouriez knew what that meant, and promptly arrested the minister and the delegates, then failing to induce his army to stand by him, rode off to the Austrians with his staff, some mercenary German hussars, and his five prisoners as hostages.

Dampierre,[1] who had been Murat's host at the supper at Valenciennes in February, took the command of the beaten and disorganised army of the north. One of his first acts was to promote Murat to the rank of captain. Joachim sends the good news to his brother André in a letter dated from Hesdin in Artois on 22 April. It is an oratorical letter with much high-flown comparison between the happy condition of La Bastide and the miserable state of the frontier villages exposed to all the horrors of war. He writes indignantly of Dumouriez. ' Our armies have abandoned the infamous Dumouriez, the moment they recognised in him a traitor, and everywhere our Republican soldiers are giving new proofs of their courage in fighting against those infamous satellites of tyrants.' He acknowledges a letter of André's, and praises him for his civic zeal, and is pleased to hear that many at La Bastide are eager to go to the front as volunteers. But he does not encourage them to act on the impulse. ' I would embrace them with all my heart,' he says, ' if they came, but let them remain as they are peaceful agriculturists. Our fields have need of their labour, and the soldiers of the Republic look to them for bread. Let them therefore remain where they are and procure it for us.' It might have been awkward for Captain Murat if a Jacobin Revolutionary Committee had seen his letter. He tells André to remain at home whatever happens

---

[1] General Dampierre was a noble, known before the Revolution as Auguste Henri Picot, Marquis de Dampierre. He threw in his fortunes with the new régime, and adopted as his surname his old title, minus the aristocratic ' de.' He had distinguished himself at Valmy and Jemappes.

## FIRST YEARS

and take care of the old father and mother. If the others will come let them ask for him at Hesdin. The victorious allies began a systematic reduction of the fortresses which the French had occupied along the border, and in the summer the advance of the Duke of York and the English to besiege Dunkirk brought the war into the neighbourhood of Murat's post at Hesdin. So far he had been engaged only in garrison duties, but an offer of promotion led him to leave his staff work and his position in the 12th Chasseurs for more active service with somewhat strange companions.

In the warfare of irregular levies, like those of the Revolutionary armies, one finds adventurers for whom campaigning is little more than an opportunity of legalised brigandage. A man of this stamp was Jean Landrieux, who had raised and commanded an irregular cavalry corps known as the *Hussards-braconniers*—the 'poacher hussars.' Poaching being at all times an irregular warfare against aristocratic privileges, the name had been assumed as not now discreditable, and indicated the source from which Landrieux drew some of his rough recruits. So far he does not appear to have served against the invaders of France, but he had put his free corps at the service of Jacobin Committees engaged in hunting down 'aristocrats' and plundering their possessions. Landrieux and his 'poachers' had drifted into Artois in April, soon after the treason of Dumouriez, and there chance had brought him into communication with Captain Murat. The Paris War Office, not entirely satisfied with Landrieux's proceedings, and engaged in organising new armies against the Allies, was anxious to give the free corps a more regular form, and turn it into a serviceable cavalry regiment. Landrieux proposed to Murat that he should be transferred to his corps with a step in rank. He would be *chef d'escadron*—*i.e.* major of cavalry, and his military training and experience would be useful in the reorganisation of the 'poacher hussars' into a respectable regiment. Murat accepted the proposal, and on 1 May, 1793 Landrieux wrote to Paris praising the civic virtues and

Republican zeal of his proposed *chef d'escadron*. The War Office did not send on the official promotion till September, but a provisional appointment was made by General Dampierre in a few days, for on 8 May Landrieux writes to Murat :—

' I beg to inform you, Citizen, that in virtue of the order of the Minister now in my hands, and at the request of General Dampierre, you have been named provisionally second *chef d'escadron* of the regiment which I command. Will you therefore be so good as to inform the general to whose staff you are attached of this arrangement, so that he may send you to your post as soon as possible. Let me know of his decision.'

The *hussards-braconniers* were now renamed the 16th Chasseurs à Cheval. Later on their number was changed to the 21st. Murat's definite commission as *chef d'escadron* in the 21st Chasseurs is dated the 23rd of the following September.

By this time he had served for some months with Landrieux's regiment which was stationed at Hesdin. He had no idea of being a party to any irregularities, and took his work seriously, exerting himself, on the contrary, to bring the ex-' poachers ' into a state of military discipline and train them into a useful cavalry unit. The result was a conflict with his commanding officer.

He saw his first active service in skirmishes with the enemy at the head of these transformed irregulars. In January 1794 he writes home from Lille that during the last three days they have been in action and ' fighting like devils ' on the outpost line where they had served for months. They had just been withdrawn to Lille. They were all in rags, and expected soon to be ordered to Dunkirk. Incidentally he mentions that during the rough campaigning of the winter he had lost three horses, and had been put to much expense to replace them. But he is anxious to help the old home, and promises to send his parents a hundred francs each month. There are complaints of the trouble and anxiety he has to suffer through the attacks of ' intriguing and ambitious men.'

The allusion was, no doubt, to Landrieux and his supporters in the regiment. In February he writes from Dunkirk asking urgently for a copy of his baptismal certificate in order to prove that he is sprung from the common people. 'They want to make out that I am a noble,' he says, 'and this puts me in a rage.' He mentions that the regiment will soon go to Holland. There is also talk of an embarkation. Perhaps there will be an invasion of England.

While Murat was doing outpost work with the 2nd and 3rd squadrons of the 21st Chasseurs, Landrieux with the 1st squadron had kept away from the front and employed himself in police duty making searches, seizures, and arrests at Boulogne, Abbeville, and other northern towns. When he rejoined, Murat showed what he thought of his methods, asserted himself as the effective commander of the regiment, if any real service was to be done, and refused to countenance Landrieux's attempts to continue his legalised plundering. It was then war to the knife between the two men. As the readiest weapon, Landrieux tried to show that Murat was not a good Republican. He had been the protégé of D'Urre de Molans, an aristocrat, nay, he was himself an aristocrat connected with the Murats of Auvergne. He denied the dangerous relationship, and the papers sent from La Bastide showed he was a son of the people. Landrieux and Murat exchanged mutual recriminations, each charging the other with being a secret agent of the Bourbon princes. Landrieux declared that his *chef d'escadron* was an agitator who was destroying the discipline of the regiment. But Murat, thanks to his hard work and his dashing conduct at the outposts, had on his side all the officers who meant business, and he sent to the War Office a statement signed by himself and nearly all his colleagues accusing Landrieux, with perfect truth, of being continually absent from the theatre of war and engaged in expeditions for his own profit. To show his own thorough devotion to the Republic he signed his name not as Murat but as 'Marat.' The result was that Landrieux was removed from the command, and for the moment Murat, *alias* Marat, was victorious.

But July brought the days of Thermidor and the swift downfall of Robespierre and the Terrorists, and the reaction in which all who had too closely identified themselves with the fallen men were in deadly danger. Landrieux tried to take vengeance on his old opponent, and that unfortunate episode of his having masqueraded as ' Marat ' helped him to trump up against Murat an accusation that he had been one of the ' Robespierrists.' He was arrested and sent to prison at Amiens, and was put on his trial for complicity in the Terror.

' The defence that Murat made before the Committee of Public Safety was skilful and energetic. He reminded his judges that the same man who had denounced him as an aristocrat was now his accuser on the charge of " terrorism." " It well befitted Landrieux, that immoral man, who had never lived but by intrigues and plunder," he said, " thus to attack one who had always walked in the straight path of virtue, who had never been absent from his post, and who had had a horse killed under him in the last campaign." If for a fortnight he had assumed the name of Marat it was only to elude the tyranny of his persecutors. If he was to be condemned for having tried " to avoid persecution by this very innocent means, they ought to punish the entire section of Paris that had adopted the name of Marat." Had he not refused to act as president of a military commission that had sent to the guillotine an officer of the regiment, Chenel, whose loss all his comrades deplored ? ' [1]

He produced a strong testimonial in his favour from the authorities of his native Department of the Lot. He was acquitted and sent back to his regiment. He had hoped to have command of it, but he had to remain for awhile only one of its squadron leaders.[2]

But his chance was coming. The regiment had been

---

[1] Chavanon de St. Yves, *Joachim Murat*, p. 11.
[2] Landrieux, though he had been worsted in his conflict with Murat, remained in the army of the Republic, and obtained promotion. In the first stage of the campaign of Italy, in 1796, we find him in command of one of Kilmaine's cavalry regiments, and closely associated with that general. He was then employed by Bonaparte in secret service work, and helped to organize Republican and anti-Austrian revolutions, in various cities in northern Italy. During these proceedings, he met his old rival Murat again. Landrieux says they met as friends, and that he

## FIRST YEARS

ordered to Paris while he was still under arrest, and it was there he rejoined it. Next year came the last struggles of the party of insurrection. On 20 May, 1795—the day of Prairal—the Jacobins and Sansculottes invaded the Assembly, and it was the *chef d'escadron* Murat who came to the rescue of the authorities with the first party of cavalry that put itself at their disposal in defence of order. Then came the Constitution of the Directory, and the Federation of the National Guard of the Sections of Paris to overthrow the 'reactionary government.' Barras was appointed commander-in-chief of the troops that had been concentrated to protect the Government, and the civilian politician, looking round for a soldier to do the real work as his lieutenant, chose young Napoleon Bonaparte for the post. The famous 13 of Vendémiaire (5 October, 1795) saw the last of the insurrections in Paris and the rise of Bonaparte's star amid the smoke cloud of the cannon that swept the streets and quays round the Tuileries and the church of St. Roch.

That many of these guns were at Bonaparte's orders, and that there was no artillery replying to them, was due to a piece of swift and efficient service done by Joachim Murat. On the eve of the great day, though still only ranking as *chef d'escadron*, he was in temporary command of the 21st Chasseurs. This was his first piece of good fortune. At midnight he had under his immediate orders 260 men; the rest were on detached duty at various points. Bonaparte had just been informed that the artillery of the National Guard was parked at the Place des Sablons under the guard of a handful of men, twenty-five at most. Murat's men were the nearest available mounted force. He was told to secure the forty guns. Off he went through the darkness at a brisk gallop and trot to the Sablons. As he entered the

even offered to lend Murat money, but he was told by the latter, that he had all he needed. Landrieux admits in his memoirs that in levying contributions he found the means of having considerable sums offered to him for his own use, and suggests that Murat and the other Republican generals in Italy found similar ways of 'making economies.' He fell into Bonaparte's disfavour, left the army, and settled in France, where, during the Empire, Napoleon's police watched him as a suspicious character.

open space he saw on the other side of it a battalion of National Guards in column marching into the square. It was the battalion of the Section La Pelletier arriving to secure the artillery. Murat formed his horsemen in line, and advancing with sabre drawn told the Nationals that if they did not at once face about and march away he would charge them and cut them to pieces. The citizen soldiers retreated before the menace of the Chasseurs. Horses were requisitioned and the guns and tumbrils were soon rumbling to the Tuileries under Murat's escort.

The bloodless victory in the darkness of the Place des Sablons had made Murat's fortune. General Bonaparte was not likely to forget the man who had armed him for the victory in the streets of Paris that was the starting-point of his career of conquest and empire. The colonelcy of his regiment was the immediate reward of Murat's prompt action. A mere chance had started him at last upon his career of success.

## CHAPTER II

### THE CAMPAIGN OF ITALY

### 1796-1798

WHILE he was still serving in the north of France Murat had written to La Bastide that, when the war was over, he would return home and, like a new Cincinnatus, put his hands to the plough and help to cultivate the family lands. The message was probably only one of those bits of pseudo-classic affectation of Republican simplicity common at the time. He was a soldier before everything else, and he said that if ' God and the bullets spared him he would go far.' Before the end of 1794 he had sold to his brother André his interest in the family property at La Bastide. His promotion to the rank of colonel, and his admission to the group of brilliant officers who were the satellites of the rising general of France would have fixed him in the career of arms, even if he had ever had any serious thought of abandoning it.

He had a new proof of Bonaparte's favour in his promotion to the rank of *chef de brigade* on 2 February, 1796.[1] In

---

[1] General Thoumas (*Les Grands Cavaliers*, i. 388) tells this story of Murat's appointment: ' The 21st Chasseurs were in garrison at Versailles, and by the orders of Bonaparte, now general of division, and commander-in-chief of the Army of the Interior, the regiment every ten days exchanged quarters with one of the regiments in barracks at the Ecole Militaire. Murat during these periods of service in Paris came into close touch with the aides-de-camp of the commander-in-chief, Junot and Marmont, and told these two officers of his desire to go to the front with them. Encouraged by them, he went to see the commander-in-chief, and with the somewhat presumptuous confidence that was characteristic of him, said to Bonaparte, ' You have not an aide-de-camp of the rank of colonel, and I propose to you that I should go with you in this capacity.' This assured self-confidence did not displease Bonaparte. He had Murat appointed to be his first aide-de-camp, and took him with him.

this position he would still be known as Colonel Murat, and in the ordinary course of events might look forward to commanding a cavalry brigade and winning his promotion to the rank of general in the next campaign. But there was something better in store for him. When Bonaparte started for Provence to take command of the army of Italy for the campaign of 1796 he appointed Murat to his staff, and during the campaign he again and again gave him the command of large bodies of troops, or sent him to superintend and report upon operations directed by others, or to conduct important negotiations. He was given abundant opportunities of distinction, and he made the most of them.

The ragged, almost shoeless, army was concentrated on the French Riviera. The Austrians and Sardinians held the passes that led over the northern Apennines. In a marvellous campaign of two weeks Bonaparte had forced the passes, separated the Sardinians from their allies, thoroughly beaten them, and forced the King of Sardinia to renounce the alliance and accept the terms of peace dictated by the victor. At Dego Murat led his first charge in a pitched battle. Bonaparte had hurried up during the action with a handful of reinforcements, among them two squadrons of dragoons. He sent Murat to them with an order to charge, and the staff officer led the wild dash into the Austrian ranks with such good effect that he was mentioned with honour in the victor's dispatch to the Directory. At Mondovi, in the final battle with General Colli's Piedmontese, Murat rallied a broken brigade of cavalry, led them again to the charge, and drove the beaten enemy across the river Ellero, fording the stream to charge them again on the further bank. Already he showed that faculty of inspiring others with his own reckless daring, that almost magnetic power of imparting for the moment his own spirit to hundreds or thousands, which is one of the secrets of the great leader.

When, after Mondovi, Colli asked for an armistice, it was Murat who was sent to the enemy's headquarters as the bearer of Bonaparte's terms. As soon as the armistice was signed he was sent to Paris with Bonaparte's dispatches

## THE CAMPAIGN OF ITALY 23

announcing the event. On 10 May, 1796 he was rewarded by the Directory with promotion to the rank of Général de Brigade. A general at twenty-eight he could hope for anything.

During the few days he spent in Paris Murat paid more than one visit to Madame Bonaparte. He had been formally presented to her after Vendémiaire, but now, when he came as the bearer of news from her husband's headquarters in the field, there was occasion for conversations in which were laid the foundations of a friendship that was soon to be of material service to the young cavalry general.

While he was in Paris Bonaparte had stormed the bridge of Lodi, occupied Milan, and driven the Austrians out of Lombardy. When Murat rejoined the army towards the end of May it was advancing to attack the line of the river Mincio, south of the Lake of Garda. The eastern bank was held by Beaulieu's Austrian army, guarding every point along the stream, and therefore nowhere strong, and everywhere weak, against the concentrated attack of their opponents.

Murat was just in time. He was given the general direction of the advanced guard when, on 30 May, Bonaparte forced the crossing of the Mincio at Valeggio. The French, striking at the chosen point of the long Austrian cordon, were able to bring some twenty thousand men into action against three thousand Austrian cavalry and four thousand infantry. Murat charged the Austrian cavalry and completely routed them. He had taken temporary command of Kilmaine's cavalry division, and thus reaped the chief honours of the day. The charge cut off the retreat of a large body of Austrians. Murat took nine guns, two standards, and some two thousand prisoners. He was specially mentioned in Bonaparte's report to the Directory, not only as the leader of the victorious cavalry attack, but also for personal acts of valour in the charge, and for having rescued a number of chasseurs who were in imminent danger of being made prisoners by the enemy.

Beaulieu retired northwards towards the Tyrol and Bonaparte began the siege of Mantua, where a strong garrison held out among the marshes and inundations that isolated the fortress. While the blockade of the place dragged on the French commander was strengthening his hold on Italy. In June he sent Murat to Genoa with a letter to the French envoy to the Genoese Republic, Citizen Faypoult, in which he directed him to warn the Senate that there must be no secret trafficking with Austria, and that there must be an end of the attacks made upon French soldiers on the borders of the Genoese territory. 'I will burn any town or village where a Frenchman is assassinated,' wrote Bonaparte; 'I will burn any house that gives shelter to the assassins.' The remonstrances of the envoy, backed by the presence of the hero of Valeggio, reduced the Senate to a state of alarm that was manifested in abject apologies.

Murat returned from his mission in the third week of June, and by an order, dated the 20th of that month, he was given the command of the vanguard of a force detached to occupy Tuscany, under General Vaubois. Murat's advanced guard was made up of a cavalry brigade (1st Hussars and 20th Dragoons) under the younger Kellerman, and a battalion of Grenadiers under Colonel Lannes, the future marshal. By a forced march and a sudden change of direction Murat surprised Leghorn, and seized an enormous quantity of supplies in the warehouses of the port, but the English merchant ships in the harbour succeeded in getting away to sea at the last moment.

Returning to headquarters on the Mincio in the beginning of July Murat was placed under the orders of Sérurier, who was commanding the besieging force before Mantua. On 16 July an attempt was made to surprise the entrenched camp that formed a huge outwork of the fortress. Murat's part in the operation was the leadership of a column that was embarked in boats to make its way through the marshes in the night. A sudden fall in the waters of the Po half-drained the marshes and left Murat's boats aground among the reeds. Marmont's memoirs followed by some of Murat's biographers, accuse him of having caused the failure of the attack by slackness in bringing up his detachment. But Sérurier's report amply justifies him. He could not do the impossible. But two days later in a successful attack on the outworks Murat showed that he could lead infantry as well as cavalry, and at the head of a column of 1000 grenadiers he fought his way at the bayonet's point into the entrenchments held by General Rukavina's Austrian brigade.

Hard work by day and night among the Mantuan swamps had, however, affected even his iron strength. He was attacked by a malarial fever and had to go into hospital at Brescia. He arrived there on 26 July. The city was held by only three companies of French infantry. Suddenly the veteran general Wurmser, who had taken over the command of the Austrian army, concentrated in the Tyrol for the relief of Mantua, sent two strong columns pouring down into northern Italy. Wurmser led the main force on the left. Quosdanovich, on the right, marched to the westward of Lake Garda, and surprised Brescia on 30 July. Murat was made prisoner, but a few days later we find him a free man at Verona. Thence, on 8 August, he wrote to Carnot, the Minister of War :—

'A burning fever had forced me to leave the army in order to restore my health. I had been four days at Brescia when the place was surprised by the enemy, who made me a prisoner of war. It is the first great misfortune I have experienced in my life. I have been unable to share the dangers of my comrades in arms during these glorious days. You will understand how much I regret it. But, notwithstanding my pledged word, I have not left the commander-in-chief, the brave Bonaparte.'

'Notwithstanding my pledged word—*malgré ma parole donnée*'—the expression suggests that Murat had regained his freedom by breaking a parole given to the Austrians, who, doubtless, thought they had to deal with an invalided officer, who would have no eager desire to be in the saddle again. But Murat had few scruples (though before the Committee of Public Safety he had boasted of never having departed from the 'straight path of virtue'), and he had an iron constitution that quickly shook off the fever. Two days after he wrote to Carnot he was hard at work again.

The ' glorious days ' he had missed while he was ill and a prisoner were those in which, within a week, Bonaparte had inflicted blow after blow on the enemy. He had temporarily raised the siege of Mantua, concentrated his forces and fallen on Quosdanovich and the Austrian right divided from Wurmser by the Lake of Garda, retaken Brescia, defeated Quosdanovich at Lonato and Desenzano, and driven him back into the Alps. Meanwhile Wurmser had got into touch with Mantua and crossed the Mincio. Bonaparte turned back upon him, beat him at Castiglione and drove him over the river and back into the Tyrol. By the end of the week Mantua was again blockaded. No wonder Murat dreamed regretfully of what he might have done in this swift succession of victories.

On 10 August he was reconnoitring with a cavalry column north of Brescia. In the following week he was at the head of a flying column—one hundred horsemen, two guns, and a battalion of infantry—disarming the district of Casal Maggiore, which had risen in insurrection when the Austrians advanced. A fine of a million of francs was levied on the district. The leaders of the rising were tried by court martial and shot. The church bells that had rung the tocsin were taken from the campanili and sent to Alessandria to be cast into field-pieces.

In the first days of September Murat was in temporary command of the fortress of Verona, where he forced the Venetian authorities to hand over to him all the supplies in their magazines. Both parties were freely violating the neutrality of the Venetian territories, and the Republic, now in its last days of helpless decrepitude, was soon to come to an inglorious end. On the evening of 3 September Murat, having handed over the garrison command at Verona to General Kilmaine, hurried off to join the army under Masséna that was marching into the Tyrol.

On the 5th Masséna occupied Trent, and Murat was engaged in the pursuit of Wurmser's rearguard to the eastward.

# THE CAMPAIGN OF ITALY 27

The Austrians made a stand at the village of Lavis on the river Avisio. The infantry stormed the bridge while Murat led the 10th Chasseurs through the river by a ford, each horseman carrying across an infantryman behind him on his horse. Wurmser, after abandoning Trent, had doubled back by the Brenta valley, marching once more to the relief of Mantua. Masséna pressed after him, and Bonaparte headed him off. Dubois, who commanded Masséna's cavalry, was killed at the battle of Roveredo in the gorges of the upper Brenta. Murat took his place; and on 8 September, when Wurmser was defeated at Bassano, led one of the decisive charges of the day. The Austrian general succeeded in reaching Mantua with the debris of his army. The blockade had been partly raised during Wurmser's dash through the Venetian territory. As the French closed in upon the place again, there was some skirmishing with the Austrians, and in an action at San Giorgio, on 15 September, Murat, while leading a successful charge, was slightly wounded—the first wound he received in action.

Having for the second time defeated an attempt to relieve Mantua and reformed the blockade, Bonaparte proceeded to reorganise his army. The cavalry was formed into two strong brigades under the supreme command of General Kilmaine. General Beaumont was given the first brigade, which was attached to the force before Mantua. General Murat was given the second, 'destined for the active operations of the army.'

The earlier biographers of Murat speak of the months that followed as a time when he had almost fallen 'into disgrace' with Bonaparte. They build up various theories to account for this state of things, some of them having recourse to the ready explanation that Bonaparte had heard rumours of his aide-de-camp having tried to be more than friendly with Josephine during the hurried visit to Paris after the armistice with Sardinia, and was anxious to keep him at a distance now that the lady had come to northern Italy. The whole supposition is quite gratuitous. The theories of Murat's 'disgrace' are partly the result of exaggerations as to his relations with Bonaparte since

Vendémiaire and in the first stages of the campaign of Italy. Murat was one of many brilliant and ambitious officers whom Bonaparte had gathered round him and used freely for his own purposes. He had not yet been admitted to the inmost circle, and consequently there was no sign of ill will or suspicion on Bonaparte's side if he kept the young brigadier-general employed for a while in ordinary work, and did not push him forward by exceptional promotions over the heads of older men, It is, however, quite possible that Murat was disappointed at being placed under Kilmaine's orders, and after the rapid rush of promotion that had fallen to his lot was impatient at not having the rank of general of division immediately offered to him. But he had risen fast enough to satisfy any ordinary ambition, and the subordination to Kilmaine was more nominal than real. The older general was almost immediately given the direction of the blockade of Mantua, and directly commanded General Beaumont's cavalry attached to the besieging force. Murat, with the second brigade, was either acting independently or attached for the time being to headquarters or to one of the generals commanding a considerable force of all arms. He had nothing to complain of.

A little later we find him in correspondence with the Director Barras, whom he had seen several times during his last visit to Paris. In one of these letters (19 Frimaire, an V, December 9, 1796), he grumbles a little, and harks back to his old revolutionary style, perhaps in the hope of thereby assuring Barras of his sound Republicanism, and so gaining his interest for a request he had made to be employed for a while in the capital. He had suggested that he might be given the command of the Guard assigned to the Directory. This would enable him to push his fortunes with the ruling powers in Paris, and prepare the way for independent command in the field. He had not foresight enough to recognise that Bonaparte, not Barras, was the man of the future.

'Things are going well here,' he wrote, ' but I can hardly believe that the Directory is not mistaken as to the principles of a number of persons whom the War Minister employs with the army. Here the talk is all of Monsieur de —— and the Baron de —— and the Comte de ——, and this in circles frequented by officers of high rank. *Je me donne à tous les diables.*' It is not easy to find an English equivalent for the last phrase. Murat swears like a trooper at the whole business to express his disgust for such aristocratic ways of talking. The supporters of the ' disgrace ' theory imagine that Bonaparte knew of this correspondence. There is no reason to suppose he did. Two years later when, with Murat's zealous assistance, he had turned on Barras, the ex-Director thought these pro-Republican letters had been written by Murat in order to mislead him and make a fool of him, with Bonaparte's consent and knowledge. This also is a baseless theory. Murat was simply playing his own game, and long before the next two years were over knew that Bonaparte, not Barras, was the man who would be useful to him.

At the end of September his cavalry brigade was attached to Masséna's corps, which was holding the western portion of the Venetian territory in order to cover the investment of Mantua against an Austrian advance in that direction. He joined Masséna's headquarters at Bassano. There were no great events till November, when Alvinzi came down from the Alps with a third Austrian army to attempt the relief of Mantua, while another army, under Davidovich, reoccupied Trent and advanced by the Lake of Garda. Napoleon drew in his outlying detachments, defeated Alvinzi at Arcola before the Trent column was in touch with him, and then drove Davidovich back into the Tyrol. The writers who hold that all this time Bonaparte was keeping Murat at arm's length, and that the young general was under a cloud of semi-disgrace, point out that nothing is heard of him during the November campaign, but the recent publication of the Murat papers gives us at least one document to show once more how misleading the negative argument can be in historical matters. For on 24 November we find Bonaparte not only writing directly to Murat but also inviting him to come to his headquarters before Mantua. ' Go to Porto Legnago,' writes Bonaparte, ' and reconnoitre the force and position of the enemy on the roads to Lonigo, Colonia, and Padua. After this you will join me during the night at Rombello, where I shall be on my way to inspect the blockade of Mantua.'

In December Murat was attached with his brigade to Augereau's corps. In January 1797, when the Austrians, under Alvinzi and Bajalich, made their fourth and last unsuccessful attempt to relieve Mantua, Murat was employed in a delicate and important operation planned by Bonaparte himself. Till the publication of the Murat papers it was thought that this bold stroke was due entirely to his own initiative, but a long letter from Bonaparte to Murat, dated 13 January, describes the plan of operations in detail, and incidentally shows how thoroughly his commander-in-chief relied upon him to deal with a main feature of his general scheme for crushing Alvinzi.

The main Austrian army was coming down from the Alps by the road that follows the Val Lagarina, a few miles east of the shore of Garda, and roughly parallel to it. Joubert held the snow and ice-covered plateau of Rivoli commanding the narrow outlet of the valley from the hill country. On 13 January Alvinzi was beginning to press him hard, and Bonaparte was hurrying to his aid with Masséna and Rey's corps. Murat had been attached to Rey's corps, but was then commanding a small detached force of cavalry and infantry with two guns, watching the western side of the lake near Salo. Bonaparte sent him, on the 13th, a detailed order for a bold stroke against the Austrian flank and rear, an enterprise which could only be entrusted to a man of reckless courage. The French had collected all the boats on the lake at its southern end, and had armed some of them as gunboats at Peschiera. Bonaparte directs Murat immediately, on receipt of his letter, to send some one to make sure that there was no important Austrian force within striking distance west of the lake. He tells him he does not think that there is any. This being verified, he is to send all his cavalry to make a forced march round the south end of the lake to join the main army. Three hours

## THE CAMPAIGN OF ITALY 31

after midnight he is to embark his two guns and all his infantry in a flotilla of boats, which is placed at his disposal. He is to cross the lake in the darkness, and at dawn disembark at some point north of Torre on the eastern shore, march into the hills and take up a position in the Austrian rear. The gunboats from Peschiera will go out and help him by threatening various points on the east shore, so as to mislead the enemy. A hundred pioneers will be sent in boats to join him, and will take with them a hundred extra tools, so that Murat, 'after working round the enemy and cannonading his flank, can entrench himself.' Bonaparte expresses the hope that he will secure plenty of prisoners. He tells him that one of his battalions, the carbineers of the 11th demi-brigade, know the ground, from earlier experience during the war. If by any mishap he fails to land in the enemy's rear, he is to try to land lower down the lake and join the left of the main French attack.

Bonaparte had rightly chosen his man. Murat crossed the lake in the night, boldly threw himself into the hills north of the Austrian attack, and after seriously alarming the enemy by opening with his two guns from this unexpected quarter, cut off the retreat of some thousands of men and made them prisoners as the Austrians gave way before Masséna's furious onset from the south. Bonaparte, in his report, paid a high tribute to the brilliant service that Murat had done him.

After the battle of Rivoli Murat returned to Salo. On 26 January he was placed under Joubert's orders, and directed to co-operate with him in an advance into the Tyrol to reoccupy Trent. On the 27th he embarked an infantry brigade and some light artillery on the lake and landed them at Torbola near its head. Thence, while Joubert advanced by the main road to Trent, Murat followed a bad mountain road up the valley of the Sarca from the head of the Lake of Garda by Arco and Vezzano, this movement enabling him to come down on the right rear of the Austrian force covering Trent against Joubert's advance on the main road. The Austrian defence collapsed. Joubert and Murat marched into Trent, and then took up a position to protect it against any attempt of the enemy to recover the place.

On 3 February Mantua had at last surrendered. Bonaparte had now all his army at liberty for active operations, and received reinforcements through the Alpine passes from Moreau's army in Germany. He was going to abandon the defensive and march on Vienna through the Venetian territory and the eastern Alps. When all was ready he summoned Murat from Trent to act with his advanced guard in the coming campaign. He joined the main army on 12 March at Castelfranco on the Brenta, bringing with him two regiments of cavalry and two guns, and was attached to Bernadotte's division, which led the advance of the main column under Masséna.

The best of the Austrian generals, the Archduke Charles, was opposed to Bonaparte. He tried in vain to bar his advance at the crossings of the Venetian rivers. The line of the Piave was forced on the 14th; the Tagliamento on the 16th: and the Isonzo on the 18th—three victories in a week; and on each occasion Murat took his full share in the fighting, being specially mentioned by Bonaparte for his conduct at the passage of the Isonzo. Bernadotte and Murat were not engaged in the fighting during the advance into the Carinthian Alps. Early in April the Archduke's army was reduced to the utmost extremity, and Austria was suing for peace.

During the negotiations Bonaparte, after sending a column to occupy Venice, established his headquarters at the château of Mombello near Milan, where Murat was with him for a while, and where, for the first time, he saw his future wife, Caroline Bonaparte. The victorious general was holding something not unlike a royal court at Mombello. The courtiers were a crowd of generals and staff officers, French, German, and Austrian diplomatists, envoys from the cities of Italy, and as an inner circle the Bonaparte family—Napoleon's mother, plain-spoken Madame Letizia, marvelling at the greatness of her son, his brother Joseph affecting

## THE CAMPAIGN OF ITALY 33

the airs of a statesman and soon to be ambassador at Rome ; Captain Louis Bonaparte recovering from an illness and inclined to talk poetry ; little Jerome Bonaparte, having a holiday from his Paris school with his school-fellow Eugene Beauharnais, the future Viceroy of Italy ; the three sisters, Elisa, lately married to the Corsican Major Bacciochi, a bad match which the family regretted ; Pauline, engaged to General Leclerc, and Caroline, still free and using her freedom in a series of reckless flirtations. Josephine was a graceful hostess, already taking the airs of a queen.

There was a succession of banquets and fêtes. Murat made his appearance at some of them. His stay at Mombello was never prolonged. He was officially still attached to Bernadotte's division which was stationed in Udine in the Venetian territory. But he had liberal leave of absence and spent most of it at Brescia, the place where he had had the misfortune of falling into the hands of the Austrians the year before. A letter of Bonaparte's, addressed to him in June, throws light on the attraction that kept him at Brescia, and also indicates a previous correspondence in which the commander-in-chief had suggested that there was work for him to do in Udine, and Murat had replied by asking if his chief had conceived an unfavourable opinion of him, apparently because there had been a hint that he was wasting his time. Bonaparte replies that he knows how to value Murat's ' military talents, courage and zeal, and has no idea that can be in the least degree unfavourable to him,' but he adds, ' I thought you would be more useful with your division than with your mistress at Brescia.' It was a reproof, not dictated by any moral considerations, of which Bonaparte then and later thought very little, but from the military commander's point of view. Bonaparte, even in the later days when he was Napoleon, had often to regret that this selfish weakness of his great cavalry leader resulted in neglect of duty. ' How many blunders Murat has committed,' he once exclaimed, ' through his way of looking for his headquarters in some château where he could meet women.' Desaix, in his journal of the campaign of 1797, noted that

c

the attraction for Murat at Brescia was a certain Madame Ruga, the wife of a local lawyer. Other gossip pointed to the Countess Gerardi, a sister of the Italian general Lechi, said to have been then the most beautiful woman in Lombardy.

A letter of introduction given to him by Josephine shows that Murat was at Mombello in the beginning of August and then made a flying visit to Rome. He can only have been there a few days, for at the beginning of September Bonaparte entrusted him with a military mission in Switzerland. The people of the Val Tellina, in the south of the canton of Grisons, had revolted and demanded the incorporation of their territory in the newly created Cisalpine Republic. There was a state of civil war in the valley, and the authorities of the Grisons had sent an envoy to Bonaparte at Milan asking him to act as arbitrator in the dispute, and meanwhile restore order in the Val Tellina. On 9 September Bonaparte issued a warning to both parties to desist from all hostilities, directing them to send deputies to state their case at Milan, and adding that in order to restore peace in the valley he was sending over the frontier a column of troops under General Murat. All disturbers of order would be arrested and severely punished. Murat moved up to Edolo on the borders of the ValTellina, with a mixed force of cavalry and infantry. He kept strictly to his mission of preserving order, and refused to hear anything of the dispute between the rival parties. That had been referred to Bonaparte, who, early in October, settled it by annexing the Val Tellina to the Cisalpine Republic.

On the eve of his advance to Edolo Murat had found time for one more visit to Brescia. There is a letter to his brother, dated from that place on 18 September, and signed ' J. Murat, le Général commandant une colonne mobile marchant en Valteline.' He complains bitterly of not having heard from him for months, and suggests that the news of his own exploits might have drawn a letter from home :—

'Six months have gone by. Your brother has faced the greatest dangers ; he has been wounded ; the public papers have eulogized him ; and you remain silent and unaffected alike by my glory and by the perils that may deprive my relatives of me. Let me tell you that I have reason to be annoyed with you, but I will pardon you everything if you still love your brother and if you are worthy of him.'

What a piece of characteristic self-sufficient vanity! He goes on to say that he hopes the coming peace will enable him to return home. He has just come from Rome, and is about to start on another expedition.

That expedition, the police duty in the Val Tellina, ended on 4 October. He had then withdrawn his brigade to Brescia and sent in his report to the commander-in-chief. Bonaparte acknowledges it in a brief note in which he says : ' I am satisfied with what you have done in the Val Tellina.' On the same day (4 October) Berthier, the chief of the staff, sends him an order to leave Brescia and take command at Treviso of the 3rd Brigade of the 1st Cavalry Division (19th Chasseurs and 5th Dragoons).

The Treaty of Campo Formio was signed on 17 October, certain points being reserved for settlement by a congress of diplomatists to be held at Rastatt in the Rhineland, where Napoleon was to be present. His progress to the congress and his reception there were a triumph. ' On 17 November,' says Dr. Max Lenz,[1] ' he began his journey to the Rhine. Wherever he appeared in Savoy, in Switzerland, he was received with public demonstrations ; he turned his attention to setting affairs in order, and negotiated and intrigued with rival parties that vied with each other in bringing their interests before him. On 25 November, before the arrival of the Emperor's envoy, he made his entry into Rastatt in a carriage drawn by eight horses, and was surrounded, courted by all the prominent men there as if he were Destiny itself. As soon as the Emperor's envoys arrived, with Cobenzl again at their head, a settlement was arrived at on 1 December. . . . The protocol was hardly signed when Napoleon, acting on the invitation of the Directory, started for Paris.'

[1] *Napoleon, a Biographical Study*, by Dr. Max Lenz, translated from the German by Frederic Whyte, p. 134.

The biographers of Murat, influenced by the 'disgrace' theory, say that he was not allowed to share his master's triumph. Chavanon and St. Yves quote a letter of Bonaparte's, dated 12 November, 1797, in which he says that he is sending General Murat on in advance to Rastatt, and then they go on to say: 'However it was not Murat but Auguste de Colbert who was actually sent as Bonaparte's forerunner to Rastatt. One may see here an indication of fresh disfavour, due perhaps to the same causes as the first. And while Lannes, Marmont, Bourrienne, Duroc, La Valette, were on their travels sharing the triumphs of their master, Murat was left for seven months dallying in Italy.'[1] In the same way M. Frédéric Masson, after speaking of Murat as in permanent disfavour with Bonaparte and probably employed in the Val Tellina only to keep him away from Milan, says: 'What is certain is that he did not go with Napoleon either to Rastatt or Paris; he remained with the army of Italy.'[2] All these theories are dissipated by one brief dispatch of Napoleon's, published in the Murat correspondence, and reproduced in facsimile as an illustration.[3] It was written on the eve of Bonaparte's departure from Milan and shows that Murat had actually preceded him. Here it is:—

'HEADQUARTERS, MILAN,
'The 26th Brumaire, year VI of the
'Republic, One and Indivisible (i.e. *Nov.* 16, 1797).

'Bonaparte, Commander-in-Chief of the Army of Italy, to General Murat.

'I inform you, Citizen General, that I start to-morrow morning at nine o'clock to proceed to Rastatt.

'Give this information to the French plenipotentiaries and those of the Emperor, who, I imagine, are impatiently awaiting me.                                                        BONAPARTE

'To Brigadier-General Murat
    at Rastatt.'

Murat stood high in the good graces of his commander. He

---

[1] Chavanon and St. Yves, *Joachim Murat*, p. 30.
[2] F. Masson, *Napoleon et sa Famille*, vol. i. pp. 315, 316.
[3] *Lettres et Documents pour servir à l'histoire de Joachim Murat*, publiés par S. A. le Prince Murat (1908), vol. i. pp. 20, 21.

## THE CAMPAIGN OF ITALY

not only shared the triumph of Rastatt but he accompanied Bonaparte to Paris. But he rejoined the army of Italy in time to take part in Berthier's invasion of the Papal States in February 1798.

After the occupation of Rome and the proclamation of the Roman Republic on 15 February, Murat was employed at the end of the same month in repressing a rising of armed peasants who objected to the new liberty forced on them at the bayonet's point. Leaving Rome on 27 February at the head of a flying column he drove the insurgent bands back on Albano, sacked the country house of the Popes at Castel Gandolfo, blew in the gate of Albano, and stormed the town with the bayonet, killing some five hundred of the 'rebels,' and then marched on Velletri, which the fate of Albano cowed into surrender without fighting. It was an inglorious warfare, recalling that of the *Chasseurs-braconniers*. He was officially thanked for his services. There is no record of his part in the plunder.

This episode closed his career with the army of Italy. In two years he had had experience of all kinds of warfare. He had commanded cavalry, infantry and small mixed forces of all arms. He had distinguished himself in a long succession of engagements and won his rank as general. Garrison duty in the Roman States and battues of half-armed peasants gave him no outlook for further progress. But now there came rumours that an expedition, long in preparation, was about to sail from Toulon, with Bonaparte in command and a career of conquest in the East for its mission. Murat was to have a place in the romantic enterprise.

## CHAPTER III

### EGYPT AND SYRIA

#### 1798-1799

A LETTER from Berthier, dated at the headquarters of the army of Italy at Milan on 11 March, 1798, informed Murat that ' by order of the Directory ' he was to travel at once post-haste to join him there, ' for an important object ' that would not admit of delay. He would find further orders on his arrival there. These further orders were contained in a note from Berthier, dated ' Headquarters, Genoa, 15 March,' telling Murat to come on to Genoa, where he would be attached to the division of General Baraguay d'Hilliers, and command a brigade of dragoons (14th and 18th regiments), and would be under the supreme command of General Bonaparte in the ' great expedition.' He was warned to keep this last information secret.

Passing through Milan in the third week of April he was presented with a magnificent sword sent him by the provisional government of Brescia, in memory of his frequent visits to their city. He had to wait some weeks at Genoa, for Nelson was watching Toulon so closely that the main body of the ' great expedition ' could not be put to sea. On 28 April the contingent at Genoa was at last embarked, and the transports slipped along the coast and anchored under the batteries of Hyères. There on 1 May came orders to return to Genoa, and disembark. There were rumours of trouble with Austria, and the ' great expedition ' might be deferred indefinitely. But a fortnight later there was a hurried re-embarkation. A strong gale from the north was driving off Nelson from the coast, but it would be a fair wind for the expedition. The main convoy from Toulon, under General Bonaparte and Admiral Brueys, sailed on the 19th. The transports from Genoa joined it at sea, and the bloodless conquest of Malta, surrendered by the knights without even a show of resistance, was the first exploit of the ' great expedition.'

Murat was ill and in bad spirits at Malta. Perhaps the voyage in the crowded transport had something to do with it. From the island he wrote to his father (15 June 1798) :—

' Malta is ours. The tricolour is flying on the ramparts of the city. We are to sail in two or three days, I do not know where, but I presume it is for Egypt. My health is not of the best. That is why I am going to ask for leave to go back to you. This will be the only way to set me up again. I have reason to believe it will be granted to me. The country is very hot, and I shall never be able to stand it. The mail is just going, and I have only time to embrace you. Assure my dear mother of all my tender love and my desire to see her and the rest of the family. Good-bye and a thousand good wishes for all. The sea did not make me sick. I am anxious to know if my little nephew has started for Paris.—Your most devoted son,

J. MURAT'

The 'little nephew' was the eldest son of his brother Pierre, for whose education he was providing. By the same post he wrote to Barras, saying he was about to ask for leave of absence.

But he changed his mind, and sailed eastwards with the expedition, which sighted Alexandria on 1 July. Murat took no part in the capture of the city, and the whole of his cavalry brigade was not landed till the 4th. On the 5th it was attached to General Dugua's division. On the 6th Dugua left Alexandria to march on Rosetta by the sandy strip of land that lies between Aboukir Bay and the lagoons of the Delta. Murat's dragoons formed the advanced guard. There were not enough horses to mount them all, and some of them had to tramp wearily on foot.

It was a trying march in the hot sand under the July sun. The men suffered terribly from thirst and heat, and after the first hour numbers fell exhausted by the desert track. Notwithstanding the fears he had expressed at Malta, Murat bore the trying experience well. Pushing on with the mounted men of the 14th Dragoons he occupied the handful of huts that formed the village of Aboukir and seized the fort on the point. Its garrison was a few watchmen, and its armament eighteen old guns of various calibres, mostly without carriages.

Next day the march was continued. There was considerable delay in ferrying the men over a broad cutting in the isthmus, through which the sea ran into the wide lagoon of Lake Edku. At first only some small native craft were available, but then some boats arrived from the fleet. Leaving Dugua's infantry to cross slowly and bivouac on the further side, Murat pushed on with the dragoons and occupied the town of Rosetta without firing a shot, the Mameluke Bey who commanded there having fled on his approach.

The rest of the column came in next day, and then Dugua marched up the bank of the Nile, leaving at Rosetta a garrison formed of Murat's unmounted men, and some invalided soldiers under Major St. Faust. Murat, in the advance up the Nile, again commanded the advanced guard now made up of his dragoons and a battalion of light infantry. The march was by the tracks through the cultivated land and under the shade of the endless palm plantations that fringe the river. On 10 July the column formed a junction at Er Ramaniyeh with the main body under Bonaparte, which had marched from Alexandria by way of Damanhour.

During the advance on Cairo Murat's brigade of dragoons remained attached to Dugua's division. It now formed the rearguard, and had the task of collecting stragglers and exhausted men and bringing them on to the army with the transport. Although the conditions of the march were better than those of the tramp across the sands to Rosetta, the men, overloaded and dressed in heavy belted uniforms fit only for Europe, suffered terribly. Some even committed suicide by drowning themselves in the river. When the Mameluke cavalry showed themselves the prospect of fighting helped to revive the spirit of the men. But the enemy steadily fell back till at last Cairo came in sight, with the great mosque crowning its citadel and the pyramids cutting the desert horizon. At the village of Embabeh the Mamelukes had formed an entrenched camp, and in front of it, on 21 July, the decisive 'Battle of the Pyramids' was fought.

On the morning of the battle Murat had a narrow escape. Soon after sunrise he had ridden out to reconnoitre the enemy's camp, accompanied only by Colonel Laugier, and a dragoon orderly. As the Mamelukes had not thrown out any outpost line he was able to come within half a mile of the camp. There he halted watching with interested curiosity the novel scene presented by the Eastern encampment, busy with preparations for battle. Suddenly some forty spearmen came galloping towards him. Had Murat and his friends tried to escape by trusting to the speed of their horses they would most likely have been ridden down by the better-mounted Arabs. Laugier had an inspiration. On his suggestion the three men, without showing any agitation, rode slowly towards a dense grove of palms. The Mamelukes at once concluded that the palm grove must be held by the French, and that Murat and his companions were trying to lure them into an ambush. They pulled bridle and turned back to the camp. As soon as they had passed the grove the three Frenchmen put spurs to their horses and rejoined their friends.

During the battle Murat was with Dugua's division, in the centre of which Bonaparte had posted himself. The division was not seriously engaged, the headlong charge of the Mamelukes breaking to pieces on the squares of Desaix and Reynier's divisions. Cairo was occupied as the result of the victory. The Mamelukes had divided, one portion of them under Murad Bey retiring into upper Egypt, pursued by a column under Desaix. The rest of them, under Ibrahim

Bey, retreated into the Syrian desert. Murat was on 27 July appointed Governor of the province of Kelioub,[1] north of Cairo in the Delta, the force assigned to him for keeping order and enforcing the payment of contributions from the villages being a battalion of infantry, twenty-five cavalry, and a piece of light artillery.

Murat had hardly begun the organization of his governorship, when news came that Ibrahim Bey was raiding towards Cairo. The Mameluke leader advanced along the south-eastern side of the Delta, keeping close to the edge of the desert, where he could always find a refuge from pursuit. On 5 August Ibrahim was in action with General Leclerc's force which covered Cairo on the north-east side. The fight took place at El-Khangah (El-Khânqâ), a few miles east of Kelioub. Murat heard the fire of the artillery and at once prepared to 'march to the cannon,' sending a message to Bonaparte at Cairo asking for reinforcements. Ibrahim drew off before Murat's arrival, but a pursuit by a large force was at once organized and for some days Ibrahim's Mamelukes had to retire along the Syrian caravan track followed up by two columns of infantry, with artillery, commanded the right column by Reynier and the left by Dugua, with a cavalry brigade under Murat and Leclerc marching at first between them and then in advance. The route was by Koraïm (El-Quaraïm) along the edge of the desert towards Salheyeh (Es-Sâlihîya). There were frequent skirmishes on the way, but after their experience of the deadly fire that had poured from the bayonet-bristling squares at 'the Pyramids' the Mamelukes had no intention of charging formed bodies of French troops. The most serious engagement was an unsuccessful attempt of Murat and Leclerc to cut off and capture the enemy's convoy of loaded camels. It led to some hand-to-hand cavalry fighting, in which the Mamelukes only gave way after they had gained time for the convoy to disappear in the wilderness of arid sands alternating with brackish swamps and lagoons, through

---

[1] Qalyûb on the modern official maps—now an important railway junction.

which the caravan track then ran. It was, however, counted a success that Ibrahim had been driven out of Egypt, and for deeds of personal valour in the convoy fight Murat was specially mentioned by Bonaparte in his report to the Directory.

The campaign against Ibrahim had lasted little more than a week. Murat was back at Kelioub on 16 August, and was soon able to report that he was 'in the enjoyment of perfect peace' with his province nearly organized, and the taxes from the villages coming in regularly. He was able to obtain a large number of Arab horses as remounts for the cavalry, and at the end of the month (29 August) Bonaparte wrote that he 'was extremely pleased with his conduct.'

In September the tranquillity of the Kelioub district was interrupted by the appearance of a body of Mameluke raiders, who were joined by some of the Arabs of the neighbourhood and formed a strong band, which made itself master of several villages along the Nile. After some skirmishing Murat and General Lanusse, in the last week of the month, arranged an expedition to break them up. Two columns each of five hundred infantry marched on the village of Dondeh, while a native boat, improvised into a gunboat by mounting four small cannon on her decks, went down the river, and entering a wide irrigation canal took up a position to cut their easiest line of retreat. Murat's column had a difficult march as many irrigation channels had to be passed, some by improvised bridges, some by fording the muddy water. It came up to the men's waists, and as they waded through it they held their muskets and cartridge boxes over their heads. The enemy was at last found in position near the village of Dondeh surrounded by inundations formed by breaking the dykes of the canals. Murat led a bayonet charge through the mud and water, and the enemy broke before his onset and lost heavily in the pursuit. Ten thousand sheep collected by the raiders and a number of good horses were among the spoils of the victory, which cost the French only four men wounded.

On the first of August Nelson had appeared before Alexandria. At sunset that evening he had swept into Aboukir Bay and destroyed the fleet of Admiral Brueys at its anchors, and then established a blockade of the coast. The ' Battle of the Nile ' had completely changed the situation by cutting the French army in Egypt off from France, and Bonaparte expected that soon a Turkish army would invade the country under the protection of Nelson's fleet. At the end of October Murat was sent to inspect the defences of the coast district, and he visited Rosetta and Alexandria. From the latter place he made a successful expedition to break up a ' rebel ' gathering at Damanhour.

During his visit to Alexandria he sent a short letter home by one of the ships that from time to time ran the blockade. It is dated 6 November, 1798, and addressed to his father :—

' I am still alive, dear father, and in the best of health. I am grieved at having no news from you. It is the only trouble I have to endure. I am not able to give you any detailed news, because I am not sure that Messieurs les Anglais will be so good as to let this letter go through. I hope to tell you everything on my return, which, however, will I hope not be long deferred. Embrace my dear mother, and tell her that what I long for most is to see her, to embrace her, and forget in her arms all the fatigues I suffer. Good-bye. Embrace my brothers and sisters for me, and believe me for life your good son,     J. MURAT

' P.S.—We have just heard a report that the Grand Turk has declared war against us. I don't believe a bit of it. However, we are prepared for all events. We do not get any news from France. Send my little nephew to Paris, if he has not gone there already.'

In the first month of the new year Murat was employed with a flying column breaking up hostile gatherings in the Delta, and scored two more successes on 11 and 20 January, 1799. Bonaparte thanked him by making him a present of a house in Cairo ' as an extra reward for services rendered during the campaign, and in compensation for the expenses incurred in it.'

The news that the ' Grand Turk ' was about to attempt

the recovery of Egypt was true. A Turkish army was assembling in Syria, and Bonaparte decided to anticipate the attack by invading that country. He gave Murat the command of the cavalry in the Syrian expedition when he marched from Cairo on 10 February.

Murat's cavalry was a force of only nine hundred men formed of detachments from all the mounted corps in the army of the East, with a battery of six horse artillery guns. With a part of this force he rode at the head of Kleber's advanced guard during the march. On 25 February the army was before Gaza. Between Bonaparte and the town there were six thousand Turkish infantry and a mass of some six thousand more Mameluke, Arab, and Albanian horsemen. When the French formed for battle Murat found his handful of cavalry opposed to this huge force of mounted irregulars, and in order to compensate in some degree for the disparity of numbers the infantry of Lannes was sent to support him.

The Mamelukes charged boldly and drove in the three foremost French squadrons, but Murat flung the rest of his sabres on their flank, while on the other side Lannes fired into them at close range. The Mamelukes gave way, pursued by Murat. Neither the Arabs nor the Albanians showed any determined front, and soon the whole six thousand were in flight. The enemy's infantry gave way as promptly before the advance of Bonaparte and Kleber with the French battalions. They fled so fast that very few were either killed or captured in the pursuit. The result of the victory was the immediate surrender of Gaza.

After four days' rest there Bonaparte marched on Jaffa and took it by assault. He then marched northwards along the coast till his advance was stopped by the determined resistance made by Djezzar Pasha's Turkish garrison and Sidney Smith's sailors at Acre.

During the siege Murat was employed in reconnaissances and raids in northern Palestine. In a first expedition he occupied the village of Shefa Amr, in the hills ten miles south-east of Acre, where Djezzar had a splendid palace which was converted into a military hospital. Then, on rumours that the Pasha of Damascus was assembling an army to raise the siege, he was sent into the hills with a column composed of 200 cavalry, 500 infantry and 2 guns. He was to place a garrison at the ruined castle of Safed, a fortress built by the Crusaders on a bold crag commanding the road from Acre to the crossing of the upper Jordan at Jisr Benât Yâcûb (the Bridge of Jacob's daughters), then to reconnoitre as far as the Jordan and discover if the Pasha of Damascus showed any signs of activity in that direction. The small Turkish garrison of Safed made a prompt retreat on Murat's approach, and he marched as far as the Jordan, sent out scouting parties on the further side of the river and satisfied himself that all was quiet in that direction ; then leaving a small garrison at Safed, he rejoined the army before Acre, after an absence of a fortnight.

He had strictly obeyed his orders, but he had not pushed his investigations far enough, and he had been further handicapped by the hostility of the people, who were all in a conspiracy of silence as to the movements of the Pasha. He ought to have placed a permanent post at the Jordan crossing, pushed at least one bold reconnaissance far on the further side, and used money freely to obtain the help of native spies. Had he done so he would have learned that while he was still at Safed the Damascus army was in full march southwards. Before he was back at Acre Junot, who held the district round Nazareth with a detached force, was fighting with the Turks, and Safed was closely blockaded by the enemy.

Bonaparte sent off Kleber's division to reinforce Junot at Nazareth, and dispatched Murat to the relief of Safed with a thousand infantry and a hundred dragoons.[1] Instead of marching directly on Safed Murat, leaving the camp before Acre on 14 April, arrived by a forced march through the hills in the afternoon of the next day at a point from which before sunrise on the 16th he was able to issue into the plain

---

[1] How the units of the French expedition had shrunk in numbers during a year of Eastern campaigning is shown by the fact that Murat's column of a thousand infantry was made up of no less than four regiments —the 4th Light Infantry and the 9th, 18th, and 55th of the Line.

between the hills of Safed and the Jordan. The dragoons galloped to seize the bridge over the river. The infantry formed in two squares moved out into the level ground. The enemy's cavalry charged them again and again, and for a while the two squares were like islands in the midst of a raging storm of horsemen. But their levelled bayonets and their steady fire beat off every attack, and at last the Turks broke, and the French, cheering wildly, advanced on the enemy's camp. It was taken almost without resistance. The son of the Pasha of Damascus had commanded the army, and his camp was a scene of oriental splendour that afforded a rich booty to the victors. They were enraged at seeing in front of the Turkish general's tent four severed heads stuck on spears—heads of Frenchmen captured in an unsuccessful sortie of the Safed garrison. The camp was plundered. What could not be removed was burned, and that evening the relieving force and the rescued garrison bivouacked in the red glare of blazing tents and huts.

Murat then marched southward by the shores of Gennesareth, occupied the city of Tiberias, and cut off numbers of the fugitives of the main Turkish army in flight from Kleber's victory of Mount Thabor.

After this success he returned to the lines before Acre and asked to be allowed to take his turn of duty in the trenches. On 6 May, in repulsing a sortie of the garrison, he had a narrow escape of being killed. His life was saved by his aide-de-camp, Auguste de Colbert, who was himself badly wounded in the hand-to-hand fight. Ten days later, after the failure of a last desperate assault, Bonaparte found himself compelled to raise the siege and begin his retreat southwards. 'Thousands of his best were left behind buried in the trenches and the galleries of the mines, and probably still more were carried off by fever following wounds and by pestilence in the hospitals.'[1]

Murat's cavalry, now greatly reduced in numbers, formed the rearguard during the retreat, which ended with the re-entry into Cairo on 14 June. He was then employed in

[1] Lenz's *Napoleon*, p. 161.

minor operations against bands of Mamelukes and insurgents in the Delta. But he was soon recalled from this irregular warfare for more serious business. On 12 July a strong Turkish army, escorted by Sir Sidney Smith's squadron, appeared in Aboukir Bay, disembarked at the village of the same name, and entrenched itself on the sandy peninsula on which it stands, with its flanks protected on both sides by the sea. Bonaparte was preparing to attack the invaders, and Murat was recalled to Cairo, where he was given the command of the vanguard of the little army assembled there.

Murat had under his immediate orders 2300 men, including a cavalry brigade formed of the 7th Hussars and 3rd and 14th Dragoons, General Destaing's infantry brigade and 4 guns. The rest of the army was made up of the division of Lannes (2700 men and 5 guns), and that of Lanusse (2400 men and 6 guns), in all 7400 men and 15 guns—less than the strength of a single division of the Imperial armies in coming days.

On 24 July the French came in sight of the Turkish lines. Saïd Mustapha Pasha, the commander of the expedition, had landed some eighteen thousand men. His camp was covered by two lines of entrenchments armed with artillery. The inner line had a high redoubt in its centre and its flanks ran down to the shore. The advanced line did not extend completely from the sea on its right to the lagoon of Lake Aboukir on its left. On the morning of the 25th the artillery of Lannes and Lanusse opened fire on the advanced line. Then suddenly Murat rode for the gap between its flank and the lake with his cavalry and horse artillery. As the infantry of Lannes and Destaing advanced to attack in front with the bayonet, Murat was on the flank and rear of the defences, unlimbering his guns and opening with case shot at close quarters. The Turkish line gave way, but the cavalry had cut off their retreat and charged them furiously as they fled. Within the first hour the whole line was in possession of the French. Of the enemy 1200 were prisoners, 1400 killed and wounded, and 5400 driven into the sea and drowned. Eighteen guns mounted on the entrenchment were

## EGYPT AND SYRIA

taken, and some fifty standards were collected as trophies —Eastern armies carry a large number of flags.

Then began the attack on the second or inner line. By occupying with his artillery a headland of the peninsula Bonaparte was able to bring an enfilading fire to bear on the extreme right of the Turkish works. The defenders threw back their right a little and thus opened a small gap, through which Murat charged with the six hundred sabres of his hussars and dragoons. He had to dash through a cross fire from the redoubt and the gunboats in the bay, but he penetrated into the enemy's lines, charged them in flank and rear, and as the infantry attack came into the works turned his cavalry upon the Turkish camp. In this last stage of the fight an incident occurred that is more common in fiction and poetry than matter-of-fact military history. The two leaders came into personal conflict. Murat found himself face to face with the Seraskier Saïd Mustapha Pasha. Both were wounded in the fight that followed, the Turk being disarmed by Murat, with the loss of two fingers taken off by a sword cut, but not before he had fired a pistol at the French general sending the bullet through his lower jaw from one side to the other. The seraskier was made prisoner and sent to Bonaparte. Murat roughly bandaged his jaw and would not go into hospital till the battle ended. Luckily for him the bullet was a small one. It had not injured the tongue, or even started out any of the teeth. His vigorous health enabled him to make a comparatively rapid recovery, all the more easily because he was in the best of spirits at the news that Bonaparte was giving him the chief credit for the success of Aboukir. The victory had been complete. Nearly the whole Turkish army had been killed, captured, or driven pell-mell into the sea. A handful of men, the remnant of eighteen thousand, were closely besieged in the fort of Aboukir. A hundred Turkish standards and thirty-two guns were taken, and among the captured cannon were found two field pieces of English make, presents from the British Government to the Sultan. Bonaparte, in a general order to the army, announced that

D

the 'English cannon' were to be presented to the cavalry brigade in recognition of its prowess, the guns were ordered to be inscribed with the words 'Bataille d'Aboukir,' and with the name of Murat, and the titles of the three regiments of his brigade (7th Hussars, and 3rd and 14th Dragoons).

In his report to the Directory Bonaparte wrote: 'The winning of the battle, which will have such an influence on the glory of the Republic, is due chiefly to General Murat. I ask you to grant this general the rank of general of division. His cavalry brigade has achieved the impossible.'

He had already promoted his enterprising cavalry leader, and Murat had received the provisional warrant of his new rank in the hospital on the very evening of the battle. It came in the form of an official communication from Berthier, as chief of Bonaparte's staff, with the heading, 'Promotion on the field of battle of General Murat to the rank of general of division,' and set forth that the commander-in-chief wished to recognize thereby the general's former services, but especially those he had rendered 'by contributing in the most brilliant manner to the glorious victory of Aboukir,' and added that the Minister of War had been informed of the appointment and asked to confirm it.

Three days later Murat was sufficiently recovered to dictate a long letter to his father from the hospital at Alexandria. He writes in the best of spirits. If the news of the victory has reached his home they will doubtless have heard of his wound. But he begs his father not to be alarmed. The surgeons say he will be well in a fortnight. There will be no permanent injury. When he comes back to Europe the fair ladies may think he is not quite as handsome, but he will be as enterprising as ever. He encloses a copy of eulogistic orders to the army reciting his services and his promotion. If his father needs help, as no remittance can be sent from Egypt, he tells him to apply to a friend who is his business man in Paris. He hopes soon to be home, and sends a thousand kisses and messages of affection to his mother. Then comes a message from the *chef de brigade* Bessières, who is in an hospital bed near him, and wishes to communi-

## EGYPT AND SYRIA

cate through the Murats with his own people at Preissac. Bessières has been wounded before the fort of Aboukir, but is doing well.

This time the long wished for return to France was near at hand. Bonaparte had news of the state into which the affairs of the Republic were drifting in Europe, and foresaw a crisis in which he would have more to gain by being in the centre of things in Paris, than isolated with the army of occupation in Egypt. The success won at Aboukir would enable him to return as a victor. He left Kleber in command of the army, and chose for the companions of his return voyage to France some of the most brilliant of his officers. Murat was one of this band of trusted adherents. In the last week of August, when he was nearly but not quite recovered from his wound, he was suddenly informed that he was to embark on a frigate in the harbour of Alexandria, to return home. He had only a few hours in which to arrange his affairs and make his preparations. On the night of 22 August, 1799, he sailed from Alexandria on board the frigate *Carrère*, commanded by Captain Dumanoir. Amongst the officers with him were Generals Marmont and Lannes. Another frigate, the *Muiron*, sailed in company, conveying Bonaparte, Berthier and a number of officers and civilians. Evading the English cruisers the two frigates reached Ajaccio on 30 September, and after a short stay there ran across to St. Raphael in the Bay of Fréjus, where they anchored on 9 October, after narrowly escaping capture by a British squadron.

Murat was back in France after a year and a half of absence. He was a general of division at thirty-two, with a record of service ending with the chief share in a decisive victory. Above all he was now in the inner circle of the ambitious soldier who was so soon to be the master of France.

## CHAPTER IV

BRUMAIRE—MARRIAGE TO CAROLINE BONAPARTE—MARENGO

1799-1800

FROM Fréjus Murat travelled directly to Paris, and arrived there showed no disposition to renew relations with his old correspondent, Barras, the chief of the Directory, for its days were numbered, and Murat was the ally of the coming man.

In the hurried preparations for the *coup d'état* of Brumaire four generals of the 'Army of the East,' Berthier, Lannes, Marmont, and Murat were employed in ascertaining the feelings and views of the officers stationed in and round Paris, and securing the support of those who responded favourably to the first cautious advances. Berthier dealt with the officers holding staff employment; Lannes those of the infantry, Marmont with the artillery officers, and Murat with the cavalry. He secured for Bonaparte the support of the three cavalry regiments then in garrison at Paris, the 21st Chasseurs à Cheval, and the 8th and 9th Dragoons. The 21st was his old regiment, which he had commanded against the street insurrection of Vendémiaire. The 8th and 9th had both been under Bonaparte in the army of Italy, and one of the colonels was Sebastiani, a Corsican devoted heart and soul to his fellow-countryman. On 19 October Murat's promotion to general of division was finally confirmed by the War Office.

On the 18 Brumaire—9 November—each of the four generals had invited eight or nine picked officers to breakfast with him. Duroc, the trusted aide-de-camp of General

Bonaparte, rode round to these gatherings, appeared for a few moments at the table, told the guests of the coming crisis and proposed that they should mount and join the general's staff. Horses had been provided and were waiting ready saddled somewhere near by. So at each halt Duroc collected a party of officers devoted to his master, and thus it was that when Bonaparte rode out to take command of the army of Paris he was escorted by a cavalcade of some fifty officers of rank whose names were already famous in the wars of the Republic.

That morning Murat was appointed to the command of the cavalry in the capital, and personally directed the mounted troops that kept order round the place of assembly of the Chambers in Paris, while the first stage of intended revolution was being carried out—the adjournment to St. Cloud, the appointment of General Bonaparte to the command of the army of Paris with orders to ' protect ' the meeting at St. Cloud, the forced resignation of Barras, and the arrest of the two other Directors.

In the next day's proceedings at St. Cloud Murat played a very prominent part. He was beside Napoleon when he came out of the Hall of the Five Hundred, complaining that he had been insulted and his life threatened. Murat not only encouraged him to a further effort, but helped him to rouse the soldiers to indignant hostility against the Assembly. When after Lucien Bonaparte had resigned his presidency and the Five Hundred were declaring Napoleon an outlaw, Murat and Leclerc were the two officers who entered the hall, sword in hand, at the head of Frégeville's grenadiers. Murat shouted, ' Citizens, you are dissolved,' and then turning to the grenadiers he told them ' to sweep all these people out of the place.' Then the levelled bayonets sent the deputies scrambling out of the windows into the garden. Later the minority met to proclaim the change of government, and the Consulate of Napoleon Bonaparte.

Long after dark that November evening there was an alarm at an old house at St. Germain, where Madame Campan, once the companion of the hapless Marie Antoinette, kept a girls' boarding-school. There was something like a scare when the place was roused with clank of sabres, ringing of horse hoofs, and loud knocking at the gate. But it was no hostile summons. Four of Murat's troopers had ridden from St. Cloud in the darkness bringing a letter to one of the elder girls, Mademoiselle Caroline Bonaparte, a letter written by Murat himself in haste to be first to let her know that her brother had become the ruler of France, with some useful help from the writer of the letter.

Murat had seen something of the lady in the days when her brother, the young victor of the campaign of Italy, was holding his court at Mombello. After the return from Egypt, she and her schoolfellow, Hortense Beauharnais, were released from Madame Campan's care for a fortnight's holiday at the house of the Bonapartes in the Rue de la Victoire. She was sent back to St. Germain two days before the *coup d'état*. Murat saw her more than once during this brief holiday in Paris, and from this time, not from the days of Mombello, we may date his courtship of Caroline. At Mombello he can only have vaguely thought of a marriage with her as a remote possibility, for he had not yet penetrated to the inner circle. Now the position was changed. The day of Aboukir had confirmed him in his own high opinion of himself, and further proved that the opinion was to some extent shared by Bonaparte. To marry into the family that was on the fair way to governing France would be to assure his future. But others were forming similar plans for themselves.

The handsome, lively, and somewhat reckless Corsican girl had many admirers among the young officers who visited her brother's house. Two of the generals, Lannes and Murat, were among them, and Josephine favoured Murat's claims. Napoleon, now First Consul, and determined not to relinquish the power he had grasped, whatever paper constitutions might say, was already foreseeing the time when he might have princes among his sister's suitors, but meanwhile, was anxious that Caroline's marriage should be so arranged as to strengthen his own position. Genera

Moreau was the one man in France who, he thought, might prove strong enough to be his rival. A week after the *coup d'état* the *Moniteur* of the 24 Brumaire (15 November) contained an announcement that General Moreau would, before long, marry one of the First Consul's sisters, and the only sister unmarried at the time was Caroline. Bonaparte must have suggested the alliance to him before making the announcement, and believed he was favourable to it, but the result of the *Moniteur* paragraph was that Moreau told the First Consul he had no aspirations to his sister's hand. The statement in the *Moniteur* was then treated as an unauthorised rumour, but the incident made the family all the more anxious to have Caroline married as soon as might be, if only to show that there was nothing in the Moreau rumour, and that no one was disappointed at the general's disappearance from the list of possible suitors.

The choice lay between two of the young generals who had thrown in their fortunes with those of the First Consul, Lannes, Governor of Paris since the eve of the *coup d'état*, and Murat, who had been appointed commander-in-chief of the Consular Guard on 30 Brumaire (21 November). Napoleon favoured Lannes, and at first spoke of the proposal of a match between Caroline and Murat as a piece of empty sentimentalism. Caroline had taken a giddy fancy for the dashing cavalry leader, he said, and did not realize that she was perhaps sacrificing a much more brilliant match in the future. But Caroline, now freed from Madame Campan's school and figuring in the court that surrounded the First Consul's wife, not only showed a strong determination to choose for herself and to choose Murat, but she found a powerful ally in Josephine, who strongly urged the young general's claims.

While the proposed marriage was still being discussed, and nothing was yet decided, Murat received the long-delayed official confirmation of the promotion to the rank of divisional general won on the field of Aboukir. His correspondence about this time shows that he was in communication with the authorities of his native Department. He presents to the First Consul an address of congratulation from the administration of Cahors; he sends that body a copy of the new constitution under which 'the French people has recovered its rights so long usurped by conspiring factions'; and he promises to use his influence to promote local interests. One important fact about his home we learn incidentally from his contract of marriage. Before the new year of 1800, and apparently some time in the latter half of 1799, his father, Pierre Murat, had died, and his widowed mother was living with André Murat, now the head of the family at La Bastide.

In the first days of January Napoleon agreed at last to his sister's proposed marriage with Murat, and the formal contract was signed on the '28 Nivôse, an VIII'—that is, 18 January, 1800—at the Luxembourg in Paris, then officially known as the 'Palace of the Consuls.' The drafting of the document shows that the Bonapartes had not yet entirely got rid of the Italian style they had used in Corsica. The First Consul is more than once mentioned as 'Napolione' Bonaparte. The destined bride of Murat, generally known by her adopted name of Caroline, is mentioned by her baptismal name (Maria Nunziata) in its French form 'Marie Annonciate.' As she is still a minor ('born at Ajaccio in March 1782') her mother Letitia signs for her. Her four brothers are parties to the contract. It is agreed that there is to be no community of goods between husband and wife, both waiving any claim the law may give them in this direction, a separate estate being constituted for the wife, and her husband agreeing that she shall have power to deal freely with her property. Her four brothers make up a sum of forty thousand francs as her dowry. Murat agrees to settle this amount upon her, and to add to it from his own resources a sum equal to one-third of it. In addition he recognizes as her personal property diamonds, jewels, and other effects, to the value of twelve thousand francs. 'Jean-Baptiste Bessière, *chef de brigade*, cousin,' signs as witness for Murat, using an unusual spelling of his name, and claiming a relationship of which we now hear for the first time.

CAROLINE BONAPARTE, ABOUT THE TIME OF HER MARRIAGE
FROM A LITHOGRAPH BY DELPECH

## MARRIAGE TO CAROLINE BONAPARTE

The marriage was fixed for 20 January, two days later. On the 19th Murat writes from his house in the Rue des Citoyennes (on the south side of the Seine), to inform his brother André of his good fortune. He is about to start, he says, for an 'estate of the Consul Bonaparte,' where next day he is to marry the great man's sister. The marriage contract was signed last evening. Will André tell his sister and his mother, and assure the latter that her fortunate son is longing to see her and hold her in his arms. He will come soon and bring his wife, who will be delighted to greet his mother. 'Dear little Caroline' is going to write to the old innkeeper's widow, and André is requested to see that there is an affectionate reply in proper form. He reports that the little nephew in Paris, the son of his brother Pierre, is doing well, then he comes back to his marriage: 'Adieu. To-morrow I shall be the happiest of men. To-morrow I shall have for my own the dearest of women.'

It was not to an 'estate of the Consul Bonaparte,' but to his brother Joseph's princely domain of Mortefontaine, nineteen miles from Paris on the way to Chantilly, that the happy pair had been invited for the celebration of the wedding. It was a purely civil ceremony. The Republican calendar, which had abolished the Sunday, was still in vogue, and the thirtieth day of the 'Snowy month' (30 Nivôse = 20 January) had been chosen for the civil ceremony, because it was a '*decadi*,' a tenth day, the day of the rest in the new system. So, too, the party did not go to church, but to the 'tenth-day temple' (*temple décadaire*) of Plailly, the village near Joseph Bonaparte's park and château. The civil officer who declared Murat and Caroline man and wife in the name of the Republic was Citizen Louis Dubos, President of the Municipal Administration of Plailly. Neither the First Consul nor Josephine was present. The Bonaparte family was represented by the mother of the bride, her brothers Joseph and Louis, and her uncle, Fesch. General Bernadotte, ex-Minister of War was one of the witnesses for Murat. General Lannes was magnanimously present to congratulate his successful rival.

The bride and bridegroom did not remain long as Joseph's guests amid the woods and lakes of Mortefontaine. Murat, within the week, took Caroline to his house in the Rue des Citoyennes, and proudly appeared with her in the salons of the Luxembourg, and the handsome pair were night after night the honoured guests at balls and parties, for, thanks to the First Consul, Paris had a court once more, and was trying to live up to its newly refurnished splendours.

The general was a striking figure. Above the middle height and with the frame of a giant, but without any clumsy heaviness, he liked to appear in one of the showy cavalry uniforms of the Consular Guard. Every movement was marked with vigour and restrained impetuosity. The dark eyes that looked out from his full good-humoured face sparkled with animation. The marks of the wound received at Aboukir were concealed by the short whiskers, black as the mass of curling locks that in the fashion of the time came down to his embroidered collar.

He did not dance. At balls he was content to hold Caroline's fan and gloves, and appear as her faithful squire. On these occasions she would sometimes wear the diamond necklace, the gift of the First Consul, but oftener her husband's present, a necklace of fine pearls that had cost Murat thirty thousand francs. She was tall, with a beautiful fair complexion, a pleasant smile, a lively engaging manner. Unflattering critics said she was not the beauty of the family, that her head was too large, her shoulders rounded, her figure too slight, her neck too thick. Perhaps her portraits flatter her, for they do not make one ready to believe such carping descriptions. She played her part as hostess at the Rue des Citoyennes in a way that was helpful to her husband's prospects.

He appears to have really been anxious to revisit La Bastide, and bring his wife with him to the scenes of his boyhood. He wrote to André to buy a house and get it ready for him, but the intended visit had to be deferred indefinitely, for within three months of his marriage he

## MARRIAGE TO CAROLINE BONAPARTE 59

received sudden orders for employment that was the prelude to active service.

In the middle of April he was directed to proceed at once to Dijon, and take command of the cavalry of the ' Army of Reserve ' which was being formed in the south-eastern Departments, with its headquarters in the old Burgundian capital. He left Caroline in Paris and was at Dijon on the 19th.

The First Consul was preparing one of the most daring strategic combinations in order to restore the military fortunes of France, and at the same time secure a long lease of power for himself. During his absence in the East, the Republican armies had suffered defeat after defeat. The Austrians had overrun northern Italy, and Masséna was with difficulty holding on to the old Genoese territory, while Suchet with a small force watched the borders of Provence. Moreau with the Army of the Rhine guarded the eastern frontiers. But amid the disasters of the preceding year the Republicans had not lost the control of Switzerland, and Napoleon meant to take advantage of this as the basis of the coming campaign of 1800. The fact that the ' Army of Reserve ' was being assembled in Burgundy, and on the shores of the Lake of Geneva, did not betray the secret of his projected enterprise. Precautions were taken to prevent any detailed information as to its strength becoming public property, and the First Consul was pleased to hear that the Austrian newspapers ridiculed the idea that any considerable force could be assembled in that quarter, treated the ' Army of Reserve ' as a myth, and explained that the most the French could do would be to assemble an inconsiderable force to guard the passages over the Alps, and perhaps reinforce either Suchet in the south or Moreau in the east to a moderate extent.

Murat as commander-in-chief of the cavalry had the title of lieutenant-general, but this did not indicate any new step of promotion. The title was a temporary and local one, assumed by a general when he took command of a group of several divisions or brigades, and thus acted as the 'lieutenant' of the commander-in-chief of all the armed forces of France—the First Consul.[1] Murat's duties were those of inspection and organization. On his arrival at Dijon he was received with enthusiasm by the regiments assembled there. His reputation as a daring and fortunate leader made him popular with the army, and his appearance was believed to be the herald of Napoleon's coming.

This was the case. Napoleon arrived at Dijon a few days after his lieutenant. His original plan of campaign had been to move the Army of Reserve into Switzerland, unite it to the troops already there under General Moncey, make Zurich and Lucerne his base of supply, and marching over the St. Gothard strike directly at Milan, forcing the Austrians to withdraw from their attacks on the line of the Genoese Apennines by thus appearing in their rear and on their line of communications. While keeping the essential principle of his plan he had modified its details, and decided to act at an earlier date than he originally intended, because in the course of April the position in north Italy and on the Riviera had suddenly become very serious. The Austrians had forced the line of the Apennines. Melas had pushed Suchet back along the Riviera to Nice, while his lieutenant, General Ott, had driven Masséna into Genoa, and was besieging him there with the co-operation of an English squadron blockading the harbour and cutting off all supplies by sea. The place was short of provisions, and the garrison was soon almost starving, but Masséna was grimly holding out though his soldiers and the population were in the direst straits.

The Austrian commander regarded an attack from the

---

[1] Murat's force was a cavalry division of four brigades, made up of a large number of regiments, some of these units being very weak. The total strength was about six thousand sabres. Two horse artillery guns were attached to each brigade. The organization was as follows:—

1st Brigade.—General Champeaux, 12th Hussars, 21st Chasseurs à Cheval.
2nd Brigade.—General Rivaud, 1st Hussars, 2nd and 15th Chasseurs.
3rd Brigade.—General Duvigneau, 5th, 7th, 8th, and 9th Dragoons.
4th Brigade.—General Kellerman, 1st, 2nd, 3rd, 5th, and 20th Cavalry of the Line.

Alps as an impracticable operation, and expected that if the much talked of 'Army of Reserve' were a reality, it would make its appearance as a reinforcement for Suchet on the French Riviera. He left the passes unguarded, except by a few weak posts incapable of prolonged defence. Napoleon ordered Moreau to cross the Rhine and enter southern Germany so as to keep the enemy occupied in that direction, while he moved the troops in south-eastern France and Switzerland across the nearest Alpine passes. He himself led the strongest column over the Great St. Bernard, mounted not on the prancing charger of David's well-known picture, but on a sure-footed mule. Murat went with him, with the two light cavalry brigades of his division. For many a mile of mountain paths the men tramped on foot leading their horses. Two smaller columns each some five thousand strong, under Generals Thurreau and Chabran went over the passes of Mont Cenis and the Little St. Bernard. From Switzerland General Moncey led fifteen thousand men over the St. Gothard, and sent a brigade of three thousand under General Bethancourt over the Simplon. If Napoleon had been opposed by a leader equal to himself these various columns would have been checked and beaten in detail before they could combine their operations in the plains of northern Italy. But he took great risks cheerfully because he knew his enemy.

As soon as the passage of the Great St. Bernard was successfully completed Murat pushed on with his cavalry and horse artillery, and on 27 May occupied Vercelli. He kept close touch with the retreating Austrian detachments, co-operating with Lannes in driving the enemy's rearguard from the banks of the Sesia, and entering Novara on the 29th.

The Austrian general, Festemberg, had halted on the Ticino to bar the way to Milan. He held the eastern bank, and had removed all the boats he could find down the river to Pavia. On 31 May Murat was on the river bank at Galliate, with his cavalry, the infantry of Boudet's division, and the artillery of the Consular Guard. An artillery duel began across the river, while Murat sent scouting parties up and down the bank to search for a crossing. The people of Galliate, or the more active party of them, were friendly to the French, and they showed them where they had some boats hidden in an irrigation canal. These were pulled out into the Ticino above the town and the crossing began. Murat had some of the grenadiers of the Consular Guard formed up on the opposite bank before the enemy discovered that the boats were at work. Turbigo, the scene of MacMahon's exploits on the day of Magenta, fifty-nine years later, was taken, and steadily reinforcing his advanced party, getting his guns across on rafts, and swimming his horses, Murat solidly established himself on the eastern bank. In the darkness at ten o'clock Turbigo was retaken by a counter-attack of the Austrian general, Loudon, but by midnight Murat had captured it again at the bayonet point, and the enemy was in full retreat southwards. Next day the French army crossed the Ticino at several points and concentrated about Buffalora; Murat with the advanced guard marching to Sedriano on the direct road to Milan. On 2 June he continued his march under a dull sky amid intense heat, and at four in the afternoon rode triumphantly into Milan amid the muttering of a distant thunderstorm.

On the news that a great army had descended from the Alps into Piedmont and Lombardy, Melas had stopped his advance along the French Riviera, and was moving towards the passes of the Apennines to meet the invader. He had given Ott orders to raise the siege of Genoa, but on 1 June Masséna, reduced to starvation point, had sent out a white flag to arrange terms of capitulation. Ott succeeded in keeping Masséna's officers in ignorance of what was happening north of the Apennines, and on the 4th Genoa surrendered, and the garrison marched out with the honours of war. Melas then diverted every available man to the scene of the coming conflict in Lombardy.

Napoleon's first object after securing Milan was to seize

## MARENGO 63

the crossings of the river Po. Murat with his cavalry and Boudet's infantry division was at the famous bridge of Lodi on the Adda on 4 June. Thence he marched next day to the left bank of the Po opposite Piacenza, starting at 3 A.M., and in the forenoon coming in sight of the outwork on the north bank, which covered the floating bridge of boats leading across the river to the city.

The place was held by a small Austrian garrison under General Mosel. He did not feel himself strong enough to hold the north bank, and when Murat attacked the bridgehead the Austrians soon abandoned it, leaving eighty prisoners in the hands of Boudet's infantry. They cut the floating bridge, but the French seized some of the boats that had formed its northern end, and collected a few others. Murat had thus a flotilla of some twenty boats in all in his possession at nightfall. With these he began ferrying his men across below the place. Next morning he stormed one of the gates of Piacenza, and at the head of his horsemen drove back an Austrian column with was coming up to reinforce the enemy. Part of the garrison held out in the citadel. In the town he captured considerable quantities of ammunition and provisions stored in the magazines, and a convoy of thirty barges laden with supplies moored at the river bank. The further trophies of the victory were two standards and thirteen guns. There were more than fifteen hundred prisoners, among them an officer with dispatches from Melas to his Government, from which Napoleon learned the news of the fall of Genoa.

Murat blockaded the citadel of Piacenza for three days, then on 9 June, Loison's division arrived to maintain the blockade, and he was set free for further active work. Before marching off he wrote a letter to Napoleon. So far he had only corresponded with headquarters, by means of official letters to Berthier as chief of the staff. While he was serving with the army, Napoleon's brother-in-law was merely 'General Murat commanding the cavalry,' and a letter directly addressed to the commander-in-chief was a military irregularity. But Murat was so pleased with his success that he could not resist the temptation to write freely about it to the great man, instead of confining himself to formal routine communications. 'I have not written to you, so far, mon général,' he says, 'for fear of offending you and General Berthier, and I suppose he shows you all my letters.' He expressed a wish to have more men at his command. He would then do still more useful work. Among the gossip of the letter there was an ungallant reference to the wife of an Austrian general of Irish descent whom he had found at Piacenza. 'The wife of General O'Reilly is here in my quarters. I am showing her all the courtesy that is due to the fair sex, though she is ugly enough.'

On the evening of the 9th, as he marched from Piacenza, Murat received orders to hand over Boudet's division to Desaix, who had just arrived from Egypt, and to concentrate all his cavalry under his own command for the coming struggle with the main Austrian army under Melas, which was now north of the Apennines. He joined the First Consul's headquarters at Voghera.

On 14 June Marengo was fought, one of the most fiercely contested battles of the Napoleonic wars. It lasted from nine in the summer morning till nightfall, and at one time it seemed that the long struggle would end in disaster for the Republic. Napoleon had personally to rally broken infantry retiring in confusion before the Austrian onset. But late in the day the arrival of Desaix with a fresh division, and a splendid charge of two of Murat's brigades, led by the younger Kellerman, turned the tide of fight, and changed impending defeat into decisive victory.

There was a relatively considerable force of cavalry engaged on both sides,[1] and the ground was favourable

---

[1] Compared to modern battles and those of Napoleon's later campaigns, the numbers engaged at Marengo were small. At the outset, the Austrians were the stronger. Taking the numbers engaged from first to last they had 28,000 men in action, including some 6000 cavalry. The French opposed to them 28,500 men, including 5200 cavalry. The losses were heavy. Four thousand seven hundred French were killed and wounded, and about 900 taken prisoners (in the first stage of the fight).

## MARENGO 65

to mounted action, the first ground of the kind Murat had seen in the campaign, rolling plains without fences, a contrast to the swampy rice-fields and endless irrigation canals and causeway roads of Lombardy. The cavalry was engaged frequently during the long-drawn contest, but generally acted in independent brigades, Murat never being able to collect his whole division for a united attack. One of his brigadiers, Champeaux, was killed while charging, at the head of his men, to cover the retirement of the broken infantry. Murat then united the 2nd brigade to Kellerman's command. He himself repeatedly charged, sword in hand, beside one or other of his brigadiers. Throughout his career, when acting as commander-in-chief of the cavalry, it was never his way merely to send orders to his subordinates to lead this or that brigade or division to the charge. He would gallop up to the head of a brigade, flourish his sword, or oftener his riding-whip, point to the object of attack, and spur forward the foremost in the wild rush to death or glory. Berthier, in his report on the battle, tells how—' The cavalry, under the orders of General Murat, made several decisive charges. General Murat had his clothes riddled with bullets,' but he escaped unwounded. At the moment when the battle seemed lost, Berthier placed a battalion of 800 grenadiers of the Consular Guard under Murat, who, as their old commander, knew them well. They stood like a 'living citadel' in the midst of the broken line, retiring foot by foot with bayonets fixed, and firing volley after volley in the faces of the Austrians, while Murat led charge after charge to relieve the pressure upon them. 'They lost 121 men killed and wounded,' says Murat in his report, 'and I owe them very special praise.'

Next day he hung on the rear of the retreating Austrians,

---

The Austrians lost 6500 killed and wounded, and 2966 prisoners. The percentage of loss was much higher than in any recent battle. At Marengo the victors lost 16·5 per cent., or, including the prisoners, 20 per cent. The Austrians lost 23·2 per cent. in killed and wounded, or, if we include the prisoners, 33·8 per cent. Compared to such losses, the heaviest losses in South Africa were trifling, and even in the battles of the Russo-Japanese War, lasting for days, the total loss seldom exceeded 10 per cent.

E

and collected a considerable number of prisoners. Napoleon recognised that he owed to him no small part of his success, and when he handed over the command of the army of Italy to Berthier, and hurried back to Paris after the victory, he took Murat with him to share his triumph in the capital.

## CHAPTER V

THE 'ARMY OF OBSERVATION'—COMMAND IN ITALY

1800-1801

ON 1 July Murat was again at his house in Paris, in the Rue des Citoyennes, and Caroline was welcoming her husband, crowned with new laurels, and her brother, now the greatest man in Europe. It is pleasant to find that one of Murat's first acts, on the very day of his return, was to write an effusively affectionate letter to his old mother, who, in the inn at La Bastide, where she lived with her matter-of-fact son André, had been reading the praises of Joachim in the bulletins of victory, and bearing as well as she could the disappointment of hearing again and again that the oft-promised visit to the old home was deferred. One wishes that General Murat had proved the sincerity of his professions of filial affection by finding time for a flying visit to La Bastide, where the house that André had bought for him was long prepared for his arrival. The letter, with its thoroughly French phrasing, is almost untranslatable. It sounds crude in English, but here is a literal version :—

'PARIS, 12 Messidor, an VIII,
'1 *July*, 1800.

' I hasten to announce to you, my adorable mother, my return to Paris. It is a long time since I have had any news from you ; but my good little Caroline who has had some, did not fail to send it on to me. You are well ; you always love me ; you love my wife ; I am the happiest man in the world ; but I shall be still happier when I have the happiness of embracing you. Adieu ; love me ; I shall soon be near you. My wife too, embraces you very affectionately.—The most affectionate of sons, J. MURAT

'My little nephew embraces you.
'A thousand messages to all my brothers and sisters.'

A week later, on 6 August, he wrote to her again, telling her, 'with more sorrow and regret than he could express,' that the promised visit to La Bastide must be once more deferred. He had been appointed to the command of a 'camp of grenadiers,' and could not go home. 'Only peace, and peace is now not far off, can give me the opportunity,' he says, 'but I swear that then no power will prevent me from coming to see you, embracing you, and never leaving you again.' Here the general 'protests too much.' There was not the slightest probability of his burying himself in a country house at La Bastide. But he goes on to give practical proof of his affection for his people. He sends his mother 4000 francs for herself, 2000 more for André, 2000 for his sister Jacquette, and 2000 for Madelon. Madelon, he suggests, can use the money to pay her debts, an allusion to some news from home. 'If you need any more,' he continues, 'write to me, and I shall at once send you all you wish for.' If his married sister, De Mongesty, wants anything, they have only to let him know. He tells his mother to take care of his nephews. When he comes he will take them with him—a flat contradiction of the promise to stay at La Bastide, written a few lines higher up. Caroline sends good wishes. 'She will soon make me the happiest of fathers, as I am the happiest of husbands,' he says. He ends by asking his mother to console herself with the assurance that in two months—and perhaps sooner—he will be with her.

Murat had been given his new command on 2 August. He was to complete the organization of a division of grenadiers and 'éclaireurs' (light infantry) in a camp to the north of Beauvais, the training being done under canvas, so as to allow the division to be prepared for campaigning, by moving its quarters from point to point and working over new ground. Probably with a view to improving his own position with Napoleon's right hand man, the future Marshal Berthier, he asked for the appointment of his brother, César Berthier, as his chief of the staff. In a letter written a few days later, he asks for a supply of tall bearskin caps for his grenadiers. He explains his ideas on the subject :—' You know that the *bonnet à poil* is the head-dress for the grenadier. And indeed, what enemy is sufficiently master of his *morale* not to be shaken by the advance of a strong body of grenadiers, with the tall caps that add a foot to their height, and give them the most formidable military appearance?' Then he asks for a standard for each battalion. 'The flag is indispensable in a manœuvre camp, and still more in action. It reanimates the courage of the soldier wearied with the fight, and there are times when, carried by a few brave men into the midst of the enemy, it can make a doubtful victory certain.' He must have bands of music to ' charm the idle hours of the soldier in camp, make him forget his fatigues during manœuvres, and intimidate the enemy in action.' Other letters deal with reports on camping-grounds near Beauvais, request the addition of engineers and ambulances to his command, and go into details as to supplies. The correspondence shows that Murat took his work very seriously; that he was not a mere dashing leader of cavalry charges, but that he was ready to deal with the drudgery of organization and training, and appreciated the importance of attention to every detail. He formed his division into an independent force of all arms, obtaining the addition to it of artillery, cavalry, and departmental corps. One of his troubles was the want of money. In a letter of 18 August, he complains that the pay of his men is six months in arrear, and that, notwithstanding a promise of the First Consul to provide the funds, he cannot get a sou. On 22 August he secures a small instalment of 10,000 francs, and next day 100,000. Then we hear of a brigade of the line arriving from Amiens. The Beauvais camp was growing into a strong force. Peace negotiations had been begun, but they dragged on from week to week and were broken off, so that it was not until after the winter campaign and Moreau's victory at Hohenlinden that the war came to an end. Murat was, therefore, doing useful work.

In October the force which he had formed and trained in two months of continual manœuvres was reviewed by the First Consul, then the camp was broken up and the troops marched southwards to Lyons to join a reserve army that was being concentrated there in view of the probable renewal of hostilities. Murat, having done his work, returned to Paris. Among his letters there is one dated from Paris, on 28 October, which shows that he was in friendly correspondence with the family of Mion Bastit. It is addressed to François Bastit, then employed in the administration of the Department of the Lot. He speaks of his hope of visiting Cahors on the conclusion of peace ; says he has just heard of the death of one of his nieces 'which has greatly pained me,' and asks François Bastit to be a friend to his old mother at La Bastide, and to all the Murat family. In a postcript Caroline sends a friendly message. Official letters to the War Minister, in the first part of November, show that he inspected the detachments from the Beauvais camp on their march southwards through Paris, and was busy making good various minor deficiencies in their equipment.

He had done his work at Beauvais very thoroughly, but he was anxious to secure the command, not of a training camp, but of a force that would be employed in the field, if the conference at Lunéville came to nothing, and war began again on a grand scale. Orders had been given to form an army of reserve in eastern France, with headquarters at Dijon, and Murat used all his influence to be appointed its commander. Early in November he heard that Joseph Bonaparte, then at Lunéville for the peace negotiations, was putting forward a rival candidate in the person of General Bernadotte, who had married his sister-in-law, Desirée Clary. He sent at once an ultimatum to Joseph. If Bernadotte was put before him, he declared that

## THE 'ARMY OF OBSERVATION' 71

he would hand his resignation of his general's commission to the First Consul. On the critical day of Brumaire Bernadotte had stood neutral, waiting prudently to see who would conquer. Murat believed that he had even sided with the hostile majority in the Five Hundred when Napoleon withdrew from their hall, after having failed to secure their support. So he wrote to Joseph :—' I will never look on quietly and see power passing into the hands of a man who, on the 18 Brumaire, was on the side of those who voted the outlawry of the family.' Now that he was the husband of Caroline, he wrote as one of the Bonapartes.

Napoleon himself suspected the loyalty of Bernadotte, and Joseph's candidate had really no chance against Murat, who, on 20 November, was appointed to the command of the 'Army of Observation' at Dijon. On the 27th, for the second time, he established his headquarters in the old capital of Burgundy. Before leaving Paris he had sent a short note to André Murat promising once more to come to La Bastide as soon as he was free.

One can trace his restless energy, his grasp of detail, his impatience for results, in the long list of letters written or dictated on the day of his arrival—requisitions for supplies from various quarters, requests for new units to be added to his command, directions for immediately placing part of his force in a position to descend into Italy at a moment's notice by moving a strong column to Chambery in Savoy. Next day he wrote a long letter to the First Consul. He explained that he had departed from the directions given to him in Paris by sending General Sarrazin's column to Chambery instead of Geneva, because the roads on that side were 'less bad,' and supplies could be more easily obtained. The only drawback was that the movement might ' reveal a few days sooner the ultimate destination of our troops ' (*i.e.* north Italy). He complains —as he had had to complain at Beauvais—that it is difficult to obtain money from the Treasury, so that the pay of the troops is in arrear, and the officers could not even settle up their local debts before marching off. Then there is a long postscript which reveals his disappointment that he is still in a subordinate command, and merely preparing reinforcements for the army in Italy, and cannot yet look forward to being *général en chef*, commander-in-chief of an independent force in the event of a winter campaign beyond the Alps. Inartistically frank flattery of the First Consul mingles with his plea for an improved position for himself. The postscript is thoroughly characteristic :—

' The brother-in law of the Consul Bonaparte has had a perfect reception here ; all the constituted authorities proclaim Bonaparte the saviour of France and the pacificator of Europe.— General Murat asks you as a favour, my General, to allow him to go with the second column. He has been welcomed and fêted here as a Commander-in-chief, and the title is given to him both in speaking and in written documents. Every moment he feels having to hear people say, " Your army will do good service "— " Your army is splendid." And all the while it is known that he is not a commander-in-chief, though it had long since been rumoured that he would have this standing. He feels himself in an uncomfortable position. Will you deign to free him from it as soon as possible ? '

Bonaparte did not act upon these suggestions. Murat had to be content with his modest functions of organization and preparation, and his orders for a march to Chambery were countermanded by the Minister of War, and Sarrazin's column directed to Geneva. His correspondence shows that he worked very hard at Dijon. He had the Alpine passes reconnoitred and something done to improve the wretched mountain roads. On 5 December he orders all stores in the magazines of Dijon to be hurried up to Geneva, and everything prepared for a march by the Val d'Aosta and over the snowy passes of the Little St. Bernard. ' The Corps of Observation is to be transferred to Italy.' Even at the last moment he has to complain of lack of equipments. He sends requisitions to Lyons for 4000 overcoats, 4000 shirts, 4000 pairs of shoes and 2000 horseshoes for the artillery and cavalry, to be supplied at once. In a letter to Bonaparte—one of the many written on that

## THE 'ARMY OF OBSERVATION'  73

busy day—he says that he will 'punctually execute' the order for the march over the St. Bernard, though he 'foresees great difficulties.' He encloses a report exposing the swindling practices of the army contractors, and sends with it a sample of the wretched material they use for the men's greatcoats.

Before he left Dijon for Geneva, Murat had a letter from the First Consul's uncle, Fesch, telling him that Caroline was well, and he need have no anxiety about her. There would soon, he hoped, be news of the birth of an heir. Then he gives him the current rumours of Paris. It was said that Murat is to command the 3rd corps of the Army of Italy, Bernadotte the 4th. The plan of campaign would be a descent from the Alpine passes as far east as the Grisons, with 'Magdonal' (Macdonald) operating through the Tyrol. It was not, however, at all certain that there will be a campaign or that Bonaparte will take the field, for there is a general expectation that Austria will make peace.

The expectation was well founded. Moreau had advanced with the Army of the Rhine into south Germany, and on 3 December he had defeated the Austrians, under the Archduke John, on the field of Hohenlinden. He followed up the retreating enemy through the snows of Bavaria, and was about to invade Austrian territory, when, on 25 December, the armistice was signed that was the prelude to the treaty of Lunéville and the temporary pacification of Europe.

But in Italy there was no armistice till the middle of January, and the First Consul had directed Macdonald from the Grisons and Brune from Lombardy to co-operate in gaining as much ground as possible from the enemy in Venetia while the state of war continued. Murat had left Dijon for Geneva on 10 December. So far he had written in an optimist spirit of the progress and condition of his force, but on the 15th, he wrote from Geneva to the Ministry of War that he could no longer be silent about the wretched state of his artillery. The roads from Dijon to Geneva were frightful. The march by the Jura had been 'the final blow'; the roads from Morey to Nyon were deep in snow and covered with slippery ice. He had requisitioned teams of oxen for the guns and wagons, but of eighteen guns he had only got six through to Nyon, the rest were still in the mountain roads struggling with 'incredible difficulties.' Twelve guns, luckily sent on to Geneva before the snow fell, had been got as far as Annecy. The transport train was in a miserable state of disorganization. The soldiers were deserting, some of them taking away the horses and selling them, the quartermaster-sergeants were rascals, and their officers not much better. All the local authorities, mayors, prefects, subprefects, seemed to be protecting and encouraging desertion. Unless the Government took rigorous measures there would soon be no recruits. The conscripts came to the depots to 'steal' a suit of clothes and go home with it. He was doing what he could to reorganize the artillery and train. 'It is cruel for me, Citizen Minister,' he concluded, 'to be forced to set such frightful pictures before your eyes, but rest assured that I shall labour without respite to reorganize this so essential part of my command.' The letter throws a light on the condition of the French armies during the winter campaign when France was thoroughly tired of the long war.

There were pressing orders from the Paris War Office to Murat to have his troops at Milan at the earliest possible date. Part of the infantry was sent over the Little St. Bernard—a difficult march. It was found impossible to get the guns over the pass even on sledges. The Simplon was reconnoitred as an alternative route, but this was found impracticable. Finally the guns were dragged over the Mont Genèvre pass and reached Milan by way of Turin. Murat arrived there in the last week of December.

Brune had begun hostilities against the Austrians under Bellegarde by advancing against the line of the Mincio, while Macdonald made a splendid march over the ice and snow of the Splügen to descend upon the enemy's flank and rear. The Austrians were forced steadily back, making no obstinate resistance anywhere. Murat was irritated at being kept idle at Milan, and being under Brune's orders as a mere subordinate commander on the line of communications. On the New Year's day of 1801 Milan heard the news of the 'Attempt of Nivôse,' the explosion of an infernal machine in the Rue Nicaise at Paris when the First Consul was on his way to the opera, with Josephine and Caroline in his carriage, on the evening of the 3 Nivôse, an IX (24 December, 1800). Murat made the news the text for a long letter to Napoleon.

The first part of it is written in the high-flown style of the Revolutionary time. He tells how the universal joy at Milan was suddenly interrupted by the terrible news. Then he goes on :—

'Ah! my dear general, you have been in danger and I have not been there to share it. This attempt has frozen me with horror. It was aimed at all your family. Ah! far from me be the heart-rending picture of what might have been—my young Caroline, on the eve of being a mother, rolled in the dust and bathed in blood; your whole family massacred on your lifeless body. Ah! pardon my begging that you will not leave me in the state in which I am! Your armies are everywhere victorious. They no longer need me and the brave men I command. Recall me to your side, and rely on them, for they are entirely devoted to me. It will be a great joy to be with you, and the scoundrels who may think of assailing you in the future will have to pass over our corpses to reach you.'

Then after this plea for a recall to Paris, there is a most unworthy attack upon his commander-in-chief, General Brune. The general, he says, seems to have lost his head, says he has enemies at Paris, expects a blow from that quarter. Can it be that the scoundrels, who have attempted the First Consul's life, have accomplices in the armies, and even among those who command them? He will name no one. If he knew them they would not long survive. But he cannot help thinking that the 'brigands' who planned the assassination, must have relied on support from men in high places after it. Then he attacks Brune's military conduct. He says he is at variance with Macdonald, and does not really command the army. Every general is doing what he likes himself. There was nearly a disaster at the passage of the Mincio. 'Brune gives me no orders,' he adds, ' and I am here waiting for yours.'

The letter shows Murat at his worst, chafing at his position, too proud to remember the claims of military discipline, grasping at any chance of leaving the army, and meanwhile trying to blacken the character of his chief by wild insinuations and reckless charges. Napoleon sent a reply that must have done something to bring him to his senses. He told him that he was an officer of the army of Italy, and must not correspond directly with him, but report to his commander, Brune. ' I do not approve of all the remarks you make to me ' is his curt dismissal of Murat's accusations. As to his desire to return to Paris he says :—' A soldier should be faithful to his wife, but should not wish to return to her until it is decided that there is no more work for him to do.'

Before this reply could reach Murat he received from the Paris War Office direct orders to march upon and occupy Ancona, which, it was claimed, belonged to the French Republic under the Treaty of Campo Formio. He was to avoid any act of hostility to the Pontifical States. He was told that Brune had been informed of this arrangement, and a letter from the general confirmed this. Murat, pleased to have something to do, wrote to him with more than mere formal politeness. But the old ill will remained. On 13 January he asked the First Consul to relieve him of his command. He was anxious to leave Italy, and to be spared the sight of the commander-in-chief's blunders. He reported to him in proper form, he said, and Napoleon need not fear that he would commit any indiscretions. Then he proceeds to be indiscreet enough :—

'However,' he continues, 'I must speak to you about his movements. I cannot endure seeing any longer the laggard and unskilful advance of the army, which only marches to victory

## COMMAND IN ITALY

because it is still guided by your genius. The army marks all its movements with new blunders, and abandons itself to the most awful pillaging. All the country from the Adda to the Brenta is ruined. The most detestable discord prevails among the generals. They all want to command, and not one of them is capable of it. Bellegarde is allowed to make a leisurely retreat, and is evacuating the country without being disturbed.'

Then he goes on to write a long hostile criticism of Brune's operations, praising Macdonald in order to blacken Brune the more by contrast. At the end of the letter he mentions that Brune has just directed him to occupy Tuscany on his march to Ancona.

Napoleon took no notice of Murat's proffered resignation of his command, and of his criticisms of his chief. He pointed out to him, however, that Brune's having entrusted him with the occupation of Tuscany was a proof of his confidence, and bade him not to delay in carrying out his orders. Murat was to proceed to Bologna, and take over the command there of the troops destined for the march to Florence and Ancona. He reached Bologna on the evening of 17 January. There was already a French force in Tuscany under General Miollis, which had repulsed from Siena a Neapolitan corps under General de Damas. An Austrian column from Ancona was reported to be at Forli. On the evening of his arrival at Bologna, Murat wrote to Miollis that the first division of his troops would be at Florence on the 30th to support him. If the Neapolitans were retiring he was simply to follow them up, and reoccupy the positions they evacuated, but not to go beyond the borders of Tuscany. He (Murat) would presently take over the command, and require all available men for the march on Ancona. The same evening he wrote to the French consul at Leghorn for information as to the movements of the Neapolitans, and, quite unnecessarily, gave him an outline of his plan of campaign, based on the supposition that he would have to fight both Neapolitans and Austrians. It was a piece of boasting, a prophecy of imaginary successes.

For there was to be no fighting. At Bologna Murat found General Levachoff on his way to Naples on a mission of diplomatic courtesy, conveying decorations to the Neapolitan court from the Czar Paul. Murat knew that the First Consul was anxious to cultivate friendly relations with Russia, so he did his best to entertain Levachoff. He wrote to Napoleon that he had got up for the Russian general a banquet and a masked ball, given him a guard of honour, and arranged that the civil and military authorities should wait upon him. Then, taking Levachoff with him, he hurried on to Florence, where he arrived on 20 January. The Russian had told him that his master had written to Bonaparte asking him to spare the kingdom of Naples, so Murat's first act at Florence was to send a letter to De Damas asking him if he still entertained hostile views towards France. The officer who conveyed the letter took with him a message from Levachoff to the Neapolitan headquarters, and the result was that General de Damas began at once the evacuation of Tuscany, retiring into the Pontifical territory.

Then came news that under the terms of the Treaty that was being arranged at Lunéville, the Austrians had agreed to hand over Ancona. All that Murat had to do was to send an officer to arrange details and choose one of his regiments to form the garrison. Thus in a few days he found himself in peaceful possession of central Italy, commander-in-chief, *de facto* if not *de jure*, and holding a kind of military court at Florence. To add to his satisfaction there came news from Paris that on the 21st Caroline had given birth to a son, the Prince Achille Murat of future years.

Murat had now for a while to play the diplomatist and the politician rather than the soldier. Peace had been arranged with Austria. The First Consul was all powerful in continental Europe. Only England still continued the struggle against him, and his policy in Italy was directed to closing the ports of the peninsula against English commerce. This was to be a first condition in the peace to be arranged with Naples. Murat was also to secure or compel the evacuation of Rome and the Papal States by the Neapolitan army. Northern Italy was already a French province under the name of the Cisalpine Republic. In central Italy, Napoleon, who was anxious to be on good terms with the Pope, and was already planning the Concordat and the restoration of religion in France as a useful auxiliary to public order, had decided that the Papal States should be respected, France being content with the occupation of Ancona. Tuscany and the minor duchies of central Italy were to be formed into a new state, the kingdom of Etruria. Murat had not yet been informed of his project. The Grand Duke had taken refuge in Austria, and the council of regency, established on his departure, had been replaced by a triumvirate of moderate men friendly to France, to the disgust of the Jacobin party in Florence. Murat reported that there was widespread misery and much disorder in Tuscany, and, after publishing a proclamation to its people promising them the inauguration of a better state of things and inviting them to co-operate with him in bringing it about, he laid an embargo on all English property at Leghorn, and announced that the ports of central Italy were henceforth closed to the British flag.

In the negotiations with Naples, Murat was supported by the friendly action of the Russian ambassador to the Bourbon court. There is no need to follow in detail the story of the exchange of projects and counter-propositions that ended in peace being signed at the end of March. Suffice it to say that the terms originally demanded by Murat, as directed by Talleyrand, were the evacuation of the Papal States, the liberation of all French prisoners and of persons imprisoned for political action on behalf of France, the seizure of all English and Turkish ships in Neapolitan ports, and an order that no further supplies should be sent from Sicily to the English fleet blockading Malta. In order to enforce the evacuation of Rome Murat pushed forward a division of French troops from Tuscany, first to Foligno, then to Perugia. Under this threat the Neapolitans began the evacuation, and yielded every point except that of the embargo on British shipping. Finally it was arranged that this should not be mentioned in the treaty of peace, but should be the subject of a separate and secret convention, the Bourbon Government obtaining this small concession by paying a million and a half of francs into the military chest of Murat's army, thus relieving him of serious difficulties in keeping his troops paid and supplied. This had hardly been arranged when the First Consul sprang a new demand on the Bourbon court—the occupation of the port and arsenal of Taranto by the French. The Neapolitans protested that the treaty had been accepted by Murat, and that this new proposition was a breach of faith, but on a peremptory order from Paris to Murat to resume hostilities and march on Naples, his last demand was also conceded.

While the settlement with Naples was still being arranged, Murat was cultivating friendly relations with the Vatican. On 23 January he addressed from Florence a long letter to Pope Pius VII. He informed him that in case of the failure of the negotiations with Naples, his troops might have to march through the Papal territory, but assured him that in that case the strictest orders would be given that property and religion should be respected, and he expressed his own desire to do everything to ' re-establish their former good relations ' between France and the Holy See.

Consalvi, the cardinal Secretary of State, thanked him for his letter, and sent one of his secretaries, Mgr. Caleppi, to Florence to discuss the situation with him. Murat wrote again to Consalvi on 2 February, telling him how pleased he was with the result of his conversations with Caleppi, which showed that there was the best prospect of friendly relations between France and Rome. He told him to assure the Holy Father that there would be no interference with the government of his States, asked that the local authorities should everywhere remain at their posts, and suggested that no Frenchman, Cisalpine or Tuscan should be allowed to remain in Rome without a passport from the French headquarters. This was with a view to preventing the extremists he had driven from Florence organizing an agitation in Rome. The First Consul did not want another Roman Republic. On 13 February, a long-standing ambition of Murat's was satisfied. He was no longer to report to General Brune. His army, in Tuscany and the Papal States, was, by a decree of the First Consul, given an independent existence under the name of the ' Army of Observation of the South,' and he himself the rank of *général en chef*. He had established his headquarters at Foligno, in the Papal States. As he himself noted in one of his letters to the Minister of War, notwithstanding all the reassuring messages he had sent to the Vatican, the presence of his troops so near Rome made the Pope and the cardinals anxious, and encouraged the Republican agitation in the city. On 18 February he wrote that, at the earliest possible date, he would retire into Tuscany and use part of his force to seize the island of Elba. Consalvi had already been urging their withdrawal. Murat, at his wits' end for money for the army, suggested to the cardinal that the retirement of his force from Foligno might be facilitated by his finding some funds for the expenses of its maintenance. The cardinal, after pleading the poverty of the Pontifical States, at length agreed to pay a hundred thousand Roman scudi, and sent Murat as a present for himself a valuable cameo. Murat sent it on to Caroline. Caleppi had invited him to visit Rome, and, as soon as the preliminary armistice was signed with Naples, the general and his chief of the staff left Foligno for the city, where they arrived on 22 February. Murat stayed at the Sciarra Palace for three days as the guest of Consalvi. He had several audiences with Pius VII, and made an excellent impression on him and on the cardinals. Consalvi wrote in praise of his courtesy, his sense of justice and his moderation. The cardinal tells in his memoirs how Murat won his heart by an act of generous consideration. Caleppi had drawn up a proposed draft of a treaty between Pius VII and the French Republic in which, in his anxiety to conciliate Murat and his master, the First Consul, he had included a stipulation that the British flag should be excluded from the Roman ports. Murat told Consalvi that the draft treaty might be taken as the basis of negotiations with France. The cardinal had never seen it till then, and said Caleppi had no authority to propose or accept the exclusion of the flag of any Christian people from the ports under the Pope's control. Pius VII, he said, considered it the duty of his office to be the friends of all, and to stand neutral in their disputes. Murat argued the point, but Consalvi stood firm. The general might easily have reported to Paris that this condition had been proposed and refused, but he took a generous course. ' Well,' he said at last, ' since this treaty causes so much pain to you and the Holy Father, let us throw it in the fire and say no more about it.'

As the result of the friendly relations thus established, the contribution of the Pontifical State to the expenses of the army was reduced to 73,000 scudi. Murat and his officers were well pleased with their visit to Rome, and accepted from Pius VII and Consalvi a number of cameos and other works of art as tokens of friendship.

He returned to Florence in the first week of March. He had already written to Ali Pasha, the ruler of Albania, assuring him that France was the good friend of the Mussulman powers, and asking him to release a number of French prisoners, taken when Ali seized the fortresses of the Illyrian coast. He had also sent off ships from Ancona with supplies of ammunition for the French army blockaded in Egypt. In a letter to the First Consul, dated 8 March, he told him that the generals and officers were all afraid of being sent to Egypt. He had assured them that there was no reason to expect this. In the same letter he reports that he had assisted with his staff at a Te Deum in the Duomo for the re-establishment of peace, he had given a banquet in the evening, there had been a general illumination, and salutes of artillery had been fired during the day.

At the end of the letter there was a message for his wife :

# COMMAND IN ITALY 83

—' Scold Caroline. She is running about to balls. She will fall ill, and I shall lose my dear good Caroline, and Achille his little mother.' The news of Caroline came in letters from uncle Fesch, who passed on to Florence all the gossip of Paris. Fesch wrote, a few days later, that he had found Caroline in tears after reading a letter from her husband. He assured Murat that she and the child were well. She could not refuse invitations to balls, but she was none the worse for the fatigue. She would soon be with him in Italy, and so put an end to his anxieties.

Peace having been concluded with Naples, and friendly relations re-established with Rome, Murat's next business was the inauguration of the new kingdom of Etruria. This short-lived State was to come into existence in virtue of a clause in the Treaty of Lunéville, which gave practical effect to an arrangement already made by Napoleon with the Spanish Bourbons—part of his policy of an alliance between France and Spain. The Duke of Parma, Ferdinand de Bourbon, was the grandson of Philip V of Spain, and was married to a Spanish infanta. Parma, Modena, Lucca and Tuscany were to form the new kingdom over which he was to reign at Florence as Ferdinand I of Etruria.

While the accession of King Ferdinand was being arranged, Murat prepared to execute another provision of the Lunéville Treaty by which Elba was ceded to France by Etruria. A summons to the Tuscan governor of Porto Ferrajo was followed by the concentration of a brigade at Leghorn. The embarkation was delayed by a mutiny of some of the troops, who thought that they were going to be shipped off to Egypt. At last, in the night of 30 April to 1 May, the expedition disembarked at Porto Longone in Elba, under General Tharreau. Longone surrendered at once, but the capital of the island refused to submit and held out till November against Tharreau's brigade besieging it by land, and Admiral Gantheaume's squadron blockading the port.

On 6 May, Caroline arrived at Florence with little Achille. Murat was delighted with the child. 'Achille is charming, he has already cut two teeth,' he says in a postcript at the end of a long official report to the First Consul. It was shortly after Caroline's arrival that he wrote (16 May) to his aged mother at La Bastide, a characteristic letter that must have delighted old Jeanne Murat, always a devout Catholic :—

'It is a long time since I have written to you, my dear Mother, but be quite sure that it is not through forgetfulness, for you are always present to my heart. And how could I forget her who gave me life, brought me up in the first years of my boyhood, and gave me the means of happiness in making me affectionate? The Holy Father has sent me a rosary for you, blessed by his own hand. What a pleasure it is to me to send you this mark of attention on the part of the Head of the Church. What a joy it will be to you to receive it. I am the happiest of men, for I have with me my Caroline and my pretty Achille. My happiness would be complete if you were near us; if I could console your old age. How I envy my brother's lot! He is with you, he sees you, he loves you, he ought to be very happy. Adieu, my dear mother. I hope to go to Barèges. Then I shall have the pleasure of embracing you. I embrace you with all my heart. J. MURAT
'I send you the portrait of the Pope.'

It was a miniature that Pius VII had given to him. So Jeanne Murat hoped again to see her son.

Caroline shared with her husband the honours paid to the representative of France during the long series of fêtes that marked the foundation of the new kingdom of Etruria. In July, Murat visited King Ferdinand at Parma. In August Florence was *en fête* for the reception of its king and the proclamation of the new constitution.

Murat had completed his work in central Italy. He had proved to the First Consul that he could render him solid service in the field of administration and diplomacy as well as at the head of his troops. The impression he had made at Rome was especially useful now that the negotiation of a Concordat with the Holy See was one of the chief points of Napoleon's policy. Consalvi's letters show that Murat was regarded as a personal friend. Among the presents sent to the general at Florence there was a valuable Raphael from the cardinal's own gallery.

After the fêtes of Florence he received, early in August, a welcome proof of Napoleon's esteem for him. He was given the command of all the troops south of the Alps, the 'Army of Italy,' and in the middle of August he was directed to make Milan, the capital of the Cisalpine Republic, his headquarters.

## CHAPTER VI

### MURAT COMMANDER-IN-CHIEF AT MILAN

#### 1801-1803

MURAT took up his residence at Milan on 20 August. Brune, whom he had so persistently attacked in his letters to the First Consul, was generous enough to write to him congratulating him on his appointment. Murat, who had learned something of diplomacy, sent a most courteous reply. 'My dear Brune,' he wrote, 'I beg that you will believe that I feel how much I am flattered in being chosen as your successor, and at the same time how difficult it is for me to replace you.' Brune was anxious that one of his divisional generals, Boudet should be given a command in the Cisalpine Republic. Murat expressed his pleasure at being able to comply with this request. He was all the more pleased, he said, because Boudet had acted with him in the Marengo campaign. But these were all empty compliments on his part, for, on 15 September, he wrote to the First Consul :—

'Brune wrote to me some time ago to ask me to employ Boudet in my command, and I thought it right to ask this of Berthier (the War Minister). Policy required me to take this step, but a sounder policy requires that I should ask you not to send him here. All the generals of the Army of Italy have been spoiled. They think they are all Commanders-in-chief.'

The episode throws an unpleasant light on the self-seeking insincerity of Murat.

He wrote to his brother-in-law reporting adversely on the civil administration of the Cisalpine Republic. The officials were not up to their work. The whole system would

# COMMANDER-IN-CHIEF AT MILAN 87

have to be changed. As to the military forces in north Italy, they were too much scattered in small garrisons. His first step was to concentrate in larger bodies both the French army and the Italian troops of the Republic, and arrange peace manœuvres for the month of September.

Murat's correspondence during the autumn of 1801, mostly dated from Milan, is chiefly made up of letters dealing with the routine business of the moment. Here and there one comes on a passage that throws light on the disturbed state of northern Italy. Murat is no longer the ardent partisan of the Revolution. He is on the side of order. The existing Government at Milan he regarded as dangerously weak and inefficient. The actual administration had offered its resignation to the First Consul, who was to elaborate a new Constitution for the Cisalpine Republic. Writing on 28 August to Napoleon Murat urged that there should be no delay in making a change.

'Here, as everywhere else, authority that cannot make itself respected produces only evil, and this evil may have unfortunate results, if steps are not soon taken to remedy it. I think, therefore, that you ought not to hesitate to accept the resignation which the Government has sent to you. It will be easy to replace them. There are here men of worth and good repute whom public opinion already looks to for this purpose. They will carry out your views and secure the prosperity of the Cisalpine. The French name will then be no longer hateful, and we shall hear no more of rich landowners and pretended aristocrats being assassinated in the name of Bonaparte.

'Berthier orders me to make this Government respected. It is as if he said to me, " Make yourself the accomplice of its follies." I cannot at all make up my mind to play such a part. It is too repugnant to my views and my duty, and would identify me too much with him. He writes letters to people here that one is sorry to read, that show his weakness, and these his correspondents publish by hawking them round the cafés. I would not mention this to you, only that Moncey has already sent you copies of some of these letters. Berthier lets these people here parade him as their supporter and to believe them one would think that he, and not you, was the protector of the Cisalpine.

Besides, I swear to you, and you know that I have no reason to mislead you, that all the Republic is waiting impatiently for a Constitution which is known to be generally based on our own. Any other of a more popular kind, and therefore more favourable to the party now in power, would be received with sorrow.'

The new Constitution which, under Republican forms, gave all effective power to the President and his colleagues, was not adopted till December, when Napoleon met the delegates of the Cisalpine State at Lyons, was himself chosen chief of the Republic, and selected as his representative at Milan and Vice-President of the Cisalpine, Melzi, the head of a noble Milanese family and a man of moderate Conservative views.

Long before the Lyons conferences Murat was able to report that there was no disorder in northern Italy, and his subordinates were carrying out the training of the troops in the various camps and garrisons. As commander-in-chief at Milan he had a very easy position, and more ample resources than had yet been at his disposal. His pay and allowances amounted to 328,000 francs a year (more than thirteen thousand pounds sterling). Except for a few days when she went to see Venice, Caroline was with him. But, in the third week of October, Madame Murat left Italy to return for a while to Paris, taking Achille with her. Murat wished to go with her, but the First Consul refused his request for leave of absence. He accompanied Caroline, however, as far as the French side of the pass of Mont Cenis. He was back at Milan on 18 October.

In the beginning of the month news had reached Milan that preliminaries of peace between France and England had been signed at London. Murat sent the news to Pius VII in a letter to Consalvi, in which he addresses him familiarly as '*Mon cher Cardinal.*' He wrote also to Elba directing the general in command of the siege of Porto Ferrajo to conclude an immediate armistice with the garrison, which was made up of a British contingent, some *émigrés* officers, and a small body of Tuscans. On the eve of the armistice the garrison had made a sortie in which life was lost on

## COMMANDER-IN-CHIEF AT MILAN 89

both sides. It was the last engagement of the war. Another letter of Murat's was addressed to General Menou, commanding the French army in Egypt. He told him that peace was concluded, and said: 'May this news find you a conqueror, or at least unconquered, as you have been till now! May it be a recompense for the glorious resistance you have made, and the undaunted courage you have shown.' The aide-de-camp who sailed from Ancona with the letter was to buy some Arab horses in Egypt for his chief. But when Murat came back from the Mont Cenis on 18 October he found and sent on to Napoleon letters, received from Alexandria by way of Taranto, that told of the defeat and capitulation of the French army in Egypt on the eve of the peace. In November he wrote a formal letter to 'the Consuls of the French Republic' stating that, while he was in Egypt, General Bonaparte had given him, in recognition of his services, a house at Cairo, which, as a result of the capitulation of the army under Menou, he could no longer hope to possess. He asked that, in compensation for this loss, its value should be paid to him, and added that, if this petition was granted, he meant to devote the money to the making of a road connecting the Departments of the Lot and the Cantal, and passing through his native commune. 'This would be his first service to the country in which he was born.' I can find no trace of the petition having had any result. Murat's first gift to his native Department was characteristically a portrait of himself, painted by a Milanese artist, which the Departmental authorities hung in a place of honour in their hall of assembly.

During the war numerous corps of volunteeers had been organized in northern Italy. These were now a subject of anxiety. Murat reported that they were at the call of any promoter of disorder. It was decided to disarm them. The operation was carried out peacefully except at Bologna, where, in the evening of 3 November, the cavalry and artillery of the local National Guard joined the free corps in resisting the order. The cannon of the National Guard were brought out in front of the town hall and loaded. The gunners stood by them with lighted matches. In the hope of inducing the French troops to side with the revolt placards were posted, headed ' Death to the chiefs of the army. Eternal friendship to the soldiers.' General Gobert, who commanded at Bologna, turned out the whole of the garrison, disarmed the National Guard, captured their seven cannon, and arrested the leaders. After this Murat ordered that National Guardsmen in north Italy should not be allowed to keep their arms at home. Muskets, bayonets, and cartridges had all to be stored in armouries, where, if need be, the troops could take possession of them. This would prevent any dangerous demonstrations when the new Constitution was proclaimed.

He was still anxious to revisit Paris, and made repeated applications for a short leave of absence, but it was not till the end of December that the First Consul thought he could safely leave his post. One reason for his wish to be again for a short time in the capital was that he was expending large sums in the purchase of property in and near Paris. The commanders of the Republican armies in the days of the Consulate found means to accumulate considerable fortunes, and Murat had been one of the most successful in this respect. He had already purchased, on 15 June, 1800, the estate of Villiers, near Neuilly-sur-Seine, as well as the old church and cemetery of Villiers. On 15 December, 1801 he bought, through his Paris agents, an estate at La Motte-Sainte-Héraye in the Department of the Deux Sèvres, which was estimated to produce an annual revenue of 32,000 francs. The price was 470,000 francs. Within four months he expended more than a million francs. His fortune was probably not entirely the result of economics on pay allowances. On 12 January, 1802 half a million was paid as the price of the Hôtel Thélusson, which he meant to make his town house in Paris. The Hôtel was one of the finest houses in Paris, a palace built in 1780 by the architect Ledoux for the millionaire banker Thélusson. With its courtyards and

## COMMANDER-IN-CHIEF AT MILAN 91

gardens it covered an extensive site with two façades, one on the Rue de Provence, the other on the Rue de la Victoire. Carriages arriving by the great archway on the Rue de Provence passed by a paved slope to a terraced road round the garden, leading to the arcade under which the guests alighted at the foot of the great staircase. Thence the carriages went down by another inclined road to the range of stables fronting on the Rue de la Victoire. The great staircase led to the reception rooms, two antechambers, two immense drawing-rooms, a concert hall, a library, and a picture gallery. From one of the drawing-rooms the windows opened on a portico of Corinthian columns, giving access to a terrace adorned with statues that looked out on a walled garden. Murat had made a good bargain in securing this palace at the price he paid for it, and he spent money freely in redecorating and furnishing it for Caroline. In the following March there was another purchase, a considerable tract of land being added to his country estate at Villiers, at the cost of 153,000 francs.

It was in the last week of December that he at length obtained leave to visit Paris. He went as far as Lyons with some of the Milanese delegates to the conference that was in session there, and was at home for the New Year.

On 4 January, 1802 he was with Caroline among the guests at the marriage of Louis Bonaparte, the First Consul's brother, and Hortense Beauharnais, the daughter of Josephine by her first marriage. It was a brilliant gathering. The civil ceremony had taken place in the morning at the Tuileries. In the evening the religious marriage ceremony took place at the old home of the Bonapartes in the Rue de la Victoire. A large room had been converted into a temporary chapel, and at the improvised altar stood the Papal Legate, Cardinal Caprara, wearing cope and mitre, with crosier in hand. Napoleon and Josephine were there, and Madame Letizia, the First Consul's mother. There, too, were Joseph Bonaparte (about to start for Amiens to settle the final treaty with England), and Lucien and the sisters of the First Consul.

With Pauline was her husband, General Leclerc, about to go to take command in San Domingo. When the cardinal had ended the ceremony of the marriage, Murat came forward leading Caroline by the hand. He told Caprara that on account of the state of affairs in France at the time of his marriage there had been only the civil formalities required by the law, and he and his wife now wished for the blessing of the Church on their union. So there was a second marriage ceremony, the effect of which, by the law of the Church, would be to remove all doubts as to the legitimacy of little Achille.[1]

Murat spent a few days at Lyons in the last week of January, and was again at Milan in the beginning of February. By a proclamation dated 2 February, 1802 addressed to the people of the Cisalpine, he announced to them that their new Constitution had been completed, and that the State had been given a new name, 'The Italian Republic.' Its founder would watch over its progress under the new regime, for 'Bonaparte' would be the head of the reorganized state. The Vice-President Melzi, who would directly exercise his authority among them, had 'been chosen for that eminent position by the voice of public opinion.' A new period of happiness had begun for them. The new name of the 'Italian Republic' would be a motive for burying in oblivion the troubles and the errors of the past. 'This name should arouse in your souls a noble pride. It forcibly summons you to the love of all the virtues, the cultivation of all the arts, which have so long adorned the happy land of Italy.'

The 'happy land' had, meanwhile, to provide on a liberal

[1] In the collection of *Lettres et Documents pour servir à l'Histoire de Joachim Murat*, there is a letter dated 'Lyon, 14 Nivôse, an X. (4 janvier, 1802).' The place (Lyon) has apparently been supplied by the editor to a letter bearing only the date. There is here a curious oversight on the part of an editor as competent and as careful as M. Paul Le Breton, for it is quite certain that on 4 January, Murat was in Paris. The letter (*Lettres et Documents*, vol. ii. p. 226) is addressed to Murat's chief of the staff, General Charpentier, and deals with various military details. It must have been written in Paris, and perhaps Murat purposely omitted to add the place to the date, as when he left Milan it was generally understood that it was only for the purpose of proceeding to Lyons to take part in the discussions on the new Constitution of the Cisalpine Republic.

scale for the pay and maintenance of its French garrison. Napoleon had said that he did not mean to send one *sou* across the Alps, and, before the ink on his proclamation was quite dry, Murat was writing to King Louis of Etruria that he must at once pay his share of the contributions. Murat was himself well provided for. Before he bade good-bye to Napoleon at Lyons, he had arranged with him that besides his pay as commander-in-chief of the French troops in Italy, raised to 40,000 francs a month, he should have an allowance of 30,000 francs a month for 'extraordinary expenses,' and a palace at Milan for his residence. Thus he had more than £33,000 sterling a year during the rest of his stay in Italy.

Unless he is greatly belied, these were not his only resources. Under the provisions of the Treaty of Amiens (signed on 27 March, 1802) the French troops were to be withdrawn from central and southern Italy. Murat was to visit Rome and Naples in order personally to direct the evacuation of the Papal and Neapolitan territories. In March, Consalvi wrote him a most friendly letter, and the Sciarra Palace was being prepared for his reception. Suddenly it was announced that his visit must be deferred. He had hurried off to Paris, where he arrived on 23 March, remaining there till 6 April, when he started on his return journey to Milan.

There is a mystery about this flying visit to Paris. It was explained at the time that it was due to anxiety about the health of Caroline, who was expecting soon to give birth to another child. But Caroline was well enough to preside as hostess at a splendid fête which Murat gave to Napoleon at his country house, the château of Villiers-Neuilly, on the eve of his return journey. Another rumour, to which Consalvi alludes in a letter to the Legate Caprara, was that Murat had been accused of receiving considerable sums in order to induce him to secure appointments for various people in the new administration of the Italian Republic, and was summoned to Paris to explain his conduct. If this was the case, he must have succeeded in clearing himself of the charge and satisfying Napoleon, for the First Consul showed him nothing but good will.

Passing through Milan, Murat reached Rome on 18 April. The Concordat had just been signed, Murat was a *persona grata* with the Pope and his Secretary of State, and the Papal court gave him a brilliant reception. A guard of honour of fifty men was stationed at the Palazzo Sciarra. On the 19th there was a dinner at the Vatican, at which he was the chief guest. The cardinals, the foreign ambassadors, and the Roman nobles were all there to do him honour. He had a long interview with the Pope, and received as a present from him a cameo set in diamonds. On the 20th he went on to Naples. There the king presented him with a splendid sword, with a diamond-studded hilt, afterwards the weapon that Murat carried in many a famous cavalry charge. The reception at Naples, however, was a contrast to his experiences at Rome. Everything was perfectly correct and polite, but the Bourbon court showed no friendly cordiality.

During this journey in Italy, while on his way back to Milan, Murat received the news that on 25 April Caroline had given birth to a daughter, who was christened Marie-Letizia-Josephine-Annunziade, the names of Napoleon's wife and mother, added to those that Caroline had received at baptism. Murat was anxious to be with his wife again, and the First Consul made no objection. He hurried north from Milan, and arrived in Paris on 25 May. He stayed in the capital till the following October.

During this long stay in France, he kept in touch with his command in Italy by correspondence. In June he wrote to his brother André, telling him that he was sending his courier, François, to La Bastide, with a carriage, which was to bring to Paris his nieces, the two daughters of their elder brother, Pierre, for whose education he was going to provide. He asked André to send with them his son, Pierre Gaetan. 'It is time,' he wrote, 'for him to begin his education. He can go through it with Achille.' Some presents were sent by the courier, and there was

## COMMANDER-IN-CHIEF AT MILAN 95

a message for the old mother. 'Tell my dearest mother that I always love her with all my heart, and that my happiness would be perfect if she could witness it and share it.' Probably he only half meant this. Jeanne Murat would have been out of her element in the splendid salons of the Hôtel Thélusson, and was happier with André in the inn at La Bastide.

One may anticipate events and note here the subsequent career of the three children, for whose education their uncle Joachim was providing. The girls had already been for some years at a country school, and Murat now sent them to Madame Campan's fashionable academy at St. Germain, where Hortense and Caroline had been pupils. The elder girl, Marie Antoinette, was married in 1808 to Prince Charles of Hohenzollern; the younger, Clotilde Jeanne, was married in 1812 to the Duke of Carigliano. André's son, Pierre Gaetan, was only four years old when he was brought to Paris to be Achille's playfellow. As the Comte Pierre Murat, he was elected to the National Assembly by his native Department in 1830, and died at La Bastide in 1847.

It was not till the autumn that Murat left Paris to return to Milan. Caroline went with him. They travelled by way of Lyons, and on 16 October, passed over the Mont Cenis. Napoleon, who had halted at the hospice of the St. Bernard during his march over the Alps, and seen the monks distributing bread and wine to his soldiers, had founded another Cistercian hospice on the Mont Cenis. Murat made a short halt there. He wrote to Napoleon of his reception by the 'good monks of the *auspice*' (his spelling sometimes breaks down over an unfamiliar word or name). They were devoted to their founder, they longed for Napoleon's portrait. He had promised to send it to them. He also suggested that some money should be sent to them. They entertained officers passing over the Mont Cenis, and even lent them money, which was not always repaid. They were at the end of their resources. At Turin the travellers were received by the civil and ecclesiastical authorities. Murat reported that with good management there would be no serious opposition to the projected annexation of Piedmont to France.

At Milan, he was at first on the best of terms with Melzi and the Government of the Italian Republic. During this stay in Italy, he wrote frequently and at great length to Napoleon. In some of the letters he writes with remarkable frankness. He warns him that there is a considerable party in Italy that is disappointed with the results of his policy. They had hoped for a united Italy, one Republic with Rome for its capital, and they saw in the First Consul a reactionist, who was not only maintaining the power of the King of Naples and the Pope, but set up a new kingdom in Tuscany, and, if he had kept the Cisalpine Republic in being, had put the aristocratic party in control of it, and given Venice to Austria, after destroying its old Republican institutions. Murat warns him that many Italians were thinking that it might be better to throw themselves into the hands of the English.

He was the declared enemy of the men who thus clung to the old ideals of the Revolution. His standpoint was that of the Italian general, Lecchi, who, repudiating the suggestion that he was in sympathy with the Italian ' Jacobins,' declared that he had benefited enough by one Revolution and did not want to see another. Under these circumstances, one would have expected Murat to remain on the best of terms with the Conservative and aristocratic Republican Melzi. But here the proud, dominating spirit of the soldier came into play. Murat would have been well pleased to reside at Milan as the French military governor of Lombardy. He chafed at his necessary subordination to a mere civilian politician. He thought Melzi was too anxious to be everyone's friend, too gentle with the ultra-Liberals, whom Murat talked of as ' Jacobins ' and ' brigands.' His personal vanity made him think that the vice-president did not treat him with sufficient consideration. He complained of want of due respect being

## COMMANDER-IN-CHIEF AT MILAN    97

shown to him and his wife at public ceremonies, and even on social occasions, at balls and banquets.

During the winter of 1802-03 there was continual friction, with repeated complaints of Melzi in Murat's letters to Napoleon. In December he had made a tour of inspection of the garrisons in Lombardy, accompanied by Caroline. Reviews in the morning, banquets and balls in the afternoon and evening, were the order of the day. When he returned to Milan the tension between him and the civil authorities began again. He felt so dissatisfied with his position that, when he read in the *Moniteur* of 7 January, 1803 the news that General Leclerc, the husband of Pauline Bonaparte, had died of fever in San Domingo, he wrote to Napoleon (14 January) offering to take his place. The command of a small body of troops engaged in bush fighting against negro irregulars in a fever haunted West Indian island would be a poor exchange for life in a Milanese palace, but Murat was for the moment anxious to risk his life in ' that dangerous climate,' to use his own phrase. Napoleon, however, did not mean to lose another brother-in-law in San Domingo, and thought Murat would be more useful to him in Europe.

In February there was a crisis at Milan. On 24 January Murat had written a long letter to Napoleon. He began by saying that, as the First Consul took no notice in his letters of any political news he sent him, he supposed he meant him to confine his attention to military reports. But nevertheless he must tell him of what was happening in Lombardy. Alarming rumours were being spread as to alleged disasters in San Domingo. Then there were reports, industriously circulated, that the Italian Republic was to be annexed to France, and that 30,000 French troops would soon arrive in Milan. At the same time a scandalous attack on France was being passed from hand to hand in the form of a poem, of which he enclosed a copy. The author was Captain Ceroni of the 3rd Italian Infantry. Before printing it, Ceroni had shown it in manuscript to Cicognara, a member of the Council of State, and to General Theullié,

G

who was regarded by Murat as one of his enemies. The poem was dedicated to Cicognara.

Ceroni's literary effort, published under the *nom-de-guerre* of Timone Cimbro, was a denunciation of the 'betrayal' of Venice to Austria. In exaggerated poetical language it spoke of the French brigand who had come, 'covered with royal blood,' crying out 'Liberty or death!' only to change liberty into tyranny, and called on the earth to open and swallow up the false benefactor and his treacherous gifts. Murat, without the slightest proof, asserted that Melzi encouraged these 'patriots,' and that he was in secret correspondence with Moreau, the First Consul's enemy. Things were in a dangerous condition, said Murat, the Neapolitan court was hostile. All the best men in Italy would rejoice at an end being put to this provisional state of things by annexation to France.

Napoleon did not like poets and phrase-makers of any kind, least of all when they were soldiers on the active list, but he did not take any immediate action on Murat's report, nor was he alarmed by further letters, in which the general tried to persuade him that a revolutionary movement was being planned in Italy. The First Consul had received reassuring news from Melzi, and was anxious to keep things quiet in Lombardy. But on 27 February Murat wrote to him that, having learned that Ceroni was on the point of publishing 'another diatribe' like the first, he had, after informing Melzi of his intentions, sent General Lecchi to arrest Captain Ceroni and seize his papers. Amongst them were letters from Cicognara, Theullié, and Magenta, the prefect of Bologna, all lending themselves to meanings hostile to the French domination in Italy. He sent on the papers to the First Consul. He further told him that Melzi was allowing the agitation the utmost freedom. At the theatre, a few days ago, the *Conspiracy of the Pazzi* had been played. The audience was an 'assembly of brigands, whose applause was vociferous' whenever a line could be given a meaning hostile to France and Napoleon. The next piece announced was *The Death*

## COMMANDER-IN-CHIEF AT MILAN 99

of *Cæsar*, and there would doubtless be similar scenes. The patriots were in correspondence with England. An Englishman had said lately that the London merchants were closing up all business with Italy, and that fifteen British ships of the line were under orders for the Mediterranean.

Napoleon was now thoroughly angry. He wrote to Murat: ' I have read attentively the papers you have sent me. You have done just what is right in arresting the officer who wrote such an infamous pamphlet.' On the same day, 11 March, he wrote to Melzi: ' If your Ministers of the Interior and of the Police had done their duty, the authors of such pamphlets would have been severely punished, and there would not have been the scandal of our seeing a French officer arresting a citizen of the Italian Republic.' Melzi made a very weak reply, excusing his tolerance of the agitation.

Napoleon sent an order to Melzi and Murat to see that Cicognara, Theullié, and Magenta were arrested, and with Ceroni brought to trial before the Council of State. On 11 April the Council condemned Ceroni to be expelled from the army, and to be under police supervision for three years; Cicognara and Theullié to loss of rank and employment, and enforced residence in a place to be named by the Government; and Magenta to removal from his office, and loss of seniority in the civil service. Melzi, in presence of Murat's attacks, sent his resignation to the First Consul. But Napoleon thought that enough had been done to bring the 'patriots' to reason, and was in a conciliatory frame of mind. He told Melzi that he must remain in office, and wrote to Murat that he must make friends with the Vice-President. He told him to send back by the messenger who brought the letter a reply that ' all is well between you and Melzi, that all quarrels are at an end, and that everything is going well in the Italian Republic.'

Murat acted on his orders, and there was a formal reconciliation. Caroline, who had kept out of the quarrel, helped to make the pacification more real by tactfully using her influence to smooth the relations between her husband and the Vice-President. When on 16 May, 1803 her third child, a boy, was born, she invited Melzi to act as godfather at the baptism, when the child received the names of Lucien Napoleon, in honour of two of his uncles, and Melzi's names—Charles Francis—as a tribute to the Vice-President.

Indirectly the renewed outbreak of war between France and England in May 1803 helped to keep the peace between Murat and the civil authorities, for he had now to occupy himself with the active organisation of the military forces of northern and central Italy. He still broke out into complaints against the Milan government in his letters to Napoleon, and he had a fierce quarrel with one of his subordinates, General Gouvion St. Cyr. In a letter to Napoleon he said Saint Cyr was simply lying, but he was not surprised at anything he did, for he came from ' the Army of the Rhine, and all these gentlemen thought they were great personages! (*de grands cires*—a poor misspelled pun that evaporates in the translation). The quarrel originated in St. Cyr reporting directly to Paris instead of to Murat's headquarters. St. Cyr was acting towards him, just as he had acted towards Brune. The affair is only worth noting as an indication of Murat's character and temper.

## CHAPTER VII

### MURAT MILITARY GOVERNOR OF PARIS

#### 1803-1805

IN August 1803 Murat was summoned to Paris. Napoleon was not only busy with plans for the invasion of England, but also engaged in the preliminaries of the proclamation of the Empire. He wanted to have the men of his inner circle at hand for eventualities. When Murat arrived in the capital on 23 August, he was still commander-in-chief of the French troops in Italy, and was not aware that he would not return to his post at Milan, and that a new and brilliant period of his career was opening before him.

His last act at Milan had been to arrange, by order of Napoleon, that a division of the army of the Italian Republic, 6000 strong, should be sent into France under the orders of General Pino. In an official dispatch, Melzi expressed his satisfaction at a step that marked the solidarity of the two Republics of France and Italy, but Murat told how the Vice-President could not conceal his disappointment on receiving the order—' he was sad, silent, with downcast looks.' It was a blow to all hopes of the independence of the Italian Republic, a proof that Napoleon regarded Milan as practically the capital of a French Department.

Until October, Murat's correspondence shows that he was still receiving reports from the garrisons of Italy, and directing its military affairs by letter. In November he spent a fortnight in his native Department, at last fulfilling his repeated promises to revisit the old home. The elections for the Corps Législatif had been fixed for the 23 Brumaire (10 November). On 29 October, Chaptal, the Minister of the Interior, informed Murat that the First Consul had chosen him to preside at the meeting of the Electoral College of the Department of the Lot at Cahors. The Electoral College was the limited body of voters that chose the deputies to the Corps Législatif, and the coming elections had a special importance, for the chief business of the new assembly would be the inauguration of the Empire. Murat's mission to Cahors was the result of a friendly arrangement with Napoleon.

At last, after twelve years of waiting, the aged Jeanne Murat welcomed her son at La Bastide. Caroline came with him, bringing her three children, to add to the joy of the old grandmother. The peasant proprietors and small farmers, who formed the family circle of friends at La Bastide, were dazzled with the sight of splendid horses and carriages and brilliantly uniformed equerries, but delighted to find that the great man, Napoleon's famous cavalry leader, the hero of Aboukir and Marengo, had forgotten no one, was ready to meet as equals the friends who had been his playfellows long ago, and anxious to know every one at La Bastide.

On 10 November, when after a public welcome by the city authorities, who had raised triumphal arches in his honour, he presided at the meeting of the electors at Cahors, he began his speech by saying that, although he ought perhaps to forget all personal matters, and speak only of the important public act for which they had been called together, he could not help trying to express to them his pleasure at being once more, after years of absence, among the scenes of his boyhood, and in the city where he had begun his education. He assured them that throughout his career his thoughts had turned to his native Department and his old companions. The days spent among them would be among the happiest of his life, and he rejoiced at seeing old friends again, and making new friends among them. The speech was enthusiastically applauded. It

## MILITARY GOVERNOR OF PARIS 103

was proposed that General Murat should be chosen as one of the four deputies of the Department. When the vote was taken it was found that he headed the list with 162 votes out of a possible 164.[1] He proposed, and had elected as the representative of the Department in the Senate, Fesch, whom Pius VII had lately made a Cardinal. The First Consul, who was reorganizing the educational system of France, had just established a lycée at Cahors. Murat secured the best appointment on its staff for the Citizen Janvier, till then acting as tutor to his nephews at Paris. After his election he spent a few more days at La Bastide, and returned to Paris on 15 November. It is not certain that he ever saw his native place again. He may have had a passing sight of it five years later, when he was on his way to Spain as lieutenant-general of the Emperor.

Napoleon did not send him back to Milan. On 15 January, 1804, he was appointed Military Governor of Paris, and Commandant of the troops of the 1st Military Division and of the National Guard. For the extraordinary expenses of his new post an allowance of 60,000 francs was granted to him, and Caroline was given an annual payment of 60,000 more from the First Consul's Civil List.

Murat, as Governor of Paris, made his town house, the stately Hotel Thélusson, his headquarters, and Caroline presided over a kind of semi-military court with a constant round of balls, banquets, and concerts. M. Frédéric Masson, with his painstaking attention to details, has given an elaborate description of the splendours of Murat's palace.[2] Parisian society talked of them as a manifestation of the growing tendency to ostentation, extravagance, and luxury. They were the expression of Murat's Gascon tendency to exaggeration and self-assertion, the same side of his char-

[1] In the official return of the election he is thus described:—
'MURAT, JOACHIM, né le 25 mars 1767, âgé de 37 ans, domicilié à Labaltide (sic), marié, ayant 3 enfants; avant 1789 étudiant à l'Université de Toulouse; depuis 1789 général en chef. Fortune personnelle: il paie 8963 de contributions; il a obtenu 162 suffrages sur 164.'
[2] *Napoléon et sa Famille*, vol. ii., pp. 201, etc.

acter that made him later on, as the leader of the imperial cavalry, invent new uniforms for his personal use, and ride into battle with a leopard skin saddle-cloth, red morroco boots, a tunic stiff with gold embroidery, a pelisse of costly furs, a cap plumed with ostrich feathers held by a jewelled brooch, a diamond hilted sabre, and gold on his spurs and the bit of his charger. Here, in the Hotel Thélusson, there was the same unmeasured display of brilliant colour and costly material. There was the series of drawing-rooms opening off each other, the first furnished and upholstered with blue velvet, and a lavish display of gold in embroidery, fringes, tassels, gilded console tables, with marble statues holding up golden candelabra, mirrors in massive gilded frames, and Turkish carpets. Then three other salons, each with its own scheme of colour, bronzes and marbles giving an air of solid wealth to relieve the mere display of silk, velvet, gilding, and embroidery. In the winter evenings the great salons were ablaze with wax lights, and bright with the uniforms of officers and the costumes of ladies who came to pay court to the sister of Napoleon, soon to be a princess. In the summer the château of Villiers was the scene of equally brilliant gatherings.

Murat had not held his court at the Hotel Thélusson for many weeks when he found himself forced to choose between being an accomplice in a crime or bidding farewell to all his growing prosperity. That he chose the former alternative, and was to some extent involved in Napoleon's culpability in the affair of the Duke d'Enghien, is I think so certain, that only partisans of Murat can seriously deny it. The only question is as to the extent to which he was involved in the tragedy.

To say that he was an instigator of, and a willing participator in the crime is most certainly to do him wrong. It is a calumny which had its origin in the gossip of the time. Madame de Rémusat echoes it when she writes of Murat: ' His part in this affair was odious. He it was who urged Napoleon on, repeating to him that his clemency would be taken for weakness, and that the Jacobins would be furious.' But Murat had no respect for the opinion of the 'Jacobins' in Italy, and still less in France, and Napoleon needed no urging.

Murat's fault was that he did not venture to make an effective resistance, and after a half-hearted opposition found a way of complying with orders that he had at first expressed his determination to disregard. Before D'Enghien was arrested at Ettenheim by a raid across the frontier of a foreign state, Murat knew of the project. He had been confidentially informed of it by the First Consul. He then understood that the Bourbon prince would have a fair trial before his peers, the military members of the Senate. He expected to be one of the tribunal, and even violated his pledge of secrecy by asking a brother general if he would act with him in the trial.

It was undoubtedly a shock to him when, after the arrest of the duke, he received a communication from the First Consul, dated '29 Ventôse, an XII' (20 March, 1804), informing him that the prisoner was to be tried by court martial at Vincennes, and that he was to see to this order being carried out. He turned to his friend Agar, who was with him, and said: 'Bonaparte wants to put a stain on my coat, but he won't succeed in doing so.'

It was early in the day. He sent for his carriage and drove to Malmaison, where there was a stormy interview with the First Consul. Bonaparte put an end to the discussion by saying, 'If you will not execute my orders I shall send you back to your mountains of Quercy.' This was the critical moment. A stronger man than Murat would have replied that he was ready to disappear into the obscurity of La Bastide rather than obey such orders. He should have insisted on D'Enghien having a fair trial. He might have further pressed for a pledge that even his condemnation should be followed by a graceful act of mercy. But he did not mean to sacrifice his brilliant prospects. He went away depressed, and troubled—*bouleversé*, to use Agar's expression; he was almost ill when he returned to the Hotel Thélusson. But the *moment to decide*[1] had passed. Henceforth there was no strong resolve, but only a feeble struggle to save his conscience by diminishing his direct responsibility.

César Berthier, his chief of the staff, was waiting for him and asked for the list of the court martial. Murat asked him why he was moving in the matter. He had given him no orders, and had said nothing about it. César replied that he had been sent by his brother, the Minister of War. 'Well,' replied Murat, 'tell your brother that I have just seen the First Consul, that I have told him I don't want to nominate the court martial, and that I will not do so.' Then Alexander Berthier himself arrived, but Murat was still struggling to escape responsibility. 'No, I will not nominate the court martial,' he said; 'let Bonaparte do so if he likes.'

Alexander Berthier went to Napoleon, and the result was that about seven in the evening Savary, the colonel of the Consular Gendarmerie, arrived at the Hotel Thélusson with a letter from Napoleon, which was an ultimatum. Without any allusion to his earlier remonstrances, it ordered Murat to appoint the court martial, suggesting the names; directed him to send a detachment of gendarmerie to garrison the château of Vincennes and 'execute the sentence,' and, so that there might be no mistake, went on to add words that proved that D'Enghien's case was already judged and his death decided upon :—

'Let the members of the court martial understand that it must complete its proceedings during the night, and order that the sentence, if, as I cannot doubt, it is a condemnation to death, shall be executed immediately, and the body of the condemned buried in one of the courtyards of the fort.'

A concluding paragraph informed him that Savary would carry out his orders.

---

[1] 'Once to every man and nation comes the moment to decide,
In the strife of Truth with Falsehood for the good or evil side;
Some great cause, God's new Messiah, offering each the bloom or blight,
Parts the goats upon the left hand and the sheep upon the right.
And the choice goes by for ever 'twixt the darkness and the light.'
                                                             LOWELL

## MILITARY GOVERNOR OF PARIS 107

Murat still tried to avoid taking any action. He dismissed Savary with the words: 'You have the First Consul's orders, sir, mine are not necessary to you. I have nothing to say to you.' Then César Berthier arrived with a draft order constituting the court martial, which had been prepared at the War Office. At first Murat refused to sign it, but (to quote Agar's narrative, which we may take to be Murat's statement of his case) 'his chief of the staff (César Berthier) pointed out to him that Bonaparte had in reality nominated the court martial as he had himself desired, for the names of its members were indicated by him (Bonaparte); that his own signature as Governor of Paris was nothing more than a formality, but a formality so necessary that he could not refuse it, without openly declaring war against the Government, and rendering inevitable a rupture, after which any reconciliation between his brother-in-law and himself would be impossible.' Murat gave way to this argument and signed the order.

After he had thus weakly yielded, several members of the court, who had been warned by Alexander Berthier, called at the Hotel Thélusson to ask for further instructions. Murat was annoyed at being thus forced to take further part in the ugly affair. He confined himself to telling them to go at once to Vincennes.

There in the darkness of the night between 20 and 21 March the deed of darkness was done. When D'Enghien had been huddled into his nameless grave in the ditch, Murat did not refuse his share of the blood money. With Savary and other accomplices in the tragedy he received a grant of 100,000 francs from the Civil List. He had his share in the reward, and cannot be wholly absolved from his share in guilt of the tragedy, which cunning Fouché described in a phrase that has become proverbial: 'It was worse than a crime. It was a mistake.'

In one way only he could perhaps have averted this blundering crime. If he had had the courage to declare that, rather than have any part direct or indirect in it, he would resign his Governorship of Paris, Napoleon might have hesitated to proceed to extremities. But he might have persisted and broken Murat's career. Murat did not take the risk. It may be true that when he heard that the sentence had been executed he burst into tears, for he was of a kindly, emotional character. It is certain that, with his easy-going conscience, he seriously thought that his abstention from direct part in the court martial saved him from any responsibility. Before his own judges at Pizzo he called God to witness that he had no part in the crime, and there is no need to suppose that he did not speak sincerely.

It is distinctly to his credit that he did his best to prevent further executions. When Napoleon was taking advantage of the Royalist plot to accuse every possible opponent of complicity in it, Murat used his influence to save more than one of the accused, and used it successfully. He even intervened in favour of Cadoudal, though without success. While trying, with Caroline's help, to secure the pardon of the Prince de Polignac and the Marquis de Rivière, he had the boldness to write to the First Consul in the hope of saving even Cadoudal :—

'George Cadoudal is guilty. But in a state of civil war one cannot talk of crimes in the strict legal sense. In the final result only circumstances determine who is guilty. Crimes committed in a time of crisis belong to the sphere of politics, not law. You are yourself a proof of what I assert. . . . George is no doubt very guilty, but he defended a cause that he believed to be just. . . . As you have pardoned MM. de Polignac and de Rivière, why not do so in George's case? He is a man of honour and of strong character. If you will pardon him I will make him my aide-de-camp, and answer for him with my head.'

One wishes he had shown such courage in the case of D'Enghien. Perhaps there was a reaction from his weakness. He was certainly greatly agitated at reports that represented him as having pressed for the death of the young duke while others were trying to save him. He

## MILITARY GOVERNOR OF PARIS 109

heard that Savary and his agents were helping to spread this false report, and in his indignation he wrote to the First Consul a letter complaining of these calumnies, offering to resign his Governorship, and ending with an allusion to Bonaparte's words at Malmaison :—

'I shall retire to my mountains of Quercy. Then people may freely circulate the story that Madame Bonaparte threw herself at your feet to obtain the pardon of the Duke d'Enghien, and that it was I that insisted on his death.'

Bonaparte sent for him and told him he was attaching too much importance to malicious gossip, and then, playing upon Murat's feelings as well as his ambitions, appealed to him 'not to desert his general, his friend, his brother-in-law at a moment when Royalist daggers were being drawn against him.' It was after this reconciliation that he gratified Murat with the pardon of De Polignac and De Rivière.

The First Consul had taken advantage of the abortive plot to destroy or banish every possible rival or opponent to his plans. The proscribed had been driven into exile or sent as prisoners to the swamps of Cayenne.

When all chance of opposition had thus been removed, the Empire was proclaimed by a plébiscite and a vote of the Senate on 18 May, 1804. Murat had been naturally a zealous promoter of the project. It was he who in the Corps Législatif had unveiled the statue of Napoleon as the law-giver of France, and spoken of the best hope of the country lying in the perpetuation of his wise and fortunate rule. As the Emperor's brother-in-law he could safely count on a rapid accumulation of honours and wealth. And he was not disappointed.

When the Marshalate was inaugurated, he was among the first to receive the new rank, and when the list of precedence among the marshals was issued his name stood second on it. Only Berthier, Napoleon's trusted chief of the staff, through whom he gave his orders to his armies, stood before Murat. Below him on the list were men who had a far more brilliant record of service and command in the field, for Murat's most important campaigns were yet to come, and so far his record of active service included only some minor operations with the army of the north, the campaign of Italy (1796), Egypt and Syria, and the campaign of Marengo. Lannes, Masséna, Ney, and others who were placed below him had fought more battles, but then they had not married a Bonaparte.

He was given the decoration of the Grand Eagle of the Legion of Honour, and the honorary title of Grand Admiral of France. This carried with it no authority over the navy, but was a courtly and ceremonial dignity, that gave him the second place among the great officers of the Empire—only Joseph Bonaparte standing before him. On occasions of high ceremony he would appear as Grand Admiral in the inner circle near the Emperor, wearing a costume designed by the artist David, hose and doublet, mantle, plumed cap, and gold sheathed court sword. The Grand Admiralty also gave him a place in the Senate.

One more coveted step in rank was at first denied him, but not for long. The decree of the Senate establishing the Empire had given to Napoleon's brothers, Joseph, Lucien, and Louis, the title of Princes of the Empire, and their wives were thus raised to the rank of princesses. At the State dinner at St. Cloud on the evening of 18 May, Caroline, hearing her sisters announced and addressed by their new title, while she was still mere 'Madame Murat,' burst into tears of angry disappointment. Next morning Napoleon reproached her with making a scene at the dinner table, and there was a lively altercation between brother and sister. 'To listen to you,' said Napoleon, 'one would think I had robbed you of the inheritance of the late king, our father.' Caroline's reply to the sarcasm was to fall down fainting. But she had gained her point. On 20 May the *Moniteur* announced that under the new régime of the Empire, French princes and princesses were to have the style of 'Imperial Highness,' and the Emperor's sisters were to have the same title. If Caroline was to be a princess her husband might feel slighted if he were not a prince, so an imperial decree settled this point, but the promotion to princely rank was due to his marriage as well as his services. 'We have desired,' said the Emperor, 'not only to recognise the services which General Murat has rendered to 'the country, and the particular attachment to our person which he has shown in all the circumstances of his life, but also to render what is due to the dignity of our crown, in raising to the rank of a prince one who is so closely attached to us by ties of blood.'

With these new honours there came new sources of revenue for the Murats. M. Frédéric Masson reckons up the new marshal's official income, and one may thus tabulate his gains :—

| | |
|---|---|
| As Grand Admiral of the Empire . . | 333,000 francs. |
| As Senator . . . . . . | 36,000 ,, |
| Grand Cross of the Legion of the Honour | 20,000 ,, |
| As Marshal of France . . . . | 40,000 ,, |
| As Governor of Paris . . . . | 60,000 ,, |
| As Commandant of the 1st Military Division | 12,000 ,, |
| Total pay and salaries | 501,000 ,, |
| Allowances.—Office expenses . 144,000 ⎫ Lodging . . 10,000 ⎬ Forage . . 15,000 ⎭ | 169,000 ,, |
| Grand total | 670,000 francs. |

This was Murat's official income. There was in addition the revenue from his investments, such as the 32,000 francs annual rental of profits from the La Motte Sainte Heraye estate. Then Caroline had a revenue of 240,000 francs allowed to her, as a princess of the imperial family, from Napoleon's Civil List. M. Masson is probably not exaggerating when he estimates the total income of the Murats in the first year of the Empire at about a million and a half of francs.

Caroline also received presents from her imperial brother,

200,000 francs as a New Year's gift, on the evening of 31 December, 1804, and when she gave birth to her second daughter, Louise Julie Caroline, on the following 22 March, the palace of the Elysée. The Emperor provided in various sums the total amount of 970,000 francs, which was required to buy out the actual tenants, for the Elysée, during the Revolution, had passed into private hands. Its grounds had been converted into a garden where concerts were given, and wooden booths and shops had been erected against its façade. It was only after some twelve months that Caroline could take possession of it—all this time was needed to secure the removal of its occupants, compensating them for disturbance, and to restore the palace and gardens to their original condition.

In the fêtes and ceremonies of the coronation in December 1804, Murat, in his twofold capacity of Governor of Paris and Grand Admiral of France, took a prominent part. As commander of the troops in Paris he was responsible for the elaborate military display, and the equally elaborate precautions of the great day. In the procession to the choir of Notre Dame, where Pius VII waited at the high altar to crown the Emperor, Murat, as Grand Admiral, carried her crown in front of Josephine. Caroline was one of the sister princesses who bore up her train. When the city of Paris gave a banquet to the Emperor and Empress, it was Murat who, as governor of the capital, received their Majesties on the steps of the Hôtel de Ville. He was the most prominent figure among the marshals at the fête they gave to Josephine at the Opera.[1]

After the coronation Napoleon went to Milan to assume the Iron Crown of Lombardy, for the Italian Republic had been transformed into the kingdom of Italy. He had thought for a while of giving this tributary crown to Murat, but hesitated, and finally abandoned the idea. He was not

---

[1] Soon after the coronation, Napoleon gave Murat the pleasure of transmitting to his brother André the star of the Legion of Honour. Later, the Emperor gave the honest farmer of La Bastide the rank of a count of the Empire. Murat provided him with the means of building himself a country house, that became the nucleus of the château of La Bastide Murat.

# MILITARY GOVERNOR OF PARIS 113

sure that the memories of troubles belonging to his brother-in-law's last stay at Milan would help to an auspicious reign. During this absence from Paris, he had occasion to warn Murat that he must not trench upon his own prerogatives even in minor matters. Murat, as Governor of Paris, had held a review at the Tuileries, in which some battalions of the newly formed Imperial Guard were in line. Napoleon wrote to him that only the Emperor was to hold reviews and inspections on the Place du Carrousel. The Governor of Paris must choose for his reviews the Champ de Mars, or the Champs Elysées, and the Guard must not appear at them. It would be better, he thought, to have manœuvres instead of reviews. In this case he might have some battalions of the Guard under his orders.

On his return from Italy Napoleon devoted his attention chiefly to the great project for the invasion of England, the formation of the Armée d'Angleterre, with its headquarters at Boulogne, the assembling of the flotilla that was to transport it across the Channel, and the naval combinations that were to give him command of the narrow seas for the brief interval that he judged sufficient for the attempt. Murat was to command the cavalry of the invading army, and, accompanied by Caroline, he paid more than one visit of inspection to the camps of the north coast. But Napoleon's admirals failed to give him the promised command of the Channel, and English subsidies helped Austria to arm, and in 1805 brought a new coalition into being against the Empire—England, Sweden, Austria, and Russia being the four parties to the combination.

When it became evident that the invasion scheme could not be realized, and that the Grand Army, organized on the shores of the Channel, would soon have to march across the Rhine to meet Austrians and Russians in south Germany and on the Danube, Napoleon sent Murat and Bertrand on a flying visit to the probable scene of the operations. Bertrand's mission was to secure the adhesion of the Elector of Bavaria to the French side, with promises of advantages after the war, and arguments that the winning side would

H

be that of Napoleon. Murat's business was to make a rapid study of the ground, and especially of the road communications between Rhine and Danube. It says something for Napoleon's opinion of his military capacity and judgment that he chose him for such an errand.

Travelling in a post-chaise with passports made out in the name of 'Colonel de Beaumont,' Murat started on August 25, 1805, and was back at Strasburg by the middle of September, having in the meanwhile covered many hundred miles on the roads of south Germany, mostly in Bavarian territory. His route was from Paris to Mayence, then one of the French Rhine fortresses, thence by Wurzburg and Bamberg towards the frontier of Bohemia, studying the possibilities of a march on Prague, and reading in his post-chaise the record of Marshal de Belleisle's campaign, the story of the victorious French invasion of Bohemia in 1741, which Napoleon had told him to take with him. Turning southwards, as he approached the Austrian frontier, he travelled by Nuremberg to the Danube at Ratisbon, then followed the course of the great river eastwards to the frontier, and its junction with the river Inn at Passau. From Passau he followed the lower course of the Inn up stream, then turned west to Munich, drove on to Ulm, soon to be world-famous, examined the roads of the Black Forest, and reached Strasburg in the middle of September, whence he sent his report to Napoleon. He had been over much of the ground on which he was to direct the marches of his cavalry corps in the coming struggle.

While Murat's post-chaise was rattling over the roads of Bavaria the Boulogne camps had broken up, and when he reached Strasburg the Grand Army was marching in parallel columns to various points along the Rhine. Murat's part in the coming campaign had been assigned to him, and it gave him brilliant opportunities of distinction. He was to be *Grand maître de la Cavalerie* a title suggested to Napoleon by the old Roman custom that placed beside the *Imperator* the general commanding in chief, a *Magister equitum* or 'Master of the Horse,' to command the cavalry.

# MILITARY GOVERNOR OF PARIS 115

It is curious to see this aping of the classical empire coming out even in minor details. Napoleon at this time still kept on his coins the old device 'République Française' on the reverse, while on the obverse appeared his medallion portrait as 'Empereur des Français,' just as the Cæsars had affected to maintain Republican forms under the Roman Empire.

In the organization of the imperial armies, each army corps included a division or brigade of three or four regiments of light cavalry. This mounted force was sufficient for scouting, outpost, and advanced-guard work, but not intended for shock tactics in the field. The rest of the cavalry was united in a corps of several divisions under the name of the 'cavalry reserve.' We would now call it the independent cavalry of the army. It was intended to be employed first in covering the main advance, and then the whole of it, or several divisions, would be temporarily attached to whichever group of army corps was engaged in a movement that would end in a decisive battle. The organization of the reserve cavalry under Murat's command in 1805, was as follows :—

Heavy cavalry—General Nansouty's Division :—
    Four regiments of cuirassiers.
    Two regiments of carbineers.
General d'Hautpoul's Division :—
    Four regiments of cuirassiers.

Dragoons—three divisions of six regiments each, and a division of unmounted dragoons organized in battalions—
    1st Division.  General Klein.
    2nd Division.  General Beaumont.
    3rd Division.  General Walther.
    4th Division.  General Bourcier (eight battalions).

Light cavalry—General Milhaud's Division :—
    Four regiments of chasseurs and hussars.

Murat had thus under his command thirty-two regiments of cavalry and eight battalions of unmounted dragoons, 22,000 men, and 14,000 horses. The large proportion of unmounted men appears to have been the result of the cavalry corps being originally formed for the invasion for England, an operation in which it would not be possible to transport a large number of horses across the Channel.

The proportion of horse artillery was very small for such a large body of mounted troops. Murat had in all only twenty-four guns. Three were assigned to each of the cuirassier divisions, and two to each division of mounted dragoons, and to Milhaud's light cavalry. This made up a total of only fourteen horse artillery guns. Ten heavier pieces were attached to Bourcier's dismounted division of dragoons.

Murat asked for and secured as his chief of the staff General Belliard. He belonged to one of the old feudal families of Poitou, and before the Revolution had been known as the Comte de Belliard. He was a young man of twenty when the Bastille was stormed, and he then threw in his lot with the Revolution, dropped his title, and the 'de' before his name, and in 1791 volunteered for the army, and was soon elected captain by his comrades. He distinguished himself in the Army of the North, and was serving on Dumouriez's staff, when Murat was a *chef d'escadron* in Landrieux's chasseurs. He was staff officer to Hoche on the Rhine, and was then transferred to the army of Italy, and in the campaign of 1796, and on the field of Arcola he was promoted to the rank of brigadier-general by Bonaparte. After serving with Joubert in the Tyrol, he went to Egypt, and accompanied Dessaix in his pursuit of the Mamelukes up the Nile to the First Cataract at Assouan. He was then governor of Cairo, and it was there he became one of Murat's friends.[1]

Whilst his cavalry divisions were moving towards the Rhine, Murat had a busy time at Strasburg. By an order, dated 30 August, Napoleon had given him the title of 'Lieutenant-General of the Emperor commanding in his

---

[1] Belliard has a statue at Brussels, in the Rue Royale, looking out upon the Parc. This commemorates his services to Belgium, whose army he organized, after the constitution of the new kingdom. He died at Brussels in January 1832.

## MILITARY GOVERNOR OF PARIS 117

absence,' and directed him to make Strasburg his headquarters, superintend the concentration of the various corps at the points where they were to cross the Rhine, make the necessary preparations for their passage over the river, see to the armament of the fortresses, and the collection of supplies for the field armies, and obtain information as to the enemy's preparations and movements. This information was supplied by the host of French agents scattered through southern Germany. It was collected and sifted by Murat's staff, and day after day a summarised report was sent on to the Emperor, with letters reporting the arrival of troops on the river, the construction of bridges of boats, the work in the Rhine fortresses, and the collection of supplies. As soon as Murat heard from Munich that the Austrian vanguard was in Bavaria, he sent the 1st Hussars, and a brigade of dragoons across the Rhine to watch the roads of the Black Forest, and push patrols forward to the Iller.

On 25 September the 5th corps under Lannes, the Imperial Guard, and the greater part of the cavalry were concentrated about Strasburg and Kehl. Bernadotte with the 1st corps was over the Rhine, moving by Frankfurt on Wurtzburg; Marmont with the 2nd corps was near Mayence; Davoût with the 3rd opposite Mannheim; Soult with the 4th near Spires; Ney with the 6th near Maxau ready to cross the floating bridges and occupy Carlsruhe. That day the mass of the cavalry reserve had crossed the Rhine and begun its march through the Black Forest. Next day, 26 September, Napoleon reached Strasburg. He had every reason to be pleased with the work his lieutenant had done. There was a review of the great mass of troops assembled round the city, and Murat left Strasburg to direct the operations of the cavalry corps.

He was about to launch out with Napoleon on that marvellous career of victory, of which the stages were Ulm, Austerlitz, Jena, and Auerstadt, Eylau, and Friedland; on many a field from the Rhine to the Danube and the Niemen he was to revel in the 'rapture of the strife,' the overwhelming rush to victory, guiding the living tide of horses and men, sweeping down all opposition, leaving the wreckage of the battle behind, driving the broken enemy before it, and returning with the trophies of captured guns and standards. A ducal coronet and a kingly crown were to be his rewards, and then Nemesis was waiting for him, the fate to which he had helped to send the young Bourbon Prince of Enghien. The firing party in the obscure Calabrian town was but ten years away in the future on that September day in 1805, when Murat watched his splendid squadrons of steel clad cuirassiers riding over the bridge of Kehl, and looked forward only to victory and a crown.

## CHAPTER VIII

### THE CAMPAIGN OF ULM AND AUSTERLITZ
### 1805

THE Austrians had given Napoleon the chance of striking a decisive blow at the very outset of the war. Anxious to force neutrality on Bavaria, they had not waited either to be joined by their Russian allies or to bring all their own forces into the field. Their Field-Marshal Mack, who had an undeserved reputation for being a great strategist and tactician, was sent forward across the Inn with 60,000 men and overran Bavaria. By the time that the heads of Napoleon's columns were on the Rhine, Mack's army was on the line of the Iller, fronting the eastern outlets from the Black Forest, with his right at Ulm in Würtemberg, at the confluence of the Iller and the upper Danube.[1]

Himself a slave of tradition and routine, Mack had not the slightest doubt that the French Emperor would begin the campaign, as French generals had begun such campaigns during more than a century, by an advance from the middle Rhine through the defiles of the Black Forest. It was Murat's mission in the first days of the advance to confirm Mack in this opinion, and accordingly he pushed his cavalry over the low hills and through the pine woods of Baden, driving back the Austrian cavalry whom he found watching the hill roads on the eastern slope of the Forest. Murat did not force them back too quickly, and the only engagements were mere skirmishes. Having formed a screen east of the Forest, he pushed out detach-

[1] See Map p. 120, Campaign of Ulm.

ments to his left to extend the screen northwards, and prevent any stray Austrian patrol discovering what was really going on in those first days of October in the region of hill country between the north end of the Black Forest and the valley of the Neckar.

But Mack feared nothing from that direction. He felt sure that Napoleon and the Grand Army were marching through the Forest defiles directly in rear of the swarms of cuirassiers, dragoons, and chasseurs that were steadily pushing back his own mounted troops. The mass of hostile horsemen swept forward clearing the country north of the upper Danube, and effectually screening from the Austrian commander the fact that Napoleon with the troops concentrated at Strasburg (the Guard and Lannes' corps), instead of moving directly eastward over the Forest hills, had swung round behind them, and with Ney's corps from Maxau was marching by Pforzheim and Stuttgart on his right, while, further north, Davoût and Soult were marching across the upper Neckar valley, and Marmont and Bernadotte were converging on Würzburg, and the Bavarians had been called up from Bamberg to join the French left column. Seven army corps were executing a great converging movement that would bring the heads of their columns, within a week, to the crossings of the Danube below Ulm, cutting off Mack from his communications and supports, and bringing more than twofold odds against him.

As he himself afterwards said, ' He was in a dream.' Suddenly on 5 October he was roused from his dreams by rumours that the country to the north-east of Ulm was full of huge columns of French troops, pressing forward towards the Danube by forced marches, and that Napoleon with the Imperial Guard had passed through Stuttgart. He drew in his troops from the line of the river Iller, and concentrated them about Ulm.

Murat having swept the Austrian advanced cavalry posts back from the eastern outlets of the Black Forest had, by Napoleon's orders, pushed forward Bourcier's

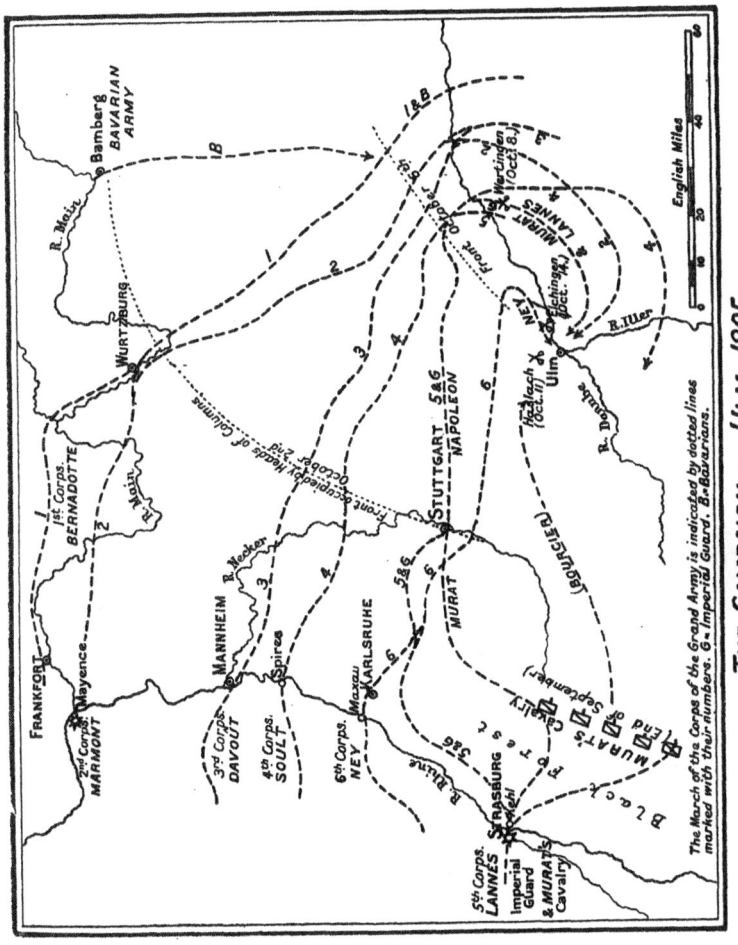

# CAMPAIGN OF ULM AND AUSTERLITZ 121

battalions of dismounted dragoons with ten guns and a few mounted men directly towards Ulm, and concentrating all the rest of his force to the left, marched by Pforzheim to join the French right, which was under the Emperor's direct command.

The cuirassier division of D'Hautpoul was detached to act with the Imperial Guard and the corps of Lannes under Napoleon; Murat with the rest of the cavalry was to cover the flank-march to the Danube. Ney's 6th corps, 20,000 strong, was placed temporarily under his orders. It was to take post on the Danube on the extreme right of the army as it passed the river, and form as it were a pivot round which the other corps swung to the east of Ulm. To Murat the Emperor wrote: 'You must flank all my march, which is a delicate operation, an oblique advance to the Danube. If the enemy means to take the offensive, I must be warned in time to adopt a decision without being forced to take the one that will suit his views.' Murat had complained that his horses were becoming tired with the forced march and continual patrol and reconnoitring work. Napoleon told him to requisition horses as remounts wherever he could find them. 'What is important for me,' he wrote, 'is to have news. Send out agents and spies, and above all make prisoners. Spare the horses which are out of condition, by using for reconnaissances only those that are strong and in good condition.'

On the 6 October the heads of all the columns were close up to the Danube, and Murat was directed to pass his cavalry across the river and clear the way for the march against the Austrian rear. There was no longer need of screening the movement. The fighting was about to begin. Early on the 7th he reached the left bank opposite Donauwerth, with Klein, Beaumont, and Walther's brigades of dragoons. The bridge had been destroyed by an Austrian detachment holding the town. Soult's corps was on the riverside with its artillery in action against Austrians. Murat with Walther's dragoons rode up the bank to the bridge of Münster where he found Vandamme's division of Lannes' corps crossing. He ordered the infantry to clear the bridge and make way for his horsemen. Then he galloped towards Donauwerth in the hope of cutting off the retreat of the Austrian detachment. He found them already retiring eastwards, and followed them up. At Rain they crossed the Lech and burned the wooden bridge behind them. Murat forded the river above the town, routed in a wild charge 600 Austrian cavalry, occupied Rain, and then leaving Walther's Dragoons to watch the line of the Lech, hurried back to rejoin the rest of his cavalry which was now crossing at Donauwerth.

On the 8th his horsemen headed the advance along the roads by the south bank of the Danube towards Ulm and the Iller valley. Ney's corps was on his right on the Danube, Lannes immediately in support of him. As soon as he found that the French had reached the Danube, Mack had decided to move out of Ulm, and fall upon them while they were engaged in crossing the river. His advanced guard under General Auffenberg (eight battalions and thirteen squadrons) had reached the town of Wertingen early on the 8th, but Mack had discovered that the French were already in force on the south bank and that he was too late. Hesitating what course to take, he left Auffenberg isolated at Wertingen.

Murat was marching that day by the Donauwerth-Wertingen road with fourteen of his cavalry regiments, and some horse artillery guns with him, and Oudinot's grenadier division, forming the head of Lannes' corps, close behind him. In the afternoon his advanced patrols came in touch with Auffenberg's outposts. With a whole *corps d'armée* following him up Murat decided on a brisk attack, and the result was the battle of Wertingen, the first serious fight of the Ulm campaign, and the first battle that was all Murat's own. It was a brilliant success. Two regiments of his hussars drove in the Austrian outposts in headlong confusion. Auffenberg and his officers were dining when the firing told them they were attacked. They hurriedly got their men into line along the little

# CAMPAIGN OF ULM AND AUSTERLITZ 123

river Sezam. Klein's dragoon brigade forded the stream above the town. Murat's aide-de-camp, Exelmans, afterwards a famous cavalry general, dismounted two regiments of dragoons, and led them across a narrow footbridge on the other side of it. Colonel Maupetit with the 9th Dragoons charged through the streets of Wertingen driving the Austrians out. Beyond the town his charge was stopped by the fire of the Austrian infantry in a line of squares, and he was badly wounded. Murat now came into action leading Klein's dragoons and the 10th Hussars in repeated charges against the infantry squares, and the Austrian cavalry. The cavalry were routed, but the infantry held their own till Oudinot's grenadiers came into action. Then square after square broke, and the Austrians fled into the woods to the west of Wertingen. Murat's trophies were eight standards, ten cannon, and 2500 prisoners.

He wrote a hurried report of his success, and sent Exelmans with his letter and the captured flags to report to the Emperor. Napoleon gave Exelmans the Grand Cross of the Legion of Honour, and sent him back to Murat with a letter of hearty congratulations and generous praise. When the first impression wore off, however, Napoleon was not so well satisfied with the victory. He said Murat ought to have used his cavalry to cut off the Austrian retreat, brought Oudinot into action against their front, and captured Auffenberg's whole division. It was hardly a fair criticism. After the event, and with all the knowledge that victory gives, it is often easy to show how a battle might have been made to yield more decisive results. But it is a different thing to decide at once amid the proverbial 'fog of war' what is to be done. If Murat had been less prompt in his attack, and had waited till Oudinot had come up, Auffenberg might have got away without losing a gun or a prisoner, after fighting a rearguard action. 'It is a little success, very pleasing to Murat who was in command,' wrote Napoleon to Joseph. Murat counted it a great success, and to the end of his life was proud of his victory of Wertingen. He pursued the enemy till dark, breaking up an attempted rally by one more charge late in the day, supported by the fire of a few of his guns. Next day Ney stormed the bridge of Gunsburg on the Danube, passed part of his corps over to the south bank, and thus came into communication with Murat, who was pressing forward by the Wertingen-Ulm road. On the 10th, Napoleon placed the whole right wing of the army under Murat's orders, and he thus disposed of the corps of Lannes and Ney as well as the cavalry.[1] Neither of the marshals liked the arrangement.

The very first order that Murat issued led to a dispute with Ney, in which the latter was right and Murat in the wrong. Murat had a meeting with Lannes and Ney on the 10th, and directed the latter to bring over all the 6th corps to the south bank of the Danube, leaving only Bourcier's battalions of dismounted dragoons to watch the north front of Ulm. Ney, supported by Lannes, pointed out that if Mack took the offensive on that side Bourcier's small force could hardly even delay him, and by a rapid march north-eastwards the Austrians would have at their mercy the supply and ammunition trains of the army, on the march to the bridges of the Danube below Ulm. Murat yielded so far as to tell Ney to keep Dupont's division on the north bank. Ney persisted that this was not sufficient, unfolded a map, and tried to make Murat realize the risk that was being taken. Murat refused to continue the discussion, and would not even look at the map. 'I understand nothing of your plans,' he said; 'it is my way to make mine in the presence of the enemy'—a foolish speech, with a dash of bad temper and self-sufficient vanity in its composition.

In the discussion Murat had urged that he had the Emperor's orders to unite the 5th and 6th corps with his cavalry. But Napoleon understood the position better

[1] Except the two divisions of cuirassiers—D'Hautpoul's division was with the Imperial Guard at the Emperor's headquarters, and Nansouty's division had been sent to Bernadotte, who with the 2nd corps and the Bavarians was marching towards Munich, to hold in check the expected advance of the Russians under Kutusoff.

than he did, and thought that Murat would realize the conditions under which he had to act. In a note to the marshal, dated the 11th, the Emperor told him that with his cavalry and the two corps he had between fifty and sixty thousand men in hand. He must march so as to be able ' to concentrate them within six hours to crush the enemy.' Next day he twice wrote to him to have a bridge of boats thrown across the Danube, so as to be in easy communication with the troops on the north bank, and to be able to reinforce them rapidly in case the Austrians tried to break out on that side. All this shows that Napoleon and Ney took the same view of the situation.

If Mack had been a more enterprising general there might have been serious results from a movement which he actually made on the 11th. Dupont closing in on the north side, supported by two of Murat's regiments sent across the new bridge, and by some of Bourcier's dismounted division, was attacked at Haslach, by a sortie of the Austrians in superior numbers. The French had to give way, and the Austrian cavalry captured a large train of supply and ammunition wagons, including part of Ney's military chest, and the infantry got possession of the north end of the Danube bridge, its guard retiring after firing the planked roadway. The French made such a good fight, and such a slow and steady retreat that Mack thought Dupont was stronger than he really was, and did not press his advantage. He halted, and contented himself with occupying the line of low hills, with the village and convent of Elchingen near the bridge head.

At the news that Mack was trying to break out of Ulm, Napoleon hurried up to the front. He unjustly reproached Ney for having exposed Dupont's division unsupported, and ordered that bridges should be thrown across the Danube in the night, and the Elchingen position retaken next day. The operation was entrusted to Ney, who was angrily eager to clear himself with the Emperor by a brilliant success. The whole 6th corps was concentrated on the north bank for the attack on Elchingen. Napoleon and his staff, and Murat with some of his cavalry rode out to watch the advance. Before putting himself at the head of his men Ney galloped up to the Emperor to receive his last instructions. Then turning to Murat he said to him, with a meaning that the rest of his hearers could not understand, ' Come, prince, come with me, and *make your plans in the presence of the enemy.*' But Murat had no part in the day's work. The heights were stormed by the 6th corps with the bayonet, and the victory gave Ney his title of Duke of Elchingen.

The corps of the French centre were now sweeping round to the south of Ulm. Ney reinforced from Lannes corps, and the Guard transferred to the left bank of the Danube, closed in on the north. On the 15th the infantry stormed the Frauenburg and Michelberg heights, driving the Austrians inside the works of Ulm. Murat with Beaumont's division of dragoons dashed through Haslach, charged the retiring enemy, cut off a battalion of infantry, and forced them to lay down their arms. Then his mounted troops completed the investment on the west side. Mack was safe in the trap his own lack of information and his indecision had prepared for him.

During the pause after Dupont's defeat at Haslach, and before Ney's victory at Elchingen, some eighteen thousand Austrians had escaped from the deadly circle that was closing on them. They were some eight thousand cavalry under the Archduke Ferdinand and Werneck's division of infantry. Mack, shut up in Ulm, capitulated on the 17th, and Napoleon could write to Josephine that he had taken the first Austrian army ' by mere marching.' The Archduke and Werneck were not to be allowed to escape. They were in full march for the Bohemian frontier, but even before Mack surrendered Murat had been sent off in hot pursuit of the fugitives.

On 18 October he was given Klein's division of dragoons, the chasseurs à cheval of the Imperial Guard, Dupont's infantry division, with the 1st Hussars attached to it, and Fauconnet's two regiments of chasseurs. Next day he

# CAMPAIGN OF ULM AND AUSTERLITZ 127

was reinforced by sending after him Oudinot's grenadiers and Milhaud with two more regiments of chasseurs à cheval. Murat executed his mission with unrelenting energy and complete success. In five days, from the 16th to the 20th, he covered with his cavalry a distance of more than a hundred miles. Some of the flanking squadrons, sent out right and left, rode even further. Eight times he was in action with the enemy, and he took more than 15,000 prisoners, 11 standards, 128 guns, and more than 1000 wagons.

There were two fights on the 16th. Klein forced several battalions to surrender at Albeck on the Danube. Twelve miles further on, at the village of Herbrechtingen, Murat came on a rearguard in battle array, with infantry and artillery. He sent his light infantry against the village, and himself charged at the head of the dragoons. He took 3000 prisoners in the fight and pursuit, and captured several guns. Next day there was another victorious fight at Neresheim, two standards were taken by Klein's dragoons, and 1000 prisoners. An Austrian general was among them. The Archduke narrowly escaped capture.

That night Murat slept a few hours at the abbey of Neresheim. At daybreak an Austrian officer with a flag of truce arrived at the abbey and reported that three battalions were close by, dead beat with marching, with no food left, and anxious only to surrender. The prisoners were secured, and the pursuit went on. Early in the day Werneck was surrounded near Nordlingen, and surrendered with seven other general officers, and all the troops with him. A large convoy escaping to the eastwards was overtaken and captured after Fauconnet's chasseurs had charged the escort. The day's captures were nearly 5000 prisoners, 5 standards, 80 guns, and 400 Austrian wagons, besides the supply and ammunition train, and the military chest captured by the enemy at Haslach. There were further captures on the 19th and 20th. The Archduke tried to delay the pursuit by sending back word that an armistice was being arranged. Murat refused to hear of it, but the report delayed Klein's dragoons for a while. The Austrians abandoned guns and wagons to expedite their march. More than once the French cavalry was in action with their rearguard. On the 20th Murat was in Nuremberg. In front were the difficult roads of the Franconian hills, and his horses were showing signs of exhaustion. He stopped the five days' pursuit. Enough had been done. The Archduke crossed the Bohemian frontier with less than 3000 men, all that was left of the 60,000 with which Mack had marched into Bavaria.

Napoleon gave Murat the praise he deserved. In the bulletin of the Grand Army, published on 22 October, he wrote: 'One is filled with astonishment at the sight of Prince Murat's march from Albeck to Nuremberg; he fought every day, and overtook the enemy, who had a start of two days.' In a later bulletin he told of the 'prodigious activity' of the pursuit, and reckoned up the captures. Eighteen Austrian generals had been taken, and three killed in action.

When Mack surrendered at Ulm, Kutusoff, with the Russian vanguard, had only reached the Inn, and was about to enter Bavaria. The slow march of the corps which were on the way to join him left him with only some 35,000 men immediately available. Even if he had been joined by the 20,000 Austrians assembled under the Archduke John in the Tyrol he was not strong enough to attack the force that Bernadotte had moved up to Munich, to protect the operations against Ulm from his expected advance. Bernadotte had with his own corps (the 1st), that of Davoût (the 3rd), and the Bavarian army. On the news that Ulm had fallen, and that Napoleon was concentrating the Grand Army about Munich for an immediate advance into Austria, Kutusoff began to retreat along the south bank of the Danube.

Murat, after giving his men a day's rest at Nuremberg, had been ordered up to Munich by Napoleon. By turning over the best of the captured horses to his own regiments, he hurriedly provided remounts to replace those that had

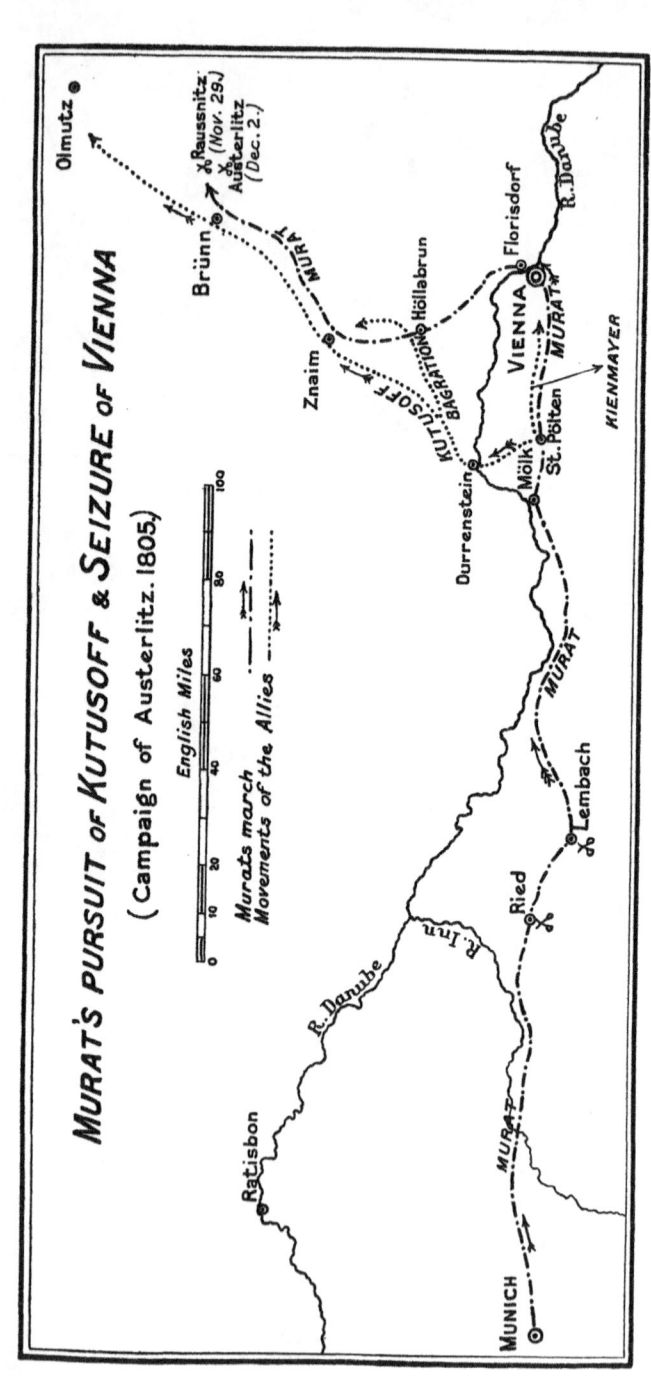

# CAMPAIGN OF ULM AND AUSTERLITZ 129

broken down in first stage of the campaign. At Munich he was directed to pursue Kutusoff, whose rearguard was still upon the Inn.[1] He set off with D'Hautpoul's cuirassier division, Beaumont and Walther's divisions of dragoons, Milhaud's chasseurs, and the light cavalry of Soult's corps. After a fight with the Russian rearguard, he forced the crossings of the Inn and entered Austrian territory on 29 October. Following up the enemy, he found next day the Russian rearguard in position at Ried (four battalions and eight squadrons strong). 'To find the rearguard and to charge it, was for the cavalry one and the same thing,' wrote Napoleon, in the bulletin that described the action. The Russians were broken and driven back, 500 prisoners were taken, and only darkness stopped the pursuit for a while. On the 31st there was another action at Lembach, with 400 prisoners taken, and in the first week of November a series of rearguard affairs, in which the cavalry secured nearly two thousand more.

On 7 November Murat occupied the abbey of Mölk, on the direct road to Vienna. The Austrian Emperor had been at the abbey that morning, and left it only a few hours before the French cavalry appeared. From Mölk Murat pushed forward a detachment towards St. Pölten, within twenty miles of Vienna. In the evening the advanced cavalry found themselves in touch with a body of white-uniformed troops of no great strength. It was Kienmayer's Austrian division covering the road to the capital. Kutusoff with the Russians had turned northwards from St. Pölten to cross the Danube at Dürrenstein, and fall upon the isolated eighth corps, which was marching along the left bank of the river.

Here Murat committed his first mistake in the pursuit. He had the corps of Lannes close at hand to support him, in dealing with Kienmayer's Austrian division. And though his real business was to keep touch with, and continually harass, the main body of the retreating enemy

[1] See map, p.129, Murat's pursuit of Kutusoff and seizure of Vienna.

I

(Kutusoff), the temptation was too strong for him when he saw the certainty that he could sweep Kienmayer out of the way, or drive him back, and in either case have the glory of occupying the capital of the Austrian Empire.

Driving Kienmayer before him from St. Pölten, Murat with the greater part of his cavalry, and a considerable force of Lannes' troops with him, established his headquarters on 11 November within three miles of the western suburbs of Vienna. He threw forward parties of his mounted troops to occupy the roads leading southward to Styria, and eastward to Hungary, and sent patrols along the Danube to collect boats for the crossing of the river. The same day he received orders from Napoleon to halt where he was for the present. 'My cousin,' wrote the Emperor (using the form of address employed in correspondence with his marshals), 'I cannot approve of your way of proceeding. You go right on in an empty headed way without weighing the orders I have sent to you. . . . You have thought only of the trifling glory of entering Vienna. There is no glory where there is no danger, and there is none in entering a capital which is undefended.'

Murat remained halted for twenty-four hours. Then came permission to advance. Napoleon had in the meantime reinforced Mortier, and made the situation secure on the north bank of the Danube, and decided that for the sake of moral effect Vienna should be occupied. He was about to establish his own headquarters in the palace of the Emperor Francis at Schönbrunn, the Versailles of Austria.

For Murat to occupy Vienna was easy enough. Kienmayer had retired across the Danube into the eastern suburb of Florisdorf. But Murat was anxious not only to enter the capital, but also to secure the great bridge over the Danube. He had heard that Kienmayer's engineers had mined it, and that a battery of artillery was in position to prevent it being rushed before the moment came when, on the advance of the French in force, the Austrians would blow it up. Seconded by Lannes he decided to get possession of the bridge by a piece of trickery.

Early on the 13th, while the corps of Lannes and several regiments of the cavalry reserve were marching into the streets of Vienna, Murat sent forward to the bridge the 1st Hussars with General Bertrand, one of the Emperor's aides-de-camp, and Major Lanusse of his own staff. Near the western end of the bridge they were challenged by a picket of cavalry. They told the Austrians that peace negotiations had begun, and asked for the officer commanding at the bridge to be sent for. Halting the hussars the two officers then dismounted, and were immediately joined by Lannes and Murat, who, on foot with their hands behind their backs, strolled slowly on to the bridge and began talking to the Austrian officers while waiting for their immediate commander, General Count Auersperg, to arrive.

At the further end of the bridge a battery of artillery was in position, pointing to the Viennese shore of the river, so as to sweep the roadway. The guns were loaded and gunners stood match in hand behind them. On the bridge sacks of sand piled up, and the canvas hose that contained the powder train, showed that it had been prepared for immediate destruction. Murat and Lannes were taking a serious risk in their adventure. Gradually moving forward they found themselves among the officers and artillerymen in charge of the battery. Murat told the Austrians that all their hostile precautions were now out of date. 'In a few days,' he said, ' our Emperors will be the best of friends, and we shall be comrades and allies.'

Meanwhile a battalion of Oudinot's grenadiers had arrived on the western bank. Some of the men hid themselves, took cover behind the poplars along the river. The rest were given the order to mark time, but as they did so came nearer and nearer to the bridge by short steps. On the bridge itself a French engineer officer, concealed by a group of his friends standing round him, cut the powder train. Auersperg now arrived, and in reply to Murat's and Lannes' professions of friendship and talk of an armistice expressed his pleasure at the news.

Then one of the Austrian officers, pointing to Oudinot's grenadiers, asked why those troops were advancing on the bridge. Lannes told him he was mistaken. The men were only marking time to keep themselves warm, for it was a bitterly cold morning. Then a number of staff officers joined the two French generals, and suddenly it was seen that the hussars were galloping on to the bridge with the grenadiers doubling behind them. The battery commander called out 'Fire!' but the order was hardly audible, for Murat had caught him by the throat with an iron grip. At the same moment Lannes and the other officers were knocking the matches out of the hands of the gunners. The hussars came riding in among the guns, with their swords sheathed. The gunners were hustled away from them, and Frenchmen and Austrians were mingled together. Murat and Lannes were complaining to Auersperg that the artillery officer had risked a horrible massacre for no purpose. The fellow ought to be court-martialled and shot, they said. Auersperg was in a helpless state of mental confusion—half believing in the armistice, half fearing that he was the victim of a trick. The grenadiers had meanwhile marched past the battery, and were in possession of the eastern bank. Masses of French troops appeared coming out of the streets on the opposite shore. Auersperg was glad enough to be allowed to take his guns away, and retired with his men into Florisdorf.

Kienmayer put him under arrest, and he was subsequently tried by court-martial for allowing his post to be surprised, and was condemned to death. The Emperor Francis commuted the sentence, and he was imprisoned for ten years in a fortress. Even in the French army opinion was divided as to the legitimacy of Murat's *tour de Gascon*, his Gascon trick. He and Lannes certainly lied boldly, and it was lucky for them that Auersperg was such a confiding fool. Marbot in his memoirs says that

## CAMPAIGN OF ULM AND AUSTERLITZ 133

their conduct was among soldiers something 'inadmissable.' Certainly it was nothing to be proud of.

Strange to say Murat, only two days later, fell into much the same kind of a snare. Napoleon had sent him across the Danube, with D'Hautpoul and Nensouty's cuirassier divisions, Walther's regiments of dragoons and the light cavalry, to regain touch with Kutusoff, ascertain whether he was retiring on Bohemia or Moravia, and follow him up. The corps of Lannes and Soult were moving behind the cavalry. On 15 November Murat came on Bagration's Russian corps in position near Höllabrun, amid broken ground where mounted troops were of little use. It was known that an envoy from the Austro-Russian headquarters was at Schönbrunn discussing possible terms of peace with Napoleon. Murat was anxious to keep Bagration near Höllabrun till the infantry of Lannes and Soult could come up to attack the position, so he entered into communication with the Russians, and told them he believed an armistice was being arranged at Schönbrunn. Bagration then informed him that Prince Winzegerode, an aide-de-camp of the Czar, was with him, and had important news. Winzegerode met Murat under a flag of truce, and surprised him by assuring him that peace was practically arranged, and then suggested that an armistice should be concluded, and the further advance of Murat's troops stopped. Murat now believed that the fiction he had sprung on Bagration was a fact, and flattered at being in communication with a direct representative of the Czar, and playing a part in the settlement of international interests, he agreed to the truce, and reported to Napoleon that in consequence of what he had heard from the Czar's aide-de-camp he had stopped the advance of the cavalry and the two corps under his orders.

Bagration had scored heavily, and Murat was 'hoist with his own petard.' A few miles to the north of Höllabrun Kutusoff's army, encumbered by an enormous baggage train, was retiring eastwards towards Moravia across the line of the French advance. Bagration had been posted at Höllabrun as a flank guard to cover this movement, and was congratulating himself on being able, by Winzegerode's smooth words to Murat, to arrest for a day or two the advance of the superior forces with which he was threatened.

When Napoleon heard what had happened he was very angry. 'It is impossible,' he wrote to Murat, 'for me to find terms in which to express to you my displeasure. You are only the commander of my advanced guard, and you have no right to arrange an armistice without my orders. You are making me lose the results of a campaign. Break off the armistice at once, and march upon the enemy.'

Murat received this letter early on the 16th, and realised that he had been duped. He called up Lannes and Soult and attacked Bagration, who retired after a hard-fought rearguard action in which he lost in the fight and pursuit 1800 prisoners and 12 guns. The cavalry could take little share in the battle, but followed up the retiring enemy, making large numbers of prisoners.

The negotiations at Schönbrunn came to nothing. Murat with the advanced guard was pressing close upon Kutusoff's retreat. On the 17th he rode through Znaim; on the 19th he occupied Brünn, which the enemy had just left. Then he pushed forward along the road to Olmutz, and next day there was a brilliant cavalry action at Raussnitz. Walther's dragoons came on a mass of 6000 of the allied cavalry, and kept them in play till Murat arrived with his two cuirassier divisions, and the cavalry of the Imperial Guard led by his countryman, Bessières. Then a series of splendid charges drove the enemy from the field.

Kutusoff, in his retreat to Olmutz, had been joined by Austrian and Russian reinforcements, while the French army, with its losses in the long series of forced marches and the detachments it had left behind, had dwindled in numbers till the advantage in that respect was on the side of the Allies. Murat's force now became a rearguard, falling back before the Allies, whom Napoleon was luring westward towards the position he had chosen for the decisive battle, along the banks of the Goldbach brook,

# CAMPAIGN OF ULM AND AUSTERLITZ

and behind the frozen lakes of Mennitz between Austerlitz and Brünn.

On 1 December the two armies faced each other on opposite sides of the long hollow of the Goldbach. There is no need to tell again in detail the story of Austerlitz, the decisive victory won next day, against superior numbers, on the anniversary of the Emperor's coronation. The numbers actually engaged were 82,050 of the Allies (including 16,500 cavalry) against 65,000 Frenchmen, of whom 15,000 were mounted troops, two-thirds of whom were concentrated under Murat on the left. He was in command of the whole left wing, including the cavalry reserve and the corps of Lannes. Opposed to him were Bagration's Russian corps, and a mass of 82 squadrons of Austrian, Russian and Cossack cavalry under Prince Lichtenstein. As the 'sun of Austerlitz' rose in its splendour, and the morning fog broke up along the Goldbach brook, the huge columns concentrated for the attack against the French right were seen descending the slopes, only to be held back hour after hour by the stubborn defence made by Davoût between the hills and the Mennitz lakes and swamps, in a defile where he could securely face superior numbers. This concentration against his right to cut him from the roads to Vienna was the manœuvre Napoleon had hoped and foreseen the Allies would adopt. It enabled him to meet them with equal numbers on the left, and with superior force in the centre, where his great attack on the Pratzen plateau broke the allied line in two, cut off the retreat of those who had attacked his right, and in combination with Davoût's dogged resistance forced the enemy back on the frozen lakes where they drowned in crowds, as the French artillery fire broke the ice under their feet.

During the long resistance of the right, and the decisive attack in the centre, it was Murat's task to keep Bagration's infantry occupied, and prevent Lichtenstein's multitude of splendid horsemen from breaking in on the flank and rear. The ground was not favourable to cavalry action, but while Lannes with Oudinot's grenadiers and Suchet and

Legrand's linesmen met Bagration's attack with a stubbornness equal to that of the Russians themselves, there were repeated charges and mêlées of the cavalry amid the broken ground. Murat was once, through a mistake he made, in imminent danger of losing liberty or life. He was standing with his staff and escort on the flank of the infantry line when a blue-uniformed regiment of cavalry came riding through the fog of battle smoke. ' Don't fire. They are our Bavarian allies,' cried Murat to the infantry. Suddenly the approaching horsemen charged. They were Russian dragoons. Murat found himself cut off with some of his staff and a handful of his escort, but fought his way through the dragoons, sword in hand, without even a wound.

The victorious advance of the French centre isolated the Russian left. Bagration began to fall back towards the heights in front of Austerlitz, and Lannes attacked in his turn, Suchet's regiments charging home with the bayonet. The furious onset of Murat's cavalry drove in the enemy's horsemen, and the French cavalry falling on the retiring columns of Bagration's corps took many standards and twenty-seven guns, and gathered up some seven thousand prisoners.

Darkness and the exhaustion of horses and men made pursuit impossible that evening. Next morning Murat failed to discover that the main mass of the Allies was retiring towards Hungary, and pursued only a body of Lichtenstein's cavalry that had taken the road to Olmutz. Before evening the pursuit was stopped. Napoleon had been asked by the Emperor Francis to open negotiations, and an armistice had been arranged. Within a month peace was concluded on terms dictated by France, and the Treaty of Pressburg was signed on New Year's Day, 1806.

We must turn from the story of battles and victories to say something of Murat's relations with his old home, for a few days after Austerlitz we find him writing from Vienna to his brother André. There is not a word about the great events of the time. He only thinks of his aged mother, whose life he knew could not now be much prolonged :—

'MY DEAR BROTHER,—As the extremely advanced age that our incomparable mother has attained must make us anticipate that she may be taken from us at any moment, I wish to remind you of the sacred duties we must fulfil in this event. I wish to preserve her loved remains and have them near me. Therefore, when you have closed her eyes, when, happier than me, you have received her last breath, have her body embalmed, and after rendering it the last funeral honours, lay it in a stone tomb which I charge you to have constructed. I shall then be able to have her remains removed later to a place I intend to prepare for them on one of my country estates. It is with tears in my eyes that I tell you of my wishes. You are too good a son and too good a brother not to do what I ask.'

Jeanne Murat died three months later, on 11 March 1806, while her son Joachim was busy with his accession to the Grand Duchy of Berg. She was tenderly cared for to the last by André and her daughters. Her body was entombed in the parish church of La Bastide. Murat erected a monument there to her memory, with the inscription :—

LA PIÉTÉ FILIALE
À DAME MURAT
1806
DÉCÉDÉE LE 11 MARS, AGÉE DE 85 ANS

Non la conobbe il mondo mentre l'abbe
Connobil'io ch'a pianger qui rimasi.[1]

---

[1] Petrarch, Sonnet LXVII.—
'The world knew her not while it possessed her.
I knew her, who remain here to weep for her.'

## CHAPTER IX

MURAT GRAND DUKE OF BERG—THE JENA CAMPAIGN

1806

ALTHOUGH Trafalgar—fought four days after the surrender of Ulm—had blasted Napoleon's hopes of victory on the sea, the crowning triumph of Austerlitz had made him the dictator of the Continent For a thousand years the chief sovereign in Europe always in precedence, often in power, was 'the Emperor.' Officially he was the civil head of Christendom. For centuries the dignity had been practically hereditary in the House of Hapsburg, but now the Emperor Francis II. yielded the precedence established by a thousand years of tradition, ceased to be the German Emperor, became merely the Emperor Francis I. of Austria and acknowledged as more than his equal the self-elected upstart 'Emperor of the French.' As the old Empire of central Europe had had its circle of vassal states, so Napoleon meant that his new Empire should have its royal and grand-ducal satellites. The Bourbons of Naples had rashly thrown in their lot with Austria on the outbreak of the war. A French army occupied Naples, and Joseph Bonaparte was proclaimed its king. Another of Napoleon's brothers, Prince Louis, the husband of Hortense Beauharnais, was made King of Holland. Prussia had hesitated during the conflict on the Danube, had more than once been on the point of joining the Allies, but had waited too long; and when the news of Austerlitz came, the Prussian Court consented to arrange by the Treaty of Schönbrunn (15 December 1805) a remodelling of Germany, the

## MURAT GRAND DUKE OF BERG

cession of various territories in the Rhineland to the nominees of Napoleon, and the formation of the 'Confederation of the Rhine,' a grouping together of the minor states of south and west Germany under Napoleon's 'protectorate.'

It was here that Murat found his reward for his brilliant services in the campaign of Ulm and Austerlitz. Napoleon had freely rewarded the cavalry officers who had distinguished themselves. The higher grades of the Legion of Honour were granted to thirty-two of Murat's colonels, and thirteen of them were promoted to the rank of Général de Brigade. What was to be done for their chief? A marshal of France could rise no higher in military rank. He must be given a sovereignty.

There was another motive for his promotion. Caroline's sisters Elisa and Pauline had been provided with tributary principalities of the Empire in central Italy. Caroline used all her influence and all her powers of persuasion to obtain a like position for herself by securing a coronet or a crown for her husband. She was probably disappointed when she learned that it was to be only a coronet, but then it might lead to a crown.

Napoleon, in planning the Confederation of the Rhine, had decided to form a new state between the frontiers of France and Prussia, and to make a French prince its sovereign. This was the reward assigned to Murat. By the Treaty of Schönbrunn Prussia had ceded to France the Duchy of Cleves, including the fortress of Wesel on the lower Rhine, and the principality of Anhalt on the northern frontier of Bavaria. The Elector of Bavaria, Napoleon's ally, whom he had made a king, agreed to take over Anhalt, and exchange for it the Bavarian territory of the Duchy of Berg, the country along the Rhine about Dusseldorf, adjoining the Duchy of Cleves. Cleves and Berg were united to form a new sovereign state, which was to be known as the 'Grand Duchy of Berg.'

On 9 March 1806 Murat, who was then in Paris, was informed by the Emperor that he was to proceed to Cologne, where he would receive from the King of Bavaria formal authorization to take possession of the territory of Berg. He was then to go to Dusseldorf, which was to be the capital of the new Grand Duchy, and would be occupied by a column of French troops under General Dupont. Simultaneously the Prussians would evacuate the fortress of Wesel, and hand it over to a column under General Beaumont.

The Imperial decree, constituting the new state and naming Murat Grand Duke, was signed on 15 March. The Emperor declares that he confers on ' his well-beloved brother-in-law, Prince Joachim,' the two duchies, to be inherited by his male heirs in the direct line, and held by him in full and independent sovereignty. The dignity of Grand Admiral of the Empire is to be hereditary in the line of the Grand Dukes. The sovereign's official title is to be ' Prince Joachim, Grand Admiral of France, and Grand Duke of Berg and Cleves.' He is now henceforth to be known as Prince Murat. Little Achille, as heir-apparent of the new state, is to be known as the ' Duke of Cleves.'

On the 16th Murat's aide-de-camp, Beaumont, took possession of Wesel. The same day Murat arrived at Cologne, where he received the formal cession of Berg from the envoys of the King of Bavaria. On the 21st the Bavarian garrison marched out of Dusseldorf, and the city was occupied by 6000 French troops under Dupont. On the 25th the new Grand Duke, wearing the uniform of a Marshal of France, and escorted by French mounted gendarmes and grenadiers, drove from Cologne along the banks of the Rhine, and was received at the barriers of Dusseldorf by Dupont and his staff, the clergy and the civil authorities. Amid the pealing of bells and the thunder of salutes, he was given the keys of the city, and then drove through streets hung with flags, crowded with cheering spectators, and lined by French infantry, to the old electoral palace in the Hofgarten in the centre of the place. In the evening there was an illumination, and next day the Grand Duke was present at High Mass in St. Andrew's Church.

## MURAT GRAND DUKE OF BERG 141

He wore this time a Court costume, the official robes of the Grand Admiral of France, with a blue mantle stiff with gold embroidery. He had a throne under a canopy, beside the altar, and after the Mass he took the oath to observe the new constitution of the state, and, speaking in French, thanked his subjects for their enthusiastic welcome, and declared that he would labour for the prosperity of the people of Cleves and Berg.

Within a week he was trying to enlarge his territory. He looked upon this sovereignty over 320,000 Rhinelanders as only the nucleus of a much larger state. Probably this was also Napoleon's view, but the Emperor counted on lapse of time giving opportunities for annexation, while Murat's restless spirit was in a hurry to begin at once. Three days after his entry into his capital he wrote to Napoleon: 'In taking possession of the Duchy of Cleves Beaumont neglected to occupy the territories of the ancient abbeys of Essen and Werden. I have ordered him to complete his task by occupying these two territories. I hope that no protest will be raised, but if there is I trust to the justice, and good will of your Majesty to support my rights.' And the same day he wrote to the Emperor's Foreign Minister, Talleyrand: 'You may look for a declaration of war as the result of this occupation. But I shall uphold my rights. Defend me, and consider that I am on outpost duty here.'

War might well be the result. Blücher had commanded the Prussian garrison in Cleves. He had chafed at the inaction of his countrymen during the war of 1805, and he had only evacuated Cleves and Wesel reluctantly, and after repeated orders from Berlin. Even then he had purposely left small posts at Essen and Werden, and kept a force of all arms near the border on Prussian territory. When Beaumont occupied the two places each with a company Blücher came back with infantry, cavalry, and artillery, surrounded Essen and Werden, blockaded the French infantry companies, and reported to his government, asking for leave to expel or capture them.

There was excitement at Paris and Berlin. But Napoleon

did not want war. 'I am annoyed,' he said, 'at the heat imported into this affair, which is not so important that it cannot be quietly arranged in a friendly way.' The situation was made more difficult by Murat asserting that when Beaumont took possession there were no Prussian soldiers in Werden or Essen. The Prussian ambassador at Paris gave Talleyrand proof that this was not true. Murat tried to excite the Emperor's personal feelings on the subject. 'Sire,' he wrote, 'I should consider myself guilty if I renounced rights I hold from your Majesty, and if I allowed your eagles to withdraw before the Prussian eagles. I await your Majesty's orders. You may rely on it, that the Prussians will not carry their point with me. Tell me to turn them out of Westphalia, and soon we shall be rid of those insolent neighbours, who need a good lesson such as your Majesty knows how to give to overbearing powers.'

With French and Prussian troops in contact in the borderland of Cleves, and Blücher and Murat both recklessly anxious for a fight, the situation was dangerous. Napoleon threw cold water on the new Grand Duke's bellicose proposals. 'What am I to say to you?' he wrote. 'You act now without any balance, now without any foresight. There was no reason to occupy Essen and Werden because the Prussian commissioner had not handed them over. But if you did occupy them it ought to have been in such force that a Prussian general with a couple of battalions could not turn you out. I have written to the King of Prussia to withdraw his troops, and you must withdraw yours. The result is that you have brought a touch of disgrace on my arms.' It took three months of negotiation to draw up a statement of the case that saved the *amour propre* of both sides, and arrange the simultaneous withdrawal of the French and Prussian troops.

While the matter was still under discussion Murat had raised new claims. The adjoining Prussian territory of the Duchy of Marck ought to be annexed to Berg. There were historical foundations for the claim, he said, and besides Marck and Berg had such intimate commercial relations that they were really one country. The Emperor refused to hear of the question being raised. In April a further diplomatic difficulty arose over a claim of Murat to levy duties on merchandise passing down the Rhine. Napoleon wrote to him that he must live in peace with Prussia, and not be such a restless neighbour. He wanted no quarrel with Berlin, he said. His policy was directed to other ends. If Murat were so precipitate in raising now one claim, now another, he would only be forced continually to withdraw from untenable positions. Nothing was lost by patience and friendly words. He must keep quiet, and above all he must be prudent in his language. He warned him that everything that he said at Dusseldorf was at once reported at Berlin, St. Petersburg, and Vienna, and often by those he thought his friends. Instead of offending the great powers by rash claims and wild talk, he must attend to the organisation of his states. Why had he not yet reported on the condition of the fortress of Wesel, and seen that it was armed, garrisoned, and provisioned ? This was the most important business he had to attend to, and yet Napoleon had not had a word from him on the subject.

Murat had visited Wesel on 3 April in order to receive the oaths of allegiance of his new subjects in the Duchy of Cleves. He wrote to Napoleon that the revenues of Berg would not enable him to maintain the fortress, and he thought it would be best to disarm it, sell off the supplies and reduce it to the position of an open town. Napoleon replied that Wesel must be maintained, and its fortifications strengthened and kept in a complete state of efficiency. It was important for the defence of the Lower Rhine and the frontier of Holland. He would himself provide all expenses, but it must be a fortress of the Empire, held by a French garrison, whose commandant would in no way interfere with the Grand Duke's subjects, the civil population.

Murat had sent for a fellow-countryman and old friend, Agar, who had been his schoolfellow at the college of Cahors, and one of his colleagues when he was elected to the Corps Législatif by the Department of the Lot. He gave Agar an estate and the title of Count of Mosbourg, and made him his prime minister, with the right of acting in his name whenever he himself was absent from the Grand Duchy. This being arranged he went to Paris on 25 April, after a stay of only a month in his new territory.

Joachim and Caroline, Grand Duke and Duchess of Berg, received the honours due to sovereigns at the court of the Tuileries on all occasions of public ceremony. But much as they liked display and ceremony, Caroline and Murat were both anxious to obtain more solid advantages, and had the influence to secure a long list of favours from Napoleon. This was why Murat had come to Paris. He could push his fortunes better there than at Dusseldorf. The organization of the new Confederation of the Rhine was being arranged. It was to be formally constituted by the beginning of July. Murat, ably seconded by his wife, urged his claims so well that it was settled that the territories of the Grand Duchy were to be enlarged, so that Murat would have some 280,000 more subjects with a corresponding increase of revenue. This was effected by the Duchy of Nassau ceding to him a stretch of territory along the Rhine, including the town of Deutz opposite Cologne, and the district of Königswinter and the Seven Mountains, and a number of minor principalities and signories, some of them then actually occupied by Prussia, becoming his tributaries.

He asked for and obtained from Napoleon, a week after, some new concessions—permission to accept the order of the Golden Fleece offered him by Godoy, the prime minister of Spain; ten thousand stand of arms, and several batteries of field pieces for the little army of his Grand Duchy; the transfer of a regiment of Polish lancers to his service; the right to remove from Bonn some scores of orange-trees for his garden at Dusseldorf; free places in the French military schools for cadets from Berg; the gift of 150,000 francs to complete the payments on account of Caroline's Paris

MURAT IN COURT COSTUME AS GRAND DUKE OF BERG
AFTER THE PAINTING BY GÉRARD

palace of the Elysée; and the possession of the château of Brühl near Cologne, famous as the place of Mazarin's exile.

Finally he raised the question of Wesel. The fortress ought to be his. He was hardly an independent ruler with a French garrison holding it. Hortense tells how he amused her one day by saying with an air of bringing forward an unanswerable argument: 'The Emperor has no right to deprive me of this fortress. It does not come to me from him, for it was a treaty with the King of Prussia that gave it to me.' On his way back to Dusseldorf in July, he wrote a formal request to Napoleon to relinquish Wesel to him, urging that it was a question that concerned the position of his duchy, not merely in the present, but under his successors. Napoleon replied that he himself was spending millions of francs on Wesel, and that such an important fortress, commanding the lower Rhine, must remain a part of the defensive system of the empire. 'As for a guarantee for the independence of your children,' he continued, 'that is a pitiable argument, at which I can only shrug my shoulders. I blush at your using it. You are a Frenchman. I hope your children will be the same. Any other sentiment would be so dishonouring to you that I beg you will never speak of it. It would be strange if, after all the benefits the French people has heaped upon you, you should be thinking of securing for your children the means of acting against France. Once more, do not talk of this to me again. It is too ridiculous.'

Murat had arrived at Dusseldorf on 25 July. There Agar informed him that the Prussians had not yet evacuated all the principalities ceded to him. At once he wrote to Napoleon that, with the ten thousand French and local troops in the Grand Duchy, he would take forcible possession of his own. On 2 August, the Emperor sent him another rebuke. 'My cousin,' he wrote, 'your idea of forcibly driving the Prussians out of the territory they occupy is a piece of sheer folly. It would be an insult on your part to Prussia, and that is quite contrary to my intentions. I am good friends with that power, and have stopped the peace negotiations with England in order that Prussia may retain Hanover. From this you can judge if I am likely to embroil myself with her for such stupidities. I cannot express the pain I feel on reading your letters. You are of a rashness that drives one to despair.'

Once more Napoleon had to intervene to check his projects, when on 1 September he convoked the States-General of Berg and Cleves, and brought forward a scheme for increasing the revenues of the Grand Duchy by additional taxation, including contributions from the princes over whose lands he had obtained suzerain rights in July, contributions against which they had been expressly guaranteed. 'Prince Murat is committing only follies,' wrote Napoleon. There might have been a serious quarrel, but just then Napoleon had other work for him to do. The Grand Duke was once more to become the dashing French cavalry leader.

Constant friction with Prussia during the summer, in which Murat's irritating action played some part, had helped the war party at Berlin, backed by the influence of the Czar, to gain the ascendant over the more prudent policy of King Frederick William. Prussia had mobilized its army and concluded a treaty of alliance with Russia in August. On 15 September, the Prussian ministry called on Napoleon to withdraw his troops from German territory. The Emperor replied by a declaration of war, and by ordering the immediate reinforcement of the French troops stationed in south Germany, which was to be his base of operations in the advance on Berlin.

On 18 September, Belliard, Murat's chief of the staff, was ordered to proceed to Würzburg. It was not till the 29th that Murat himself was told to go there. He was to do the same work that had been entrusted to him at the outset of the campaign of 1805. As lieutenant-general of the Emperor, he was to supervise the concentration of the Grand Army in northern Bavaria, organize the supply and intelligence services, and on the arrival of Napoleon take command of the Cavalry Reserve. The organization of the cavalry was much the same as in the preceding year. There were D'Hautpoul and Nansouty's cuirassier divisions (together ten regiments), four divisions of dragoons commanded by Klein, Grouchy, Beaumont and Sahuc, and each six regiments strong; a brigade of two hussar regiments under Lasalle; and a regiment of chasseurs under General Milhaud, intended to be the nucleus of a division of light cavalry—thirty-seven regiments in all, at the outset of the campaign. Later, a division of four regiments of cuirassiers under General Espagne was brought from Italy, and a fifth division of dragoons was formed under General Becker, by taking two regiments each from the divisions of Sahuc and Grouchy.

On 30 September, Murat's advanced cavalry was on the Prussian frontier. There was a pause of a few days. On 7 October, the Emperor issued his proclamation to the army ordering the general advance. Next day Murat was over the border, and pushing his patrols boldly into the Thuringian hills, behind which the Prussian and Saxon armies were concentrating. That day he forced the crossing of the Saale, and occupied Saalburg after a sharp fight. Next day, he helped to rout a Prussian detachment at Schleitz. These actions were small affairs, but they were the first successes that influenced the spirits of both sides in the opening campaign.

Napoleon wrote to Murat a criticism on his conduct of the advance through the hills that showed how the master was more prudent than his enterprising subordinate. He told him he was scattering his regiments too much both in the advance and in action. He should always keep a solid striking force in hand.

On the 11th, the pine-clad hills of the Thuringian forests had been left behind. Lasalle by a lucky stroke captured a large Prussian convoy of five hundred wagons, including a useful pontoon train. Next day Napoleon wrote to Murat, 'Inundate the plain of Leipzig with your cavalry, instead of only sending a few patrols in that direction.' He was anxious to make sure that his right front was clear of the enemy. It was presently to be his right rear as the Grand Army swung round facing westward towards Jena and Auerstadt, to attack the masses of the enemy reported in that direction. The result of the cavalry being thus flung out to the north-east was that it was only by hard marching they arrived in force on the battlefields of 14 October. At Auerstadt, where the more serious action of the two was fought (though the presence of the Emperor has made Jena the more famous), Davoût had only the cavalry attached to his army corps, some 1700 sabres. More than 8000 were in action with the Emperor at Jena. At the close of the day, Murat with D'Hautpoul and Nansouty's cuirassiers and Klein's dragoons thundered into the streets of Weimar, on the heels of the enemy, and collected thousands of prisoners in the gathering darkness of the autumn evening.

## CHAPTER X

### THE PURSUIT AFTER JENA—WARSAW—THE EYLAU CAMPAIGN

#### 1806-1807

PRUSSIA had been living for twenty years on the fame of Frederick the Great. Her power had been shattered in two weeks. It was now Murat's task to destroy whatever fragments were left of it, in one of the most marvellous pursuits recorded in military history.

The beaten army was streaming away to the westward in several columns, which presently turned first northward and then north-westward. Napoleon, advancing directly on Berlin with the main body, detached two corps to support Murat's pursuit.[1]

On 15 October, the day after the battles, Murat fell on the rearmost body of the enemy outside Erfurt, capturing in the first rush a large convoy of supplies and 800 prisoners. Riding round the town, he cut off the retreat of some thousands of the enemy who had crowded into its streets. General Mollendorf and the Prince of Orange-Nassau, who were in the town, refused Murat's summons to them to surrender, and tried to obtain conditions which he rejected. It must be 'surrender at discretion,' or he would attack. With only his cavalry in hand, he knew that to storm Erfurt would be a risky enterprise. But Ney's corps arrived to his support, and then the German generals surrendered, with 14,000 men, half of them wounded from the battlefield, and more than 100 guns. Then Murat,

[1] See Map p. 150, The Pursuit after Jena.

leaving Ney to dispose of the prisoners, continued the pursuit.

He had already pushed Klein's dragoons and Lasalle's light horsemen forward in advance. They had got in touch with a column of 15,000 men under the Grand Duke of Weimar. Unable to stop the march of this large force, they hung on its flanks and rear. Murat had discovered that the main body of the enemy under Prince Hohenlohe had turned northwards by the Gotha-Magdeburg road. He therefore contented himself with keeping Weimar's retirement under observation, pushing on between him and Hohenlohe, so as to prevent their junction, and following up the latter, collecting numbers of prisoners in repeated attacks on the rearguard.

On the 20th, Murat was before the fortress of Magdeburg. Hohenlohe had crossed the Elbe there, and was retiring north-westward. Blücher and Weimar were crossing the river lower down. Murat summoned General Kleist, the commandant of the fortress, but the Prussian declared he would hold out to the last. A division of Ney's corps was left to blockade the place, and Murat with the main body of the cavalry division turned eastward along the south bank of the Elbe. The heads of the French columns advancing on Berlin were reaching the crossings of the river above Magdeburg. Murat's mission was to cover the advance, push on to Berlin, and regain touch with the retreating enemy to the north or north-west of their capital. The whole of his cavalry was across the Elbe on the 22nd, and pushed on by forced marches towards Berlin. Lasalle's light cavalry occupied the suburb of Charlottenburg. Grouchy and Beaumont's dragoons, and D'Hautpoul's cuirassiers arrived in quick succession. The fortress of Spandau, which protects the capital on the westward, was summoned. The commandant refused to surrender to a mere mounted force, but capitulated next day on the appearance of Lannes' corps. The same day (25 October), Napoleon rode in triumph into Berlin.

Reports of spies and messages from the cavalry detachments

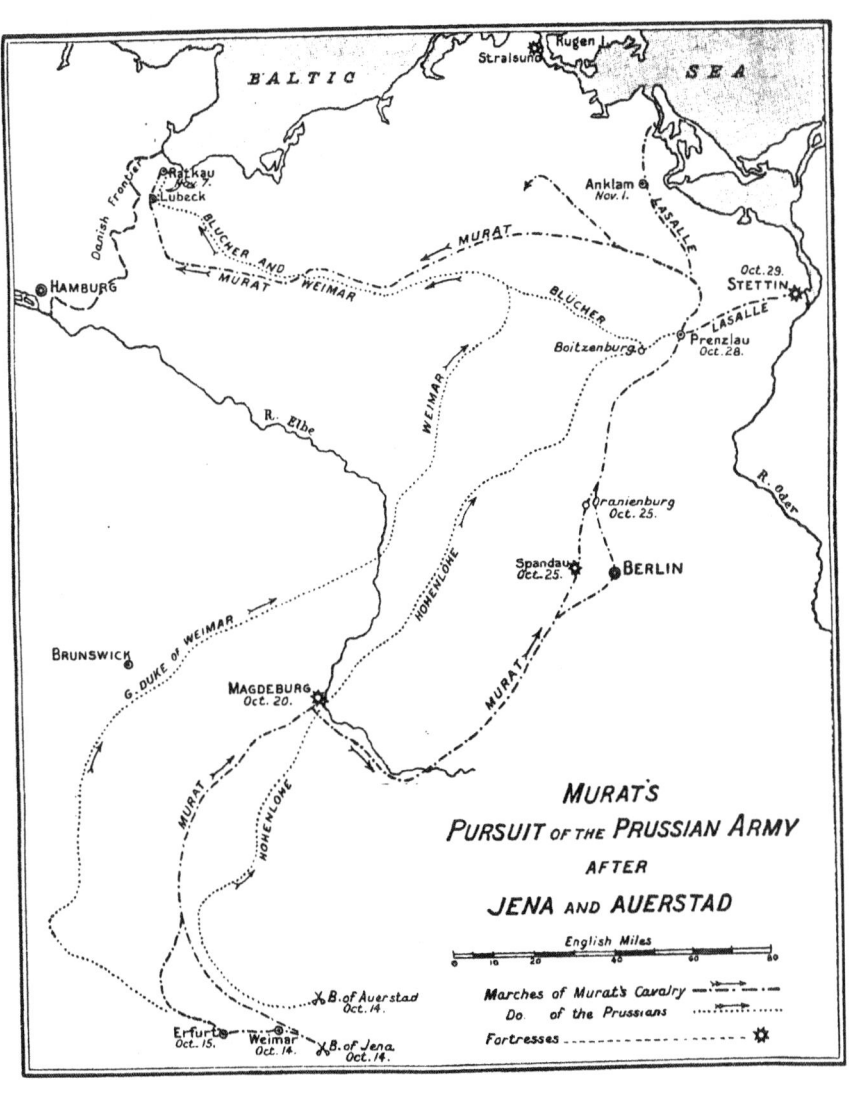

## THE PURSUIT AFTER JENA

that were keeping in touch with the enemy's retreat showed that Hohenlohe was trying to work round to the north of Berlin, in order to reach east Prussia by way of Stettin. Lasalle with Murat's advanced guard had pushed on to Oranienburg, north of Berlin, early on the 25th, and the same afternoon his patrols, sent out on all the roads radiating from the city, were again in touch with the enemy. Murat was hurrying to his help, followed by the infantry and artillery of Marshal Lannes. On the 26th, Lasalle routed Schimmelpfenning's cavalry division, which was acting as a flank guard to Hohenlohe's retreat. Next day, Hohenlohe was marching directly eastward on the main road towards Stettin, and Murat gradually closing on him by following a line of march that would bring him across his track at Prenzlau. Milhaud's chasseurs, thrown out to harass the flank of the Prussian army, were attacked by superior numbers near Boitzenburg and driven back, but Murat, hurrying in the direction of the firing, came to Milhaud's rescue with two regiments of cavalry and a horse battery, checked the pursuit, and cut off and captured some of the cavalry of the Prussian Guard.

Hohenlohe marching in the darkness before dawn, in the hope of shaking off Murat's pursuit, was entering Prenzlau, early on 28 October, when the French cavalry came galloping into the streets and headed him off in the suburbs of the town. During the morning there was hard fighting in and around the place; Murat, by repeated attacks with his cavalry and horse artillery, keeping the Prussians engaged till Lannes could come up. Before the infantry appeared, he had secured the outlets of Prenzlau towards Stettin, and flung a screen of patrols out on every road round the town. As the heads of the French infantry columns came in sight, he summoned Hohenlohe to surrender, and after a fruitless attempt to obtain favourable conditions the Prussian general capitulated. Prince Hohenlohe, Prince Augustus of Prussia, 14,000 infantry, and 2000 cavalry became prisoners of war, and forty-five standards and sixty-four guns were the trophies of the day.

Next morning, Milhaud captured six regiments of cavalry and three battalions of infantry that had separated from the main body, and Murat sent Lasalle with two regiments of hussars to summon Stettin. After some hesitation, the governor surrendered the fortress on condition that his garrison was to march out with the honours of war. Lasalle had sent back to Murat, asking him to hurry up some of Lannes' infantry, but when the time came for the march out, not an infantryman had appeared. The Prussians, once outside the place, seeing that they had been bluffed into surrender by a handful of hussars, got out of hand and prepared to resist. Bayonets were being fixed and cartridges handled when Lasalle charged into them, scattering them in all directions. At this moment Victor arrived at the head of a division of infantry, and the skirmish ended by the Prussians throwing down their arms.

On receiving the news of the surrender of Hohenlohe's army, and the capture of Stettin, Napoleon sent Murat his warmest congratulations. 'My brother,' he wrote to him from Berlin on 30 October, 'I must compliment you on the taking of Stettin. If your light horsemen can capture fortified places in this way, I shall have to disband my engineers, and melt down my siege guns. But you have still to catch General Blücher and the Duke of Weimar. March down the Oder, and pursue them at the sword's point even to Stralsund. There must be no rest till these two columns have laid down their arms.'

Blücher had united the two columns, and abandoning the idea of directly reaching East Prussia, was marching through Mecklenburg, intending to reach Stralsund and the Isle of Rügen, and thence transfer his troops by sea to Königsberg. By a forced march in the two last days of October, Murat headed him off, Lasalle taking 3500 prisoners at Anklam. Cut off from Stralsund, Blücher turned westward, marching towards the free city of Lübeck and the Danish frontier. Murat's cavalry were at his heels, and in frequent action with his rearguard, while the corps of Bernadotte and Soult followed by forced marches. On

## THE PURSUIT AFTER JENA 153

5 November, Blücher reached Lübeck. That morning Murat's cavalry charging his rearguard captured a battery of eight guns. The magistrates of Lübeck protested against the entry of the Prussian army into their city; but Blücher took no notice of their proclamation of neutrality, and marched in with bayonets fixed. The unfortunate city, which had no part in the quarrel, was attacked on 6 November by the infantry of Bernadotte and Soult, after Murat had driven the Prussian rearguard into the streets. Blücher was forced to abandon Lübeck. To prolong the resistance there would have been to be invested, for Murat's horsemen and light artillery were working round the outskirts of the place. Leaving 2000 killed and wounded in the streets, and 6000 prisoners and most of his guns in the hands of the French, Blücher retreated to Ratkau, on the Danish frontier. He hoped to be allowed to take refuge in Denmark, but he found a Danish army corps barring his march in battle array. Here the protest against a violation of neutrality was backed up with cannon and bayonets, and Blücher with men and horses weary with the long retreat, and most of his guns and ammunition convoys lost, was in no position to carry matters with a high hand, as he had done at Lübeck. Murat's cavalry were already forming to make the furious charge that would prelude the advance of Bernadotte and Soult's columns, when Blücher sent a flag of truce to ask for terms. In the afternoon of 7 November, the old veteran of Frederick's campaigns surrendered with 15,000 men, and Murat wrote to the Emperor, ' Sire, the fighting is over, because there are no more combatants left. The cavalry corps is about to start on its march to rejoin the Grand Army at Berlin.'

The pursuit had lasted three weeks. It is true that again and again it was the arrival of the infantry that compelled the surrender of the enemy, but it is none the less true that it was Murat's untiring energy that had found and kept touch with them, headed them off, and held them till the slower marching corps sent to support him could

arrive and complete the work he had begun. Some
50,000 prisoners and 200 guns had been taken. The
defeat of Jena had been turned into a disaster. Prussia
no longer had an army, except a handful of troops in East
Prussia.[1]

As in the year before, the tardy movements of the Russians
had left their allies to be destroyed singlehanded by Napoleon
in the first weeks of the war. They were now coming into
the field, and moving towards the Vistula. At the end of
October, Benningsen had about 60,000 men concentrated
round Grodno, and Buxhowden 50,000 at Wilna. Reinforcements to the extent of 20,000 more were marching
up from the Turkish frontier. In all the Czar would put
about 150,000 men in the field for the winter campaign in East
Prussia, and on the Polish borders. His unfortunate ally,
King Frederick William, had only left of his army Lestocq's
corps (20,000 men) in East Prussia, and small garrisons
in Dantzic, Graudenz and Thorn.

The Grand Army had been reinforced by Mortier's corps
(the 8th), and a new corps, the 9th, formed of south German
troops, under the command of the Emperor's youngest
brother, Prince Jerome Bonaparte. Magdeburg had surrendered to Ney; Davoût had been sent to occupy Posen.
The Grand Army 200,000 strong, with its headquarters at

---

[1] General von Horsetzky, in his *Feldzüge der letzten Hundert Jahre*
(Wien, 1894), thus tabulates the marches of Murat and the main body of
the Cavalry Reserve in this famous pursuit:—

Oct. 14. On the battlefield of Jena.
 ,,  15. At Erfurt.
 ,,  16.  ,, Langensalfza.
 ,,  17.  ,, Nordhausen.         200 kilometres (125 miles) in six days.
 ,,  18.  ,, Halberstadt.
 ,,  20. Before Magdeburg.
 ,,  22. At Dessau.
 ,,  25.  ,, Spandau.             270 kilometres (168 miles) in eight days.
 ,,  28.  ,, Prenzlau.  Hohenlohe surrenders.
 ,,  29.  ,, Stettin. Surrender of Stettin.
 ,,  30.  ,, Friedland and Anklam.
Nov. 4.  ,, Schwerin.             320 kilometres (200 miles) in ten
 ,,   6.  ,, Lübeck.              days.
 ,,   7.  ,, Ratkau.              Surrender of Blücher.

Total about 800 kilometres (500 miles) in twenty-four days. Some
regiments and divisions had covered greater distances; there were
sometimes marches of 40 to 50 miles.

# THE PURSUIT AFTER JENA

Berlin, was concentrating for its next task. It was to meet the Russians beyond the Vistula, and at the same time dispose of the Prussian garrisons in Silesia, and liberate Poland by driving out of it the small Russian army of occupation. Prince Jerome was given the easy task of the conquest of Silesia. Murat was given the hardly more difficult but the more important mission of carrying the Emperor's eagles into the heart of the old Polish kingdom.

The army with which he was to invade Poland was formed of Davoût's corps (already in movement on Posen, which it occupied on 9 November), the corps of Lannes and Augereau, and the main body of the Cavalry Reserve, some 80,000 men in all. Some of the cavalry divisions that had done the hardest work of the pursuit were left behind. The others were given German remounts to make up for their losses. The cuirassier divisions had not been employed in the forced marches in the north, and had had a long rest. Three divisions of cuirassiers, two of dragoons, and the light cavalry of the 3rd corps formed the mounted force, with which Murat pushed on in advance of the infantry columns on the road to Warsaw, after having spent a week with Napoleon at Berlin.

There he had heard from the Emperor something of his plans for the future. The prospect of the Grand Duchy of Berg developing by annexations into an important state on the east bank of the Rhine, and of Murat's coronet becoming a crown, was made impossible by the long settled scheme of marrying Jerome to a Würtemberg princess, and creating a kingdom for him in Westphalia, which would include some of the very territories Murat had hoped would be his own. Berg and Cleves were prospering under the administration of his friend Agar, Count of Mosbourg, but Murat had no great longing to return to his obscure court of Dusseldorf, where he had only spent a week of his reign. The coming march into Poland, the occupation of Warsaw, Napoleon's yet undefined plans for restoring the Polish nationality, opened out a wider horizon for Murat than a petty state in the Rhineland.

For some weeks to come he looked on Poland as his future kingdom. Prince Jerome, notwithstanding the Westphalian project, was dreaming the same flattering dream; but Murat knew nothing of this, and if he had known would not have considered Jerome's ambitions a serious obstacle. In the old days, the Polish nobles had more than once chosen as their elected king a brilliant soldier. For a nation of horsemen, what better candidate for the crown could there be than the famous cavalier who had proved his prowess on so many battlefields, and whose accession would make a sister of Napoleon Queen of Poland?

From the very beginning of the Warsaw campaign Murat was preparing for the part he hoped to play. It was then he adopted, instead of the uniform of a French marshal, a gorgeous costume of his own invention, intended to make him appear like one of themselves when he met the Polish nobles in their semi-oriental state apparel. When on 28 November he rode into Warsaw, at the head of the 1st Chasseurs and Beaumont's brigade of dragoons, his charger's bit and stirrups were of gold, his saddle cloth a tiger skin, and he himself was ablaze with gold and colour. He wore red leather riding boots, white breeches, a tunic that showed only a mass of gold embroidery, a diamond hilted sword of scimitar shape, suspended by a jewelled baldrick, a pelisse and shako of costly furs, the latter with ostrich and egret plumes held by a diamond clasp. The people received him with the wildest outburst of enthusiasm. 'He entered the old capital of Poland,' writes the Duchess d'Abrantès, 'a splendid type of that chivalrous valour, which is the distinctive characteristic of the Poles. He pleased that brave and most impressionable people, which was ready to follow with ardent devotion a young prince, who they knew would ride into an enemy's batteries as lightheartedly as other men would go to a ball.'

The advance on Warsaw and the occupation of the city were not opposed. The garrison had retreated across the

Vistula into the Praga suburb, and destroyed the bridge. They retired when the French crossed the river above and below the city, but during the first days of the occupation, while Murat held a kind of military court in Warsaw, hostile sentinels watched each other from the wharves on opposite shores of the Vistula.

Murat had at first every reason to suppose that his dreams would be realized. The Polish nobles formed a brilliant circle at his receptions, and spoke freely of their hope of seeing the kingdom restored under a prince of the Emperor's family. Prince Poniatowski, the brother of the last Polish king, and one of the soldiers of the wars of the partition, came to Warsaw to greet Murat as the personification of his country's hopes, told him that he had no thought of himself aspiring to the crown his ancestors had worn, and gave the French marshal the sword of the heroic King of Poland, Stephen Bathori. In a letter addressed to Murat he wrote :—

'We have treasured religiously the arms of the great men who once made Poland illustrious, and we consider it a duty to place them in the hands of those whom public opinion marks out as belonging to the foremost rank of men. On these grounds it is that I venture to ask your Imperial Highness to accept the sword which I take the liberty of offering to you. It was kept by the last kings of Poland. It formerly belonged to Stephen Bathori, one of the most valiant of our sovereigns, and was used in some of his most brilliant victories. Entrusted to your Highness's hands it will resume after a lapse of centuries the glorious task in which it has already been employed, and will perhaps fight once more for our Fatherland.'

On the blade there was this inscription :—

'OFFERT PAR JOSEPH PONIATOWSKI
A JOACHIM, GRAND-DUC BERG.
STEPHANUS BATORI REX POLONIÆ,
A.D. 1575.
MUTATO HEROE PRO PATRIA TAMEN, 1807.'[1]

[1] 'Presented by Joseph Poniatowski to Joachim, Grand-Duke of Berg. Stephen Bathori, King of Poland, A.D. 1575. With another hero, but still for the Fatherland, 1807.'

The gift of the historic sword in such circumstances might well seem to Murat an earnest that the sceptre of Poland would soon be in his grasp. In his letters to Napoleon from Warsaw, without actually declaring himself a candidate for the Polish crown, he showed plainly enough what his hopes were. He told of his enthusiastic welcome, of the friendship shown to him by the nobles and the leaders of the people, of their devotion to the Emperor personally as their deliverer, of their hopes of seeing at an early date Poland reconstituted ' as an independent nation, under a King of foreign birth, given to them by his Imperial Majesty.'

But Napoleon had not as yet decided anything, and he had still to fight for the possession of the Polish territory. The Russian army under Benningsen and Buxhowden was marching on Warsaw. In the middle of December, the heads of the Russian columns were on the river Narev, north-east of the Polish capital, and Napoleon, who had established his headquarters at Warsaw, had assembled the Imperial Guard, four corps of the Grand Army, and Murat's Cavalry Reserve on the line of the Vistula, north of the city and its tributary, the river Ukra, and then advanced to meet the enemy on the Narev.

For the first and last time in his military career Murat was forced to let his cavalry divisions take the field without him. He was ill at Warsaw, when after struggling through rain and sleet, over muddy tracks where the guns' wheels sank in the ground, the opposing armies met at Golymin and Pultusk, and as the result of a day of hard fighting, on 26 December, the Russians began a retreat, in which they abandoned some of their artillery simply because the teams could not drag it through the deep mud. Murat, still very unwell, had hurried up from Warsaw when he heard fighting was imminent, but did not arrive till after the double battle of the 26th. This time there was to be no pursuit; the weather and the state of the roads made it all but impossible. He spent a few days installing the cavalry in rough wooden huts erected along the outpost line, so as to form a chain of posts against Cossack raids,

# WARSAW

and then, leaving the command on the spot to Nansouty, returned to Warsaw.

With the New Year of 1807 came snow and hard frost, and the country became again practicable for movements on a large scale. In January, there were tidings that the Russian retreat had been turned into a march first north-westward, then westward round the French positions, so as by a wide sweeping circular movement to enter East Prussia, pick up Lestocq's corps, and fall upon Bernadotte on the Emperor's extreme left. Napoleon, leaving a small force on the Narev to protect Warsaw from raids on that side, ordered the Grand Army to concentrate northwards, with its centre at Allerstein. Elaborate measures were taken to conceal the stroke which the Emperor was meditating. Benningsen was to be allowed to continue his march against Bernadotte on the left, under the impression that he was going to surprise an isolated corps, and when he was thoroughly committed to the movement, Murat's cavalry was to break in on his right rear, and cut off his communications with Russia, the mass of the Grand Army following up the blow. A piece of carelessness revealed the plan to the enemy. The practice of using cipher for important dispatches was not used in the Grand Army, and success had made individual staff officers careless. A young officer conveying written orders, in which the coming operations were clearly indicated, was travelling in a sledge without an escort, just inside the outpost line, and felt so secure that he was actually sleeping rolled up in a rug, when, after dark, he was captured by a prowling patrol of Cossacks that had stolen through between the pickets. The captured dispatch told Benningsen what he had to expect. He countermanded the orders already issued, and began to retire northwards towards Königsberg, with his rearguards on a line facing the advance of the Grand Army from northern Poland.

The French followed him up in three columns, Ney on the left, Davoût in command on the right, Napoleon himself in the centre, with the main body of Murat's cavalry preceding him. It was a trying march, for with the end of January the intense cold of the winter had begun, and men and horses plodded wearily over snow covered tracks. Benningsen had decided on making a stand at Preuss Eylau, with Königsberg in his rear. In the first week of February, as he concentrated on his chosen battle ground, his rear-guards showed a bolder front to the French advance. On the morning of 6 February, Murat, with the advanced cavalry, came on a strong rearguard drawn up to oppose him near the village of Hof. There had been a partial thaw when the sun rose, and the hollow of the brook behind which the Russians were waiting was converted into a swamp. From the brook the ground rose gently to a belt of dark pine woods, along the margin of which twelve battalions were in line, with some guns on a rising ground to their left, and bodies of cavalry showing on both flanks.

Murat had nothing but his horsemen and light artillery in hand; but a few miles away the corps of Soult and Augereau, under the Emperor's personal command, were coming up in a long marching column. It would have been common prudence to content himself with merely skirmishing with the enemy, and keeping them under observation till the infantry and field batteries were ready to come into action. But this was not Murat's way. For him 'to see the enemy and to charge him, was the same thing.' Reckless of the force opposed to him and the strong position it held, he flung his horsemen into action. Even before his main body had come up, his advanced guard, formed of Colbert's dragoon regiments, was sent struggling through the thawing marshes along the brook, and launched upon the enemy in a reckless charge, from which it came back with many empty saddles. Colbert's men rallied and were joined by Klein's division, and then charged again, riding for the batteries on the left. They got in among the guns, temporarily captured four of them, and then were driven back by the fire of the infantry. While they were still in action the 1st Cuirassiers arrived, the leading regiment of

## THE EYLAU CAMPAIGN

D'Hautpoul's division, and covered the retirement of the dragoons.

So far there had been only failure. Murat had brought his light artillery into action. D'Hautpoul's cuirassier division had come up and formed in a long line. They had just rolled their cloaks and waited breathing their horses, a splendid mass of steel-clad horsemen. The 1st Cuirassiers reformed after their charge had joined the division. On their flank, Legrand's éclaireurs, the vanguard of the infantry, had come up. Suddenly, like a flash of light and colour, Murat in his brilliant Polish costume came galloping to the front of the cuirassiers. Reining up his horse for a moment, rising in his golden stirrups, and without drawing his sword, he yelled out, ' Charge ! ' pointing with a jewelled riding whip to the enemy's left. Then he spurred forward with D'Hautpoul racing after him, and the cuirassiers breaking into a steady gallop, knee to knee, waving their long swords and shouting ' *Chargez! Rallions au prince!*' Legrand's light infantry were thrown forward, after the rush of horsemen, forming a long firing line to their left. Murat, still with sword undrawn, led straight for the guns. The storm of the charge burst into and over the batteries, and thundered round the squares on the Russian left. Everything gave way before it. As the cuirassiers, after rushing the guns, turned upon the infantry, square after square broke. Klein and Colbert, eager to avenge their earlier failure, led their dragoons again into the battle. Legrand's firing line closed on the enemy. The Russian cavalry, coming to the rescue of the broken infantry, were themselves driven back by the heavy charge of the cuirassiers. Murat was in the thick of the victorious mêlée. One would have thought that his very dress, his gold and diamonds, would have made him the centre of fierce attacks by the enemy's best swordsmen, but he came out of the fighting without a scratch, though his fur pelisse was torn with bullets. The Russians retired through the woods, leaving more than 1200 killed and wounded on the ground: 800 prisoners,

9 guns, and 4 standards were in the hands of the victors.

Next day Murat found the allied army waiting for battle north of the little town of Eylau. Benningsen had 65,000 men under his command including 22,000 regular and Cossack cavalry. The allied army was almost entirely Russian, for the Prussian contingent had only 5600 men in line. Napoleon had some 70,000 men within striking distance, of whom about 24,000 were cavalry. The fighting began on the 7th, but it was not till the 8th that the engagement became general.

It was one of the most fiercely contested of Napoleon's battles, one of those, too, in which he narrowly escaped defeat. It was fought in a driving snowstorm that limited the view over the field. It was not till the afternoon that Napoleon was able to meet the enemy with anything like equal numbers. In the morning he could oppose only 200 guns to Benningsen's 450, but the Russians suffered heavily from the ricochetting fire of the French guns, for their infantry was formed in three successive lines, each of great depth. At first Napoleon could bring against them only the corps of Soult and Augereau and six divisions of Murat's cavalry (Colbert and Bruyère's hussars and chasseurs, Grouchy, Klein, and Milhaud's dragoons, and D'Hautpoul's cuirassiers). The rest of his corps were marching towards the sound of the cannon, with long miles of snowy roads to traverse before they could fire a shot.

The critical moment of the day was that when Augereau's corps, with the snow driving in their faces and half blinding them, were assailed in front by the Russian infantry and artillery, enfiladed by other batteries thrown against their flank, and charged by a mass of Russian cavalry. Augereau himself was hit. Every one of his brigadiers and colonels was killed or wounded. His two divisions were seen retiring through the darkness of the snowstorm, some of the regiments actually breaking into confused masses that might soon be a rabble of fugitives.

Murat was beside Napoleon, who with his staff and

MURAT WITH NAPOLEON AT THE BATTLE OF EYLAU
FROM THE PAINTING BY BARON GROS IN THE LOUVRE, PARIS

## THE EYLAU CAMPAIGN 163

escort had posted himself on a rising ground near the cemetery of Eylau. Through a lull in the storm the Emperor caught sight of Augereau's broken line, and pointing to the Russian attack, said to Murat : ' *Nous laisseras-tu dévorer par ces gens-là ?* ' ' Are you going to let those fellows eat us up ? '

His answer to the appeal was the famous charge that saved Augereau's corps from utter destruction. Six divisions of cavalry were hurled upon the advancing Russians in three successive waves. First came Murat, leading the two divisions of light horse ; then Grouchy with the three divisions of dragoons ; last, D'Hautpoul at the head of his regiments of cuirassiers. A mass of some 18,000 horsemen rolled down upon the Russian centre, breaking through two successive lines of infantry that had hurriedly formed squares to meet the attack. In the fog of the snowstorm some of the Russian regiments were ridden down before they could form. In other cases squares were broken up. Sixteen standards were taken. The first rush of the charge only stopped when it came upon the third line, the Russian reserve. At this final stage of the attack Napoleon sent Bessières with the mounted grenadiers, and the Chasseurs of the Guard, his own escort, to Murat's help. This fresh onset broke even the third line, and then the victorious cavalry came riding back. They had disengaged Augereau's beaten infantry, and forced Benningsen to devote all his energies to reforming his own line, and reduced him for a while to a purely defensive attitude. Murat had successfully charged an army and averted a disaster.

When darkness ended the fight the armies were still in contact. During the afternoon Napoleon had been strongly reinforced, and could expect further help early next day. Benningsen had had every available man in action, and did not expect that his wearied troops would be able to hold their own against superior numbers if the battle were renewed. He had lost 18,000 men, including 9 of his generals, and 24 guns had been captured. Before sunrise on the 9th he was retiring on Königsberg.

Murat followed him with his cavalry, their ranks sadly thinned by the losses of the day before, and by the numbers of men and horses that had succumbed to the terrible weather. He came on the enemy's rearguard near Wittenberg, about six miles from Königsberg. But this time there was no fighting. Murat, surprised that he heard no firing when his advanced patrols approached the Russian outposts, rode forward and saw his hussars fraternizing with the Cossacks. They had come out to meet the Frenchmen, making signs of friendship, and were now exchanging drinks of brandy and vodka and cigars. A Russian general came forward, and shook hands with one of Murat's officers, and said the war was over; they were all tired of killing each other. Some of the Cossack troopers shook hands with the hussars, saluting them by saying, '*Braves Français!*' but they had no more French at their command. There was a tacit truce, and some officers of Russian regular cavalry rode out to fraternize with the Frenchmen.

That Murat accepted such a situation is a plain proof that his own horses and men were near exhaustion point. He wrote to the Emperor: 'I feel sure that the enemy will not hold on to Königsberg; indeed, I expect he has already left it. This afternoon I took the courtesies of the Cossacks and of their lancers and hussars to be a good-bye to us. I would bet that I am not mistaken.'

However, he was wrong. The Russians were not yet abandoning East Prussia, and there would still be hard fighting before the war ended. But neither side was in condition for fighting amid the ice and snow of the Baltic coast country. For the first time in his career Napoleon was glad to break off the struggle for a while, retreat from a field of victory, and place his army under shelter in the towns and villages and in huge camps of wooden huts, till the spring. The old custom of going into winter quarters, supposed to have disappeared with the eighteenth century, had been perforce revived.

## CHAPTER XI

### HEILSBERG, FRIEDLAND AND TILSIT—THE SPANISH ADVENTURE

#### 1807-1808

DURING the winter, while the 10th corps (Lefèbvre) besieged Dantzic, the rest of the army had a long rest in its cantonments along the line of the river Passarge. The cavalry corps was on the left about Elbing. Remounts were collected, recruits were brought from the depots in France, and by the spring Murat had 20,000 effective and well mounted men under his command. As the weather improved, there were manœuvres of large bodies, and in a final review before the Emperor at Elbing, Murat was able to show him 18,000 men manœuvring with clock-work precision. A general reorganization of the whole army had been in progress during the winter. By the beginning of May Napoleon had, besides Murat's cavalry, 150,000 men in his camps along the Passarge, and some 75,000 more in Poland, and in Silesia, and other parts of Germany.

Benningsen had remained during the winter at Königsberg, where Frederick William of Prussia was holding his court under the protection of his ally. The Russian general had also been reinforced, but to a much less extent than his opponent. He had at most a little over 100,000 men at his disposal in the spring. There were many complaints that he did not attempt something against the French, while Dantzic still held out, but he waited from week to week in the hope of further reinforcements. It was not till the end of May 1807, when Dantzic had fallen and

Napoleon was concentrating his army to advance on Königsberg, that at last Benningsen moved.

Murat, after the great review at Elbing, had gone to Dantzic on 28 May to visit Lefèbvre and see the captured fortress. It was there he received a message from the Emperor's chief of the staff, Berthier. It informed him that Ney's corps, the only one on the north bank of the Passarge, where it formed an advanced outpost line for the army, had been suddenly attacked in force. The Grand Army was concentrating for the counter-attack, and Murat was to bring up all his cavalry from Elbing by way of Mohrungen.

Ney made a dogged resistance at Guttstadt, and though he lost some ground, he gained time for the concentration. Benningsen, on the morrow of his first success, found that a superior force was gathering to crush him, and began his retreat north-eastwards. Lestocq's Prussians fell back on Königsberg, the main Russian army retiring on Heilsberg, where there was a partly entrenched position in which they intended to make a stand. Murat had crossed the Passarge, on 9 June, following up the Russian rearguard, and reoccupying Guttstadt. Next day, with the advanced-guard made up of Soult's infantry and artillery, Espagne's cuirassiers, and twelve regiments of light cavalry under Lasalle, he came in sight of the position of Heilsberg.

The Emperor had already decided to force Benningsen to abandon the lines of Heilsberg by sending Davoût to work round his left, and threaten his flank and rear. Murat, without waiting for this movement, and on his own initiative, attacked at once with the advanced-guard. The result was heavy and unnecessary loss before the Russians evacuated the position. The cavalry was engaged with a superior force of eighty Russian squadrons, and there was hard hand to hand fighting. Murat had a narrow escape. Charging beside Lasalle, at the head of the hussars and chasseurs, he had his horse killed under him. He caught and mounted a riderless horse, but was hardly in the saddle again when he was cut off and surrounded by a party of Russian dragoons. He was fighting for his life, when Lasalle in person arrived to the rescue, cutting down several of the enemy. A few minutes later, Murat saved Lasalle's life in the mêlée. 'We are quits now, my dear general,' he said, grasping his hand. It was because Murat, Prince of the Empire, Grand Duke of Berg, and Marshal of France, was thus ready to risk his life and fight like a man in the ranks, that all who followed him felt an admiring devotion for their daring leader.

But with this dash and daring there was the lack of sound judgment that had produced the premature attack on Heilsberg, and equally brave but less reckless officers wondered at the risks he took. Thus in relating another incident of the same day, the charge of Espagne's cuirassier division, Colonel de Gonneville, who commanded one of these magnificent regiments, with all his admiration, cannot refrain from well founded criticism: 'The Grand Duke of Berg,' he says, 'came up from our right rear followed by his staff. He dashed at full gallop across our front, bending forward on the neck of his horse, and as he passed rapidly by General Espagne he shouted to him the one word—"Charge!" Fifteen squadrons, without support, were being set in motion to attack sixty squadrons of splendid cavalry, by this brief order, without further explanations, and it seemed to me all the more strange because to close with the enemy we had to pass a difficult ravine in twos and fours, and reform under fire within two hundred paces of his front lines.'

The charge was successful simply because with that strange lack of enterprise, which so often characterised Russian cavalry,[1] they waited for the cuirassiers to reform instead of charging them while they were still engaged in the process. The losses of the day were heavy. The comparatively small force engaged had 7000 men killed and wounded, and the cavalry had a large part in these

---

[1] Compare, for instance, the mass of Russian cavalry at Balaclava, remaining at the halt to receive Scarlett's charge of the Heavy Brigade.

losses. In their charge across the ravine, one of the cuirassier regiments, the 6th, lost seventeen officers out of twenty-two, and in the evening reorganized as two weak squadrons under the command of a lieutenant Napoleon was justly displeased with such unnecessary expenditure of life. Perhaps this was why he diverted Murat's energies to a subordinate operation, sending him with the left wing (the corps of Soult and Davoût), to follow up the detachment of the allies that was retiring on Königsberg.

This was why Murat had no part in the final victory of Friedland on 14 June. On the morning of the battle the Emperor had sent an order to him and to Lannes to rejoin the Grand Army, leaving Soult before Königsberg. Next day Murat overtook the cavalry which was pursuing the Russians, and commanded the pursuit as far as the Niemen.

When on the morning of 19 June he came in sight of the frontier river at Tilsit, Bagration, who commanded Benningsen's rearguard, had passed his troops across with the exception of his Cossack cavalry. These were the only Russians on the left bank. Murat was forming his horsemen in two lines to charge them, as a prelude to an attempt to force his way over the river into Russian territory, when a staff officer rode out from the enemy's ranks with a flag of truce. He handed to Murat a letter from the Czar addressed to Napoleon. The Emperor had come up with his staff and his escort of the cavalry of the Guard. Murat gave him the letter, which proved to be a request for an armistice. The war was at last ended.

Then came the negotiations that led to the famous meeting of the Emperors on the raft in the middle of the Niemen, and the Treaty of Tilsit, with its public and secret articles—the practical recognition of Napoleon as the dictator of the Continent, the alliance of Alexander with him as his helper in projects for the reshaping of the world.

Murat cherished to the last a hope that out of the new combinations the Emperor was elaborating there would come a throne for himself—perhaps in Poland. Early on the morning of the meeting between the emperors he put on his splendid Polish dress, and went to greet Napoleon. Perhaps the Emperor disliked this reminder of Murat's ambitions, for he turned abruptly on him saying: 'Go and put on a general's uniform. You look like a circus rider' (*Vous avez l'air de Franconi*). Murat obeyed, and appeared in the brilliant group of marshals that surrounded the Emperor on the bank of the Niemen wearing the uniform of a cavalry general, with the Legion of Honour, and the Golden Fleece that had been sent to him from Spain by Godoy. The Czar gave him the Cross of St. Andrew to add to his decorations—a poor substitute for the crown of Bathori and Sobieski. Prince Jerome Bonaparte had been given the new kingdom of Westphalia, under the arrangements of Tilsit, a kingdom that Murat had dreamed of as a possible development of his Grand Duchy on the Rhine. Napoleon had found kingdoms for all the three of his brothers who consented to be his satellites—Joseph in Italy, Louis in the Netherlands, Jerome in Holland. Joachim Murat, his brother by marriage, who had done more dangerous work for him than all three, had only his coronet and a handful of German subjects. He looked for compensation of some kind, and when he returned to Paris with the Emperor, he persistently devoted himself to bargaining for such increase of his territory in the Rhineland as would make Berg a state of some importance, and give him a more ample revenue.

He did not stop on his way to visit the duchy. He was quite content to leave its government in Agar's hands. His home was not at Dusseldorf, but in Paris, where Caroline had been holding a court of her own at the Elysée during his long absence. She shared her husband's ambitions, and had for a while hopes of being welcomed at Warsaw as the Queen of Poland. She had used all her influence to forward his projects with the Emperor's friends and advisers. At the Elysée, she dispensed an all but royal hospitality, and she was a prominent figure at every great social gathering in Paris, where her elaborate costumes and her display of jewels outshone all competitors. If the gossip of the day did not wrong her, she had more than one lover, among them Junot, then governor of Paris. Napoleon was inclined to believe the story, and had an angry scene with Junot on his return. Murat either did not hear the stories that were public property, or refused to attach any importance to them. When Caroline welcomed him home, husband and wife became fast allies in the promotion of their common interest with reference to the Grand Duchy.

From August 1807 to January 1808 there was a prolonged discussion between Napoleon and his Foreign Minister, on the one side, and the Murats on the other, as to questions of territorial compensation for the Grand Duke, and a minor dispute as to his position at the Imperial Court. To take the less important question first, Murat protested that as it had been agreed that in the Confederation of the Rhine, the Grand Duke of Berg should have royal honours, he and his wife should take rank at the Tuileries next after Napoleon's crowned brothers, and their wives. Napoleon had decided that princes and princesses of the Imperial family, when in Paris, should rank according to their seniority in the family itself. The result was that Murat, though an independent sovereign, ranked as the husband of Caroline after Borghese, the husband of her elder sister, Pauline, who was a mere titular prince, without an inch of territory. Napoleon rejected his plea for precedence. In reply to a final appeal of Murat's he wrote to him :—

'Your rank in my palaces is fixed by the rank you hold in my family, and your rank in my family is fixed by that of my sister. I cannot allow you to hold the position of a foreign prince at my court . . . A foreign prince only comes to Paris as an occasional visitor, and does not habitually reside there. I can the less consent to it, because if you were treated as a grand duke, you would lose thereby, as I have decided that the long established usage in France is to be followed, and that the brothers and sisters of the emperor are to take the precedence of grand dukes and grand duchesses. A different

## HEILSBERG, FRIEDLAND AND TILSIT 171

decision would be contrary to the prerogatives of France and the dignity of my crown. The grand dukes have replaced the electors, and the electors always came after the royal family ... You are too much attached to the glory of my family not to feel how disagreeable it would be to Frenchmen to see the Grand Duchess of Hesse-Darmstadt, the Grand Duke of Würzburg, the Margrave of Baden, take precedence of my family in Paris. This is so absurd that it has never entered into any one's head; and the title of brother and sister which I use to such dignitaries is only a courteous fiction, which gives them rank next after my real brothers and sisters.'

Murat was silenced and not satisfied. But he and Caroline, if they could not have royal honours at the Imperial court, could yet assert their ideas of their dignity by a more than royal ostentation, a display of wealth and state that rivalled that of the Emperor and Empress and outshone all others. At the Elysée, and during the stay of the court at Fontainebleau in the late summer, their banquets and receptions were the talk of Paris. The dinner service was of gold; the rooms were lavishly adorned with masses of costly flowers, a crowd of servants in liveries of red-and-gold waited upon their guests.

The festivities for the marriage of Murat's niece Antoinette, the daughter of his brother Pierre, celebrated at Paris in the autumn, were even more elaborate than the fête which Caroline gave on the occasion of Jerome's marriage with Catherine of Würtemberg. Antoinette Murat, daughter of a small farmer, became the bride of a prince. She was married to the heir of the Catholic branch of the Hohenzollerns, Prince Charles of Hohenzollern-Sigmaringen.[1]

Napoleon, during the long debates on the future of Berg,

[1] The marriage was a very happy one. On his wife's death in 1847, Prince Charles wrote to one of the Murats, that she had been 'an angel of goodness, and the faithful companion of his life,' in which her loss made a blank of everything. Her eldest son, Prince Antony of Hohenzollern, was the father of that Prince Leopold of Hohenzollern whose candidature for the Spanish throne led to the Franco-German War of 1870. By her marriage with the Prince of Hohenzollern-Sigmaringen, Antoinette Murat was also the grandmother of the King of Roumania, Queen Stephanie of Portugal, and the Countess Marie of Flanders, mother of the present king of the Belgians.

remained on the best of terms with his brother-in-law. On the occasion of Antoinette's marriage, his wedding presents were the title of princess for the bride, granted when the marriage contract was still being arranged, and the gift of a fine house in Paris, the Hôtel de Breteuil, in the Rue de Rivoli. He took Murat with him on a flying visit which he made to northern Italy in December. And finally, in the affair of Berg, he did not treat him ungenerously.

The arrangement arrived at was that three outlying portions of the old Prussian territory, which historically were part of the Duchy of Cleves, but were surrounded by the territory of Louis' kingdom of Holland, forming *enclaves* inside the Dutch frontier, should be ceded by Murat to Holland. He was also to cede to France the fortress of Wesel. In return he was to receive a considerable territory on the German frontiers of his Grand Duchy. Murat raised persistent objections to the cession of Wesel. There was even a moment when he indulged in gasconading talk about throwing himself into the fortress with his little army of Berg and Cleves, and defying Napoleon to take the place from him. 'We shall see,' he said, 'if the Emperor will venture in the face of Europe to besiege me there, and if he does I shall hold out to the last extremity.'

Notwithstanding such foolish outbursts, the affair was at last arranged. Murat ceded the scraps of outlying territory—Huyssen, Sevenaer, and Malbourg—to Louis, and Wesel to the Emperor, and obtained possession of the abbey districts of Elten, Essen, and Werden—the same that he had disputed with Blücher in 1806—the Prussian territory of La Marck, the city of Münster, and the Prussian part of the territory depending on it, and the territories of the counts of Lingen, Solms, and Tecklenburg, which had been Prussian for a century. In all he was given an addition to his Grand Duchy of 146 square miles, and 362,000 inhabitants, raising the total number of his subjects to nearly a million and a quarter.

The treaty was signed on 20 January, 1808. In

# THE SPANISH ADVENTURE 173

February Murat was preparing to leave Paris with Caroline, visit and take formal possession of his new territories, and transfer his capital from Dusseldorf to the city of Münster, when all his plans and the whole course of his life were changed by an unexpected order from the Emperor.

After the Treaty of Tilsit, England was the only enemy that still opposed Napoleon's ambitions. By a secret article of the treaty, Denmark was to be forced into the Franco-Russian alliance, its fleet seized and the Sound closed against the British flag. England, warned by a secret service agent, anticipated the blow by attacking Copenhagen and seizing the Dano-Norwegian fleet. Having been disappointed in the north, Napoleon set himself to secure the Mediterranean ports, and those of the Spanish Peninsula. The Ionian islands were handed over to a French garrison by Russia. The Illyrian ports were occupied in the Emperor's name. Pius VII refused to close his harbours against the British flag, and the Papal territory was invaded and annexed to the Empire. Portugal still clung to the English alliance, and a British fleet was in the Tagus. Napoleon arranged with Godoy, the dissolute and venal dictator of Spain, in whose hands the feeble king, Charles IV, was a mere puppet, a treaty for the partition of Portugal. Part of the kingdom was to be annexed to the Empire. Godoy was flattered with the prospect of the remainder being formed into a principality for himself. A French army under Junot marched through Spain, invaded Portugal, and occupied Lisbon. The royal family took refuge on board a British fleet, and sailed for Brazil.

On the pretext of supporting Junot's expedition, strong French detachments were posted in northern Spain. To weaken the Spanish power of resistance, the best of the Spanish warships were 'invited' to join the French squadron at Toulon, and a Spanish army was transferred to northern Germany to do garrison duty with their French allies. It was generally expected that Napoleon's policy would be to bring Spain into the imperial system, not by annexation, but by a marriage between a French princess and Ferdinand, Prince of the Asturias, the heir of the old king. Then there would be the control of Spanish policy by French advisers, a treaty of offensive and defensive alliance and commercial treaties that would place the development of Spain's resources in French hands. The imperial troops in northern Spain were therefore to be considered as friends and allies. But there was a widespread suspicion that the Emperor had not yet revealed his real policy, and that these allies might prove to be invaders in disguise.

By the beginning of 1808 the French army of occupation in Spain had grown into a formidable force. General Dupont was in Leon, with his headquarters at Valladolid; Marshal Moncey was in Old Castile, with his headquarters at Burgos; a division under General Mortier was in Navarre and Biscay; a whole army corps under General Duhesme was in Aragon and Catalonia. These commanders were allowed to believe that, now that Junot had secured Portugal, they would soon be engaged with an allied Spanish force in an attack upon the English at Gibraltar. Each had so far acted independently, reporting to and receiving orders from the War Office in Paris. But the time had come to give a central direction to the French forces in Spain, by appointing a commander-in-chief, and at the same time send to Madrid a lieutenant of the Emperor, on whom he could rely to support energetically the further developments of his Spanish policy. Napoleon chose Murat for this double mission.

The secret was kept up to the very last moment. Murat, busy with his preparations for his journey to Dusseldorf and Münster, had an interview with the Emperor on the morning of 20 February, in which not a word was said about Spain. In the evening he was handed two letters, one from Napoleon, the other from the Minister of War. The minister's letter informed him that he was to start that same night for Bayonne, in order to take over the command of all the French forces in the Spanish Peninsula.

## THE SPANISH ADVENTURE  175

The Emperor's letter appointed him his lieutenant-general in Spain, and enclosed detailed instructions as to the first steps he was to take. He was cautioned that the utmost secrecy was to be observed, but he was not given any information as to Napoleon's ultimate intentions. It was enough for him to know what was to be done immediately.

Murat was startled at what looked like hostile projects against Spain, when he read in the Emperor's instructions :—

'You will write to the (Spanish) commandant-general of Navarre that it is necessary for you to occupy the fortress of Pampeluna. I am at peace with the King of Spain, but since our common interests have obliged my armies to enter Spain, it is necessary that their communications should be well secured. After the citadel of Pampeluna, the most important is that of San Sebastian. You will have it occupied as well as all the fortresses between Valladolid, Pampeluna, and France. If the commandant-general of Navarre refuses to hand over the fortresses to you, you will use the troops of Marshal Moncey to compel him. As for the rest, there is no need of your entering into any communications with the Spanish court till I direct you to do so. The principal thing, before all else, is to occupy the citadel of Pampeluna. . . . As soon as the citadel is occupied by my troops, you will order the 3rd division of Marshal Moncey's corps to march from Vittoria to Burgos, so that Vittoria may be cleared for the reception of my Guard. If there is any delay about getting possession of the citadel of Pampeluna, you will have to move this division of Marshal Moncey's up to the place and make a serious demand for the citadel to be handed over to you.'

There was no time to ask for further explanations. There was a hurried farewell to Caroline, and while Paris slept, Murat drove out of the southern barriers on the road to Bayonne and the Pyrenees, wondering whether peace or war was before him.

## CHAPTER XII

### MURAT LIEUTENANT-GENERAL OF THE EMPEROR IN SPAIN

#### 1808

MURAT remained at Bayonne till 7 March. From his headquarters there he directed the movements ordered by the Emperor and collected reports of the military position in Spain, but he felt his position very embarrassing in the absence of all knowledge as to the ultimate trend of Napoleon's policy. From Bayonne he wrote to him :—

'I thought I had deserved a little confidence on the part of your Majesty, and perhaps I ought not to have expected to find myself here without being able to know beyond a certain point what preparations I am to make for the military movements in which I may have to take part. For it is not easy to organize a transport train, when one does not know whether it is to be prepared for a long expedition or for an affair of a few days.'

Pampeluna had admitted a French garrison to its citadel. At San Sebastian difficulties were raised, and Murat feared that he would have to precipitate matters by the use of force. To avoid this he had recourse to a piece of trickery. He wrote to the Duke of Mahon, the governor-general of Guipuzcoa, saying that on account of the healthiness of San Sebastian he proposed to establish a military hospital there, and would send some depot companies to the citadel to carry out the work.

The duke replied with a polite letter objecting to the proposal. Murat wrote to him again insisting on his project. The French army, he said, had entered Spain as friendly allies. The sick were not safe in the villages, exposed to the attacks of evil disposed persons. They must be in an hospital, inside the walls of a fortress, and it would be a scandal if this were refused. At the same time, he moved towards San Sebastian some detachments of the Imperial Guard which had just crossed the frontier. The duke had only four hundred men in his garrison, and he yielded to the veiled threat, for he feared to provoke a conflict. He stipulated that if the court at Madrid did not approve of his action the French were to evacuate the citadel. In his report to Napoleon, Murat joked about the simplicity of the Spanish grandee, who expected that once in the citadel the French would pay any attention to orders from the imbecile king of Spain.

Godoy had been for a long time one of his correspondents. He had sent him the Golden Fleece long before this, and invoked his protection with the Emperor. Writing to Napoleon from Bayonne, Murat acknowledged that till now he had been mistaken about Godoy's position. ' The last news from Madrid, he said, ' announces that the alarm there is at its highest, and that the Prince of the Peace (Godoy) is generally detested by all Spaniards, a thing I did not believe till now.' The queen, generally believed to be Godoy's mistress, was, he said, involved in the hatred felt for the prime minister. As for the king, he counted for nothing and inspired only contempt. The discontent with the Government was in fact so deep and widespread that ' there would be an insurrection, only that the people are fully persuaded that your Majesty will change the administration.' Deputies had been chosen by the people of Guipuzcoa and Navarre to meet Napoleon on the frontier and offer him the keys of their cities. ' These provinces already regard themselves as French. Public feeling could not be in a better disposition.'

On 3 March Murat received orders to move his headquarters from Bayonne to Vittoria. The Emperor impressed on him the necessity of seeing his troops had plenty of camp-kettles and good boots, but gave him no information as to his plans. On the 11th Murat wrote from Vittoria: 'I hasten to report to your Majesty my arrival at Vittoria, and the extraordinarily friendly reception I have had all the way from the frontier to this city. A lieutenant of yours coming to Spain to take possession of it in your name, and with the consent of all Spaniards, could not be better received. I was met at the frontier by a deputation of the States of Guipuzcoa, and as I entered the territory of each commune, the magistrates came to assure me of their feelings of devotion and admiration for your Majesty. In a word, and to sum it all up, I found on my journey the people lining the roadsides. Their outbursts of rejoicing were almost like madness. From village to village, all along the way from Irun to Vittoria, there was nothing but dancing and shouts of " Vive Napoléon ! " '

He had not been two days at Vittoria when he was told to move on to Burgos. He had the same friendly reception there. Napoleon had written that he would soon arrive himself, and Murat informed the authorities at Burgos that they might expect the Emperor before the end of the month.

But now Murat's reports began to be less optimistic. There was disquieting news. The court of Madrid was becoming seriously alarmed at the steady flow of French reinforcements over the Pyrenees, the occupation of the northern citadels, and the seizure of the citadel of Monjuich, on the heights above Barcelona, by a sudden movement of the French, an act of violence the commandant feared to resist. Godoy had ordered Solano's division of Spanish troops, which had marched into Portugal with Junot, to return at once to Spain, and he had said openly that the French were acting as enemies, and it was time to prepare for resistance. Duhesme reported from Barcelona that French and Neapolitan soldiers had been stabbed in the streets. Napoleon treated this report as of no importance. He wrote to Murat: 'There is no dis-

# LIEUTENANT-GENERAL IN SPAIN 179

content at Barcelona. General Duhesme is an old woman. The Neapolitans have had a few stabs with the stiletto. It is the way of the inhabitants. For the rest, people are well disposed, and when one has the citadel one has everything.'

But the agitation at Barcelona was really serious. In the evenings groups of Spanish soldiers paraded the town, joining the people in hostile demonstrations against the French. Elsewhere there were reports of assassinations of French soldiers, and a proclamation was issued, impressing on the officers the necessity of enforcing the strictest discipline and avoiding all causes of offence to the inhabitants. Napoleon, disregarding all reports of disaffection, and considering that once he had command of the capital, he would be master of the country, had already, on 7 March, written to Murat to occupy the passes in the mountains between Burgos and Madrid, and transfer his headquarters to the latter city. On 16 March Murat reported from Aranda that in conformity with these orders, Moncey's corps had occupied the Somo Sierra, and that two divisions under Dupont would be at Guadarama on the 19th. Next day, the 17th, from Fresnillo de la Fuente, he reported that he had news from Madrid of much excitement there on, rumours that the royal family were about to imitate the Braganzas, and leave the country, embarking at Cadiz; that the king had tried to allay the agitation by a proclamation protesting that he would not leave Madrid, but Murat suggested that this might be a device of Godoy's to keep things quiet till he could take the king away to Seville or Cadiz, and that the movement of Solano's corps from Portugal was connected with some such scheme.

While Murat was writing these letters, the agitation had ended in a popular rising against Godoy. The court was at Aranjuez near Madrid. On the 17th the people crowded round the palace and the house of Godoy. The soldiers fraternized with them. Godoy's house was stormed, and the minister was roughly handled, and barely escaped with his life. On the 18th the king published a proclamation, depriving him of all his dignities. Then, as the armed agitation continued, he announced his own abdication in favour of Prince Ferdinand.

Murat, continuing his advance on Madrid, heard the first news of the Aranjuez revolt at Castillejo on 19 March. The information he received pointed to Beauharnais, the French ambassador at Madrid, having used his influence on the side of Ferdinand. Murat's letter to the Emperor was full of anxiety and perplexity. He told of his sorrow at the prospect of bloodshed, and his fears that Europe would say that the approach of the French troops had been the signal for the rising, and that the ambassador had encouraged it. 'I represent your Majesty here, Sire,' he wrote, 'I command your armies, and assuredly no one in Europe will believe that I am at their head without knowing your plans.' He appealed to Napoleon to remember that his own imperial fame was involved, and begged for some clear direction as to the course he was to follow. Next day, in another letter written from Buitrago, after referring to reports of mob violence at Madrid and Aranjuez, he wrote:—

'What afflicts me most deeply, is that all these disorders are committed to the cry of ' *Vive l'Empereur! Vive l'Ambassadeur de la France!* ' I am sure your Majesty will be as pained as I am. It is my duty for the honour of the French name to put a stop to such horrors, and thus to remove every pretext for malevolent attempts to accuse us of having incited them.'

He went on to say that he hoped Ferdinand would maintain the French alliance, but if he chose it would be just as easy for him to provoke a revolt against it. Once more he asked for directions as to the attitude he was to adopt towards the Spanish court when he reached Madrid. 'If your Majesty,' he wrote, 'would only repose more confidence in me, one word as to your real plans would suffice. I would answer with my head for their accomplishment.'

Napoleon, who knew what he wanted, took the news of the Aranjuez outbreak much more calmly than his lieutenant. He told him he could not understand his fears for the future. He could only repeat to him that he must 'solidly establish' his troops in occupation of Madrid, give them a rest, and see that discipline was maintained, and abundant supplies collected. 'Treat the king well and the Prince of Asturias and everybody. Tell them you know nothing, and are waiting for me. What has happened at Aranjuez is very lucky, and the certainty that the king will not go away is a great gain. I await your news from Madrid'; and in a second letter he said: 'You are always complaining that you have no instructions. Nevertheless I am continually sending them to you, when I tell you to give your men a rest, complete their supplies, and do nothing to prejudge the question. It seems to me that you have no need to know more.'

On the same day that he wrote thus to Murat, Napoleon offered the Spanish crown to his brother Louis. He wrote to him that there had been an insurrection at Aranjuez, the king had abdicated, and the 'Grand Duke of Berg' would by this time be at Madrid with 40,000 men. He intended to make a French prince king of Spain. Would Louis accept the crown? In that case Holland would be annexed to France. The whole matter might be arranged in a fortnight or it might require some months. Louis was to take no one into his confidence as to this offer, 'for things like this must be accomplished facts before one admits to anybody that one has even been thinking of them.' Louis after some hesitation replied that he preferred to remain king of Holland.

On 23 March Murat entered Madrid at the head of his troops. Early in the morning he had reviewed them on the heights overlooking the city, drawing up his whole force in battle array. It was not a mere piece of display, for he was thus ready to convert a friendly parade into an attack, if there was any show of opposition. But he was able to report to the Emperor, that 'the army was received with the liveliest demonstrations of friendship. The inhabitants of all classes offered wine to the troops.' The fact was, that the people of Madrid, knowing that Beauharnais was the friend of Ferdinand, thought that the French army had come to secure his succession to the throne.

On 27 March, before the news of the entry into Madrid had reached him, but when he knew by previous letters that it had already taken place, Napoleon wrote to Murat :—

'My brother, I have received your letter of 20 March, by which I see that you will be at Madrid on the 23rd. I shall therefore soon have news from you from that city. I can only repeat to you the orders I have already given to concentrate the corps of Generals Moncey and Dupont at Madrid. . . You may post some men at the Escurial; but you ought to let all your forces be seen at Madrid, especially your fine regiments of cuirassiers . . . You will maintain public order at Madrid, and prevent any arming of the people. Use M. de Beauharnais for this purpose till my arrival, which you may announce to be imminent.'

The date and contents of this letter, and of the next to be quoted, are very important in connexion with a question to be presently discussed. On 30 March the Emperor wrote, with reference to the events at Aranjuez : ' I thoroughly approve of the course of conduct you have adopted in presence of unforeseen circumstances.'

On 3 April Murat acknowledged, with hearty thanks, the Emperor's letter of 27 March. On the 5th he wrote to Napoleon :—

' I have received your Majesty's letter of the 30th. It has made me very happy, for it has given me the certainty that my conduct in the most delicate circumstances in which I have ever found myself in all my life, has been approved by your Majesty.'

Now with these four letters before one, is it possible to believe that after writing the letter of 27 March, and before writing that of the 30th, Napoleon wrote to Murat a long letter, severely blaming his conduct, discussing the Spanish situation, and his own plans at length, telling Murat that his advance on Madrid had been too precipitate, and had provoked disorders that would wreck all his projects, blaming him for calling up Dupont's divisions to the capital, throwing on him the responsibility of all that happened, and of troubles yet to come, —in a word making him, with a strange prophetic insight into the future, the scapegoat of the whole Spanish failure?

This document is an alleged letter of Napoleon to Murat, dated from Paris on 29 March, 1808. It was first published after the Emperor's death, by Las Casas in the *Mémorial de Ste Hélène*, a work based on notes of conversations with the Emperor during the first year of his detention on the island. Las Casas introduces it with the following paragraph :—

'Here is a letter of Napoleon on the Spanish affair, which throws more light on it than volumes could do. It is admirable. The events which followed make it a masterpiece. It shows the rapidity, the eagle glance, with which Napoleon judged men and events. Unhappily it also shows how often his highest conceptions were ruined by the executive acts of his lieutenants, and in this respect the letter is a precious historical document. Its date makes it prophetic.'

It was reproduced in Montholon's *Récits de la Captivité*, and other memoirs of the time, and finally accepted as a genuine document by Thiers in his *Histoire du Consulat et de l'Empire*. It was included in the great collection of the correspondence of Napoleon I, published by order of Napoleon III, but with a note to the effect that 'neither a minute of it, nor the original, nor any authentic copy' could be discovered, and that it was taken from Las Casas and Montholon's memoirs.

Thiers was puzzled at its flagrant contradiction to the undoubtedly authentic letters of the Emperor to Murat, and tried to suggest a theory to account for this. But no theorizing can make it fit in with known facts. And the letter itself bears its own condemnation. It is dated from Paris, but on 27 March Napoleon was not there. He was writing other letters from St. Cloud. Its opening words mark it as a fabrication; by whom or when fabricated, is a mystery. Napoleon is made to address Murat as '*Monsieur le grand duc de Berg.*' He never began a letter to him thus. Up to August 1806 he always in his letters addressed Murat as *Mon cousin*, after that as *Mon frère*. In the alleged letter, he refers to his foreign minister as *Mon ministre des affaires étrangères*; but this was the style adopted years later under the Restoration. In the days of the Empire in Napoleon's authentic correspondence, it is always, '*Mon ministre des relations extérieures.*' We may take it to be certain that the letter was never written by Napoleon,[1] never received by Murat. Napoleon, instead of sending him long disquisitions on the affairs of Spain, left him in the dark as to his projects, and merely ordered certain military movements; instead of blaming him for 'a too precipitate advance,' he sent him orders to march upon Madrid, and congratulated him on his occupation of the capital. Long years after this the supposititious document was produced by men who were anxious to show that their hero could not make a mistake, and who tried to prove that Murat had shipwrecked his plans for Spain.

Far from this, Murat, though kept in ignorance of Napoleon's intentions and suddenly confronted with a most perplexing situation, had acted with remarkable discretion, and at the same time began to divine the general drift of the Emperor's policy. It certainly was no fault of his that this policy ended in disaster.

He had been told to act with reserve towards the court, and avoid committing himself to any of the rival factions. On the eve of his entry into Madrid he received an appeal from the king's daughter, the Infanta Maria Louisa, ex-queen of Etruria, whom he had known in Italy. She implored his protection for her parents, the king and queen, and

---

[1] See the elaborate and convincing discussion of this matter by Comte Murat—*Murat, Lieutenant de l'Empereur en Espagne*, pp. 145 *et seq.*

## LIEUTENANT-GENERAL IN SPAIN 185

for the fallen minister Godoy. She told him that the abdication of Charles IV had not been a free act, but had been compelled by the violence of Ferdinand and his partisans, which had gone so far that the king believed his life was in danger. She appealed to Murat to intervene on behalf of the royal family, and suggested that he should come to Aranjuez to hear from the king and queen what had happened.

Murat sent his aide-de-camp, General de Monthyon, to Aranjuez to report on the situation there, directing him to avoid giving any compromising pledges, but to assure the old king that he would be safe under the protection of the French army, and dissuade him from a project of retiring to Badajos, which the Infanta had mentioned in her letter. Some biographers of Murat say that it was he who suggested to the king that his abdication should be withdrawn. This idea, however, was the king's own. He had recovered from his first fears when he found himself in touch with the French army, and he then regretted and withdrew his act of surrender. Monthyon, when he rejoined Murat's headquarters, reported that the king was anxious for the fate of Godoy, now a prisoner in the hands of the new government, and furious against his son, whom he accused of conspiring against his life and throne.

It was now that Murat devised a project for giving the Emperor the opportunity of disposing as he wished of the Spanish crown, and making the royal family themselves co-operate in smoothing the way for Napoleon's ambitions. Reassured by Monthyon, King Charles had abandoned the first idea of flight to Badajos, and said he was ready to entrust himself to the protection of the French arms. Murat was at the same time in communication with Ferdinand's party. On the eve of the French entry into Madrid, the Duke de Parque had arrived at Murat's headquarters at the château of Chamartin, to offer him the compliments of the prince, and to announce his accession to the throne under the title of Ferdinand VII.

Murat knew that Beauharnais, the French ambassador, was in friendly relations with Ferdinand, but did not know what were his instructions from Napoleon, and how far the ambassador was acting on his own ideas, how far on those of the Emperor. It was a difficult position. He took care to acknowledge the Duke de Parque's communication in guarded phrases that committed him to nothing.

To the Emperor he wrote :—

'The sight of a king stripped of his crown, will excite sympathy, and it will even be directed against his son, whom people can hardly avoid regarding as a rebellious son, if, as the letter of the queen [1] seems to show, and as is generally believed, it is true that he forced his father to abdicate the throne. If he (King Charles) comes to my headquarters, I shall send him to your Majesty, and then Spain will be really without a king, for the father will have abdicated, and you will be in a position to refuse recognition to the son, whom one may regard as a usurper.'

Having thus summed up the situation, he sent Monthyon back to the king and queen with a draft of a letter, which he suggested should be sent by Charles to Napoleon, in case he wished to make an effective protest against his forced abdication, and the revolution which had placed his son on the throne. The king and queen eagerly accepted the suggestion, and sent him the formal protest to be forwarded to the Emperor, together with a statement that 'for the sake of the happiness of his people' King Charles now placed his crown in the hands of his Imperial Majesty, and left it to him to dispose as he judged best of the future of Spain.

Murat at the same time tried, through the French ambassador, to persuade Ferdinand to defer his entry into Madrid as king. But the prince, nevertheless, made

---

[1] This was a narrative forwarded by the ex-queen of Etruria, and written by the queen of Spain in the form of a letter to her, beginning, 'My dear daughter, You will explain to the Grand Duke of Berg the position of the king, my husband, etc.' It was preceded by a few lines addressed to Murat by the queen of Etruria.

a state entry on 24 March, the day after the French had marched in. Ferdinand was enthusiastically received by the people. He set at liberty a number of political prisoners, ordered a series of bull fights, to celebrate his accession, announced that in order to give abundance of employment, public work would be begun on new canals and roads, and directed that the French officers and soldiers should everywhere be treated as friends. In reply to a message from Ferdinand, Murat had expressed his regret that he could not meet him till he had received formal orders from the Emperor to recognize his accession. But Ferdinand, thanks to the ambassador Beauharnais, did not doubt that this recognition would be given, and sent his brother Don Carlos to Paris to obtain it.

Meanwhile the people of Madrid thought that the French general and his army were supporters of the new régime. Murat reported to the Emperor that day after day cheering crowds assembled in front of the palace where he had his headquarters, and when he rode out he was greeted with continual *Vivas*. Deputations of nobles, clergy, and people had waited on him, expressing their adniration for Napoleon as the protector of Spain, and their desire for his promised visit to Madrid.

On 30 April the Emperor wrote, that he thoroughly approved of the line of conduct Murat had adopted. He directed that King Charles should be lodged at the Escurial, the great palace of Philip II, twenty-seven miles north-west of Madrid, and that he should be regarded as king of Spain until the imperial decision as to who was to replace him. Murat suggested that Ferdinand should be invited to leave Madrid and go north to meet Napoleon on his way to the capital; that as soon as he left Madrid, King Charles should be brought there, and that it should be officially announced that he remained king until the Emperor arrived to decide as to the succession; and that as public feeling was hostile to the queen and Godoy, she should go to stay at some convent, till things were quieter, and Godoy should be kept in prison.

On 1 April the Emperor wrote to Murat, announcing that he was at Bordeaux; on the 4th that he was at Bayonne, and two days later, he ordered the Prince of the Peace, Godoy, to be sent into France. He did not adopt the programme that Murat had forwarded to him. He had plans of his own, and perhaps did not like to see his lieutenant assuming to direct events. He told him not to talk about his arrival at Madrid, though he had already sent General Savary there ostensibly to see that all was ready for his coming. He now intended to settle the affairs of Spain on French soil at Bayonne.

Twice he took occasion to find fault with his lieutenant on minor matters. The sword of Francis I, surrendered at Pavia, had been kept as a trophy at Madrid for more than two centuries. Murat suggested it would be a graceful act to restore it to France, represented by Napoleon. To the deputation which presented it to him to be sent to the Emperor, Murat made a high flown speech. Even the bravest might suffer misfortune, he said, and there was no disgrace in the French king having succumbed to Spanish valour at Pavia. In sending back his sword to the Emperor, they marked the new friendship of France and Spain, and linked together the glories of Charles V and Napoleon.

The Emperor, when Murat sent him the sword with a report of his oration, replied that he had taken a lot of trouble over a matter of trifling moment. What was the sword of Francis to him? Francis I was 'only a Bourbon,' besides he had been defeated by Italians. What had the Spaniards to do with it? The Emperor's history was not reliable. Francis was not a Bourbon but a Valois king, and the Spanish infantry decided the day at Pavia. In another letter he told Murat he must not allow a Spanish mob to interfere with the discipline of his army. This was when a couple of soldiers, who had quarrelled with some Spaniards, and been arrested by a French patrol, were rescued by a crowd that took them to Murat's headquarters, and asked and obtained their pardon.

Savary's mission to Madrid was to invite Ferdinand to go to Bayonne to meet the Emperor there, and discuss the affairs of Spain. Savary had been well chosen for the purpose, for he was more of a police officer than a soldier, and at Bayonne Ferdinand would be as much a prisoner as a guest, though the prince, when he started on his journey, flattered himself that he was crossing the Pyrenees to obtain recognition of his claims. Murat was at the same time directed to see that the king and queen should also go to Bayonne. This was easy to arrange, for Charles IV no sooner heard of his son's departure than he was anxious to see the Emperor, to prevent Ferdinand using his influence against him, with the Dictator of Europe. Before starting on his journey the old king was allowed formally to nominate a council of Regency to govern in his absence. The general commanding the French troops in the north of Spain had orders to conduct the Spanish royal family by force across the frontier if Charles or Ferdinand showed any hesitation about completing their journey. The French guards of honour and escorts provided on their way were really in the position of gendarmerie conducting prisoners of state, though, as it happened, there was no need of the iron hand ever coming out of the velvet glove.

On 20 April Ferdinand reached Bayonne. On the 21st Godoy was sent there under the escort of Murat's aide-de-camp, Manhès. Next day the king and queen started on their journey escorted by General Exelmans.

Murat was now in control at Madrid. He announced that the royal family were gone to meet the Emperor as friends at Bayonne, and that the affairs of Spain would soon be settled. To distract the minds of all classes from politics, he organized a series of fêtes and bull fights, and he reported to the Emperor that all was quiet, and that the people would accept his decision.

But in the last days of April there were signs of coming trouble. There were disturbances at Burgos and Toledo. In Madrid, itself, disquieting reports circulated. Men began to say that Ferdinand had been lured into a trap, that the French were not allies but would-be masters. One of Murat's aides-de-camp was stabbed in the crowd after a bull fight, and ran his assailant through, and a riot was averted with difficulty. But even after this Murat did not expect anything serious. It was a complete surprise to him when on 2 May—the famous *Dos de Mayo*—still an honoured anniversary in Spain, Madrid suddenly blazed out into revolt.

Murat, with the regular soldier's contempt for anything that an undisciplined mob could do, had not paid sufficiently serious attention to the reports he received from day to day, as to the state of the capital. He had tried to maintain amicable relations with the Junta or Administrative Commission that Ferdinand had left to represent him at Madrid, and had even drawn on himself blame on Napoleon's part for being too complaisant to them. At the end of April he had received orders from the Emperor to send to Bayonne the ex-queen of Etruria, and all the princes and princesses of the royal family. The Junta showed a strong disposition to oppose the departure of the ex-queen and the Spanish Prince Don Francisco, who was to travel with her. They had already sent a secret message to Ferdinand that the time was come to break with the French, and convoke the Cortes in some place not occupied by the invaders, and there was a plot in progress for Ferdinand's escape from Bayonne. On 1 May the Madrid Junta yielded to Murat's insistence that the ex-queen and the prince should set out for France next day. But there is no doubt that certain members of the Junta at once set to work to spread among the people the report that two more of the royal family were about to be carried off into captivity by the French.

Murat received reports that numbers of peasants were flocking into Madrid, and that at the cafés where they met and drank together they paid no reckoning. One of his aides-de-camp, Rosetti, had become very friendly with his Spanish host, and the Spaniard advised him if possible, to obtain employment that would take him away from the city for a few days. But on the evening of 1 May, though there were the usual crowds in the streets, there were no signs of unusual excitement.

Next morning it was different. A great crowd of townsfolk and peasants gathered before the royal palace. The crowd became very excited when three carriages drew up before the main entrance. Presently one of them drove away, conveying the ex-queen of Etruria, but still there was no opposition. The rumour ran through the people that the two others were intended for Don Francisco and his uncle Don Antonio, and that the departure was delayed by the younger prince refusing to leave the palace. At this moment Major Lagrange, one of Murat's aides-de-camp, rode into the open space before the building. There were shouts of 'They are taking them away from us,' and the people rushed upon the officer. He would have been murdered if the French guard posted at the palace had not dashed out to save him. Shots were fired at the soldiers. They replied with a volley. Immediately the city blazed out into revolt. Everywhere armed crowds gathered and attacked the posts of the French troops, and the houses where Frenchmen were lodging. A massacre of the foreigners began.

Murat had only a small force actually in Madrid. He had near his own residence two squadrons of the cavalry of the Guard, a troop of Mamelukes, some companies of French marines, and a company of Basques. The French army, nearly fifty thousand strong, was outside the city in three camps more than two miles from the barriers. Murat mounted and put himself at the head of his small force, and sent his aides-de-camp galloping to bring in reinforcements. The cavalry soon came spurring into the city. Guns rattled after them. The infantry columns were not far behind.

Murat's first efforts were devoted to clearing the long street that runs through Madrid, from west to east, dividing it into two parts, and forming the line of the Calle Mayor, Puerta del Sol, and Calle de Alcala. This thoroughfare would then be a base for attacks on the crowds in the cross streets. There was desperate fighting with no thought of quarter on either side. At the military hospital the French invalids were murdered in their beds. At the monastery of Atocha, where the monks joined the insurgents in firing from the windows, the Mamelukes of the Guard forced the gate and killed every one in the building. There was savagery on both sides.

As soon as he had set his troops in movement, Murat had written to the Junta, telling them they must assist him in restoring order.

'God knows' (he wrote) 'that it is only the enormity of the outrages committed that has decided me to use force. Because that at my disposal is so imposing, I have been all the more reluctant to appeal to it, and I have endured many seditious provocations that ought to have been sooner repressed; and I would reproach myself for my patience had it not been inspired by the noblest motives. But from this moment all tolerance ends. Tranquillity must be re-established, or the inhabitants of Madrid must expect to endure the consequences of revolt. Every gathering must disperse on pain of being destroyed. Till now I have reposed confidence in your words; the time is come for you to justify me in this, by fulfilling the grave duties that the circumstances impose upon you.'

Fortunately for him the Spanish garrison mostly remained confined to barracks, and took no part in the movement. Only the artillerymen at the arsenal opened the gates to the mob, allowed them to obtain arms and ammunition, and brought some of their guns into action against the French artillery, which was sweeping the streets with grape-shot. There were four hours of hard fighting before the French began to get the upper hand. Most of the insurgents refused to surrender, and even when a few men were driven into a corner they would

## LIEUTENANT-GENERAL IN SPAIN 193

dash in among the bayonets, knife in hand, hacking and stabbing till they were struck down, or would fire a last shot point blank at the nearest officer. At first, those who surrendered mostly gained little by it. They were marched to the nearest square and shot by order of a drum-head court-martial.

Two prominent members of the Junta, D'Azanzza and O'Farrill, had risked their own lives in saving those of Frenchmen, and in persuading parties of insurgents to disperse. Between four and five o'clock they came to Murat and promised that, if the French would cease firing, they would personally answer for the armed crowds breaking up before dark. Murat welcomed their offer, and sent his chief of the staff, General Harispe, and several other officers to assist them in their mission of peace. Harispe was directed to put a stop to any further summary executions. It was thanks to this intervention that, after hours of bloodshed, the fighting ended.

Murat sent off a long report to Napoleon, dated ' 6 p.m. 2 May.' He estimated the numbers of the insurgents at 20,000. He gave special praise to General Grouchy for his services during the day, and assured the Emperor that all danger was now over, and the city would be disarmed. In this letter Murat only said that there had been great loss of life, but gave no details. Subsequent estimates are hopelessly contradictory. A manifesto issued by the friends of the revolt stated that the Spaniards lost about 200 killed and wounded, and the French 1500. The *Moniteur* declared that the French loss had been trifling, twenty-five killed and forty-five to fifty wounded, while the rebels had fallen in thousands. Murat, in a subsequent dispatch, stated that about 200 rebels had been summarily executed, and some 1200 more killed in the fighting. The truth will never be known. All that is certain is that the rebels paid dearly for their attacks on the invaders.

Murat expressed the opinion to Napoleon that, though the

event was unfortunate, it would ensure the peace of the capital, and he hoped of the kingdom also. He represented the outbreak as the work of the '*canaille*,' and told how Spaniards of the better class repudiated it. Don Antonio, a prince of the royal house, had said, ' We are delighted with what has happened. They will not be able to tell us now that an army can be destroyed by a mob of peasants with sticks and knives.'

Napoleon was not displeased at the news. It was his theory that nothing strengthened a Government so much as an abortive insurrection. He could not foresee that the *Dos de mayo* was the first wild flicker of a flame that would soon set Spain ablaze from the Pyrenees to Tarifa.

Murat felt that the day's work had made him undisputed master of Madrid. He had demanded from the Junta that he should be accepted as its president, and given command of the Spanish troops in the capital, and he had taken up his quarters in the royal palace. To Napoleon he wrote :—' The results of the 2nd of May assure your Majesty of a decisive success. That day the Prince of the Asturias lost his crown. His party is completely beaten, and now ranges itself on the side of the conqueror. Your Majesty can dispose of the crown of Spain without any chance of peace being disturbed. Every one is resigned and waiting only for the new king whom your Majesty is about to give to Spain.'

He had won Spain for Napoleon. He was the ' conqueror ' of 2 May, and he looked forward confidently to being chosen to found a new dynasty at Madrid. He had no suspicion that Napoleon had already decided that his brother Joseph should exchange the crown of Naples for that of Spain. But on the very day when Murat's cannon were sweeping the streets of Madrid, Napoleon was writing to him from Bayonne :—

' I intend that the King of Naples shall reign at Madrid. I will give you the kingdom of Naples or that of Portugal. Reply to me at once what you think, for all this must be arranged in one day. You will meanwhile remain as Lieutenant-General of the Kingdom. You will tell me that you would prefer to remain at my side, but this is impossible. You have several children, and besides with a wife like yours you can come away if war recalls you to me; she is quite capable of being at the head of a regency. I may tell you besides that the kingdom of Naples is much finer than Portugal, for Sicily will be added to it and you will then have six millions of subjects.'

A year ago Murat would have gladly exchanged the Grand Duchy of Berg for Naples, even without the vague prospect of having Sicily also, in case the Emperor succeeded in driving the English and the Bourbons from Palermo. But now, when he was dreaming of being proclaimed King of Spain and Lord of the Indies, the offer of a choice between Naples and Lisbon was a bitter disappointment. He received the Emperor's letter on 5 May, and replied the same day, with effusive professions of devotion to his master :—

'SIRE. I have received your letter of 2 May, and torrents of tears flow from my eyes as I reply to you. Your Majesty knew my heart well when you thought that I would ask to remain beside you. Yes, I ask it; yes, I implore it as the greatest favour I have ever received from you. Accustomed to your bounties, accustomed to see you each day, to admire you, to adore you, to receive everything from your hands, how can I ever, alone and left to myself, fulfil duties so important and so sacred ? I regard myself as incapable of it. I beg as a favour to be left with you. Power does not always mean happiness. Happiness is to be found only in affection. I find it when with your Majesty. Sire, after having expressed to your Majesty my sorrow and my desires, I must be resigned, and I place myself at your orders. However, using the permission you give me to choose between Portugal and Naples, I cannot hesitate. I give the preference to the country where I have already commanded, where I can more usefully serve your Majesty. I prefer Naples, and I must inform your Majesty that at no price would I accept the crown of Portugal.'

It is a characteristic letter. Murat's strong feeling of disappointment finds vent in the exaggerated outburst of affection for Napoleon, but does not prevent him from making his choice. He would not hear of Portugal, because at Lisbon he would be overshadowed by Joseph Bonaparte at Madrid. Napoleon received the letter on the 8th or 9th, and at once summoned his brother from Naples to Bayonne to receive the crown of Spain from the assemblage of Spanish notables, whom the Emperor had gathered there to keep up the fiction that the new king was the choice of the nation, on which he was to be imposed by the arms of France.

There was a last hope that Murat might still obtain what he had hoped for. A friend of his, Laforêt, had replaced Beauharnais as French ambassador at Madrid, and wrote to the Minister of Foreign Affairs, De Champagny, that 'the Grand Duke of Berg' was popular in Spain, and the people would welcome him as their king in preference to the King of Naples. Champagny gave Napoleon the letter, and the Emperor wrote to Laforêt that he was the dupe of flatterers, and went on to say, ' There would not be a single voice in favour of the Grand Duke, and there could not be. The Spanish nation was still in that state of hatred and humiliation to which recent events had reduced it, and its own *amour-propre* must make it desire less than any other the Grand Duke, who in one day had confounded its pride and shattered all its hopes.'

The letter reached Laforêt on 23 May, and he showed it to Murat. Its language seemed a poor appreciation of his services on the 2nd of May. It may have been a coincidence or it may have been the effect of disillusion and disappointment, but, whatever the cause, Murat fell ill. For nearly two days he would see no one. The doctors said it was the result of over-work. Laforêt wrote to Napoleon begging him to send the sick man an encouraging letter, and hoping his own correspondence had not led to the illness of the Grand Duke.

While Murat was still suffering, news came day after

day of risings in the provinces. Unable to deal with the situation, he wrote from the château of Chamartin, near Madrid, a letter to Napoleon, asking him to name some one to replace him, and give him leave to return to France, and rest and restore his health at the wateringplace of Barèges in the Pyrenees. Savary took over the command at Madrid, and Murat, travelling incognito, passed almost unnoticed through the north of Spain, carefully guarded from the very people who had hailed his coming with acclamations a few months ago.

Joseph was meanwhile making his progress from Bayonne to Madrid, escorted by a French army that had to disperse a gathering of his subjects in the pitched battle of Medina de Rio Seco in order to open a way for him to his capital.

## CHAPTER XIII

### JOACHIM NAPOLEON, KING OF NAPLES

#### 1808-1812

AT Bayonne, on his way to Barèges, Murat met the Marquis de San Gallo, King Joseph's Minister of Foreign Affairs in the Government of Naples. His first act of sovereignty was to confirm him in his office, and give him full powers for the transfer of the crown of Naples. Thus, freed from the necessity of himself attending to a host of details, he went to the Pyrenean watering-place. In a few weeks he was restored to health. 'The fountain of youth is probably here,' he wrote on 14 July. 'The waters here are really miraculous.'

At the moment of resigning the crown of Naples, Joseph had given the kingdom a new constitution, modelled on that of France, with a consultative chamber and a show of popular institutions. Everything else was arranged between San Gallo, Champagny, and Napoleon while Murat was taking the waters of Barèges. He had to make some sacrifices. The Grand Duchy of Berg reverted to Napoleon, but Murat stipulated that certain charges on its revenues that he had granted to friends and relations should continue, amongst others, 3000 francs a year to his neice, the Princess of Hohenzollern-Sigmaringen, and 12,000 to Agar, Count of Mosbourg, who was presently to leave Dusseldorf for Naples. As, with his kingdom, Murat would enter into possession of palaces by the Mediterranean, he was required to renounce, in the Emperor's favour, his palaces and estates in France, Villiers-Neuilly,

La Motte Hèraye, the Hôtel Thélusson, and Caroline's claim to the Élysée. He was to take a new name, and to be known to his Neapolitan subjects as 'Gioachimo Napoleone.'

In the decrees and treaty that made him a king, his official style was ' Joachim-Napoléon, par la grâce de Dieu et par la constitution de l'État, Roi des Deux Siciles, grand amiral de l'Empire.' As yet only the continental territory of the 'Two Sicilies' was to be his. The real Sicily was in the hands of the Bourbons and the English. Effectively he would be only King of Naples, and the name of Napoleon, added to his own, emphasized the fact that he would be only a tributary king, little more than a crowned prefect of the Empire. He was courtier enough to accept his new name as an honour. ' The crown that your Majesty has just given to us,' he wrote to the Emperor, ' is no doubt a great gift, but you will permit me to rank still higher the honour you have done me in allowing me to bear your name. I appreciate all the value of this distinguished favour. I know what I am pledged to by the glory of this name. Your Majesty will never have to regret having made me one of your family.'

The new reign was to date from 1 August, 1808, and on that day King Joachim Napoleon was proclaimed by the Council of State at Naples, a Te Deum was sung, and there were illuminations in the evening. But though Caroline was anxious to pose as a queen among her new subjects, Murat was in no hurry to end his holiday. From Barèges he went for a few days to Cauterets, and then to stay with Lannes at his château of Bouillas. On 4 August he arrived at Paris. The Emperor had written to him two days before that he need not go at once to Naples. The weather was hot, and he might find it trying in southern Italy. He should take care of his health, for that was all important.

But when, a few days later, Napoleon himself arrived in Paris, he had changed his mind, and he urged Murat to start at once for Naples. Perhaps the reason was that Joseph had by this time discovered that with his new kingdom he had taken over a civil war in full working order, and was regretting his bargain, and asking to be allowed to go back to Naples. Napoleon was, therefore, anxious to instal Murat there as soon as possible, so as to put an end to Joseph's appeals. On 18 August the Emperor told him he must begin his journey south at once. On the 21st, Caroline and Joachim Napoleon appeared at a ball at the Hôtel de Ville as king and queen of the Two Sicilies. Next day Murat started on his journey. Caroline followed him a fortnight later.

At Milan he had a talk with the Viceroy Eugene on the affairs of Italy and their future relations. At Rome he was received by General Miollis, and the French army of occupation was under arms in his honour. Pius VII, stripped of his temporal power, was still at the Vatican, but Murat did not visit him, for the Pope had shown no willingness to recognize him. The seizure of Rome had broken off all friendly relations with the Imperial family.

On 6 September he entered Naples. He rode into the city wearing his brilliant battle uniform, but accompanied only by a single aide-de-camp, the young Chef d'escadron La Vauguyon, the son of a noble family of the 'emigration' that had made its peace with Napoleon. La Vauguyon was soon to be a general of the Neapolitan army. A cavalry escort rode with the king and his companion. Naples was *en fête*, and had erected triumphal arches, and hung its house-fronts with tapestry. On the Piazza del Mercatello two statues had been erected, one of Napoleon, the other of Caroline as the goddess Juno. Under an arch on the Piazza di Foria, the municipality presented an address of welcome. At the church of Spirito Santo, Murat dismounted and assisted at a Te Deum sung by the archbishop, Cardinal Firrao. The crowds in the streets and squares greeted the new king with an outburst of southern enthusiasm, and in the evening the city was a blaze of light, rockets shot up from the sea front, and the ships and fishing-boats hung out Chinese lanterns.

Next day Murat met his ministers and Departmental officials, and began to look into the affairs of his kingdom. He soon found that he could not do much till his man of business, Agar, arrived from Dusseldorf, where he was winding up the affairs of the grand duchy. King Joseph had not left King Joachim an easy task. The transfer of the crown had been accompanied by a simultaneous transfer to Spain of most of the French soldiers and civilians who had helped the Emperor's brother to govern his kingdom.

Murat was naturally first interested in finding out what kind of an army he had at his disposal. The result of his inquiry was disappointing. All the best regiments had been sent to Spain to swell the ranks of the Imperial army of occupation in Catalonia. Joseph had taken away the Royal Guard—Frenchmen, dressed as Neapolitans, and now to adopt a Spanish uniform. For a while the new king would have to be content to have detachments of the French army of Italy keeping order in his dominions. As for the navy, his flag would fly only on a frigate, the *Cerere*, a corvette or armed yacht, and a few gunboats. The treasury was empty. Joseph had spent money freely and run into debt. He had inaugurated ambitious public works—roads, bridges, harbours—and there was no money available to keep them going. The treasury officials produced endless accounts to show that everything had been done according to the solemn laws of routine and red tape, and that if there was no money and much debt, no one was to blame for the financial chaos, that, in fact, there was no chaos, but orderly and systematic embarrassment. Murat puzzled over returns and balance-sheets, and told them he did not pretend to understand accounts, but money must be found, and as for public works, he would see that henceforth nothing was undertaken till there were funds in hand to pay for it.

For the moment, with the Civil List represented by

claims the treasury could not meet, he was forced to fall back on his private resources. He and Caroline had been used for years to handle money freely and spend it lavishly. Till Agar arrived to put the finances in order, they had to fall back on their personal credit. To make matters worse, Napoleon, after taking over the French estates of the Murats, was not even paying King Joachim what was due to him as Marshal of France and Grand Admiral, and the French treasury was sending to Naples demands for the payment of the French troops in the kingdom, including arrears that Joseph had allowed to accumulate year after year.

Murat had already reason to feel that he was not being generously or fairly treated by his Imperial brother-in-law. And to add to his discontent with his new position, Napoleon began to find fault with his public acts and write to him as if, instead of being ' King of the Two Sicilies,' he were only a French Governor of Naples. He had made up his mind that he would be really a king, and a popular king. During the very first month of his reign at Naples he had issued a series of decrees that at once secured for him the hearty loyalty of most of his new subjects. The ports were closed against the British flag under the general regime of the Continental blockade, and to prevent smuggling there were harassing restrictions on the fisheries, which were such an important national industry. These Murat at once abolished, to the joy of all the coast population. Another decree put an end to the military tribunals and the state of siege in Calabria. There was an amnesty for all deserters from the army. Political exiles were recalled and were to be allowed to return on taking an oath of allegiance. During Joseph's reign the property of relations of the *émigrés* (that is, those who had gone to the Bourbons in Sicily) had been seized by the State. This property was now restored. Hundreds of prisoners under sentence of death for rebellion were reprieved, and all prisoners were liberated who were confined for minor offences. At the same time the rations of the Neapolitan soldiers were improved, and it was announced that all arrears of pay would soon be met, and, meanwhile, the men would be paid regularly on a more equitable scale. A royal guard of Neapolitans would be formed, several new regiments raised. These decrees were hailed with a grateful enthusiasm that augured well for the new reign.

Marshal Jourdan, who had acted as Joseph's chief of the staff, had followed him to Spain. Murat appointed the Marquis de Perignon commander-in-chief of his army, and secured as executive commanders the French generals Cavaignac, Campredon, Lamarque, and Manhès. Salicetti, a Corsican, and a friend of the Bonapartes since early days at Ajaccio, was named chief of the police. Agar came to take charge of the finances and repeat the administrative success by which he had distinguished himself in the grand duchy. The rest of the ministers were Neapolitans.

Murat had hardly arrived when he was busy with military projects. Notwithstanding his limited resources he effected his first conquest in October, 1808. All through Joseph's reign the Bourbon flag had been kept flying on the island of Capri, at the very entrance of the Bay of Naples. Sir Hudson Lowe (the future gaoler of Napoleon) was in command of a mixed garrison of 2000 English and Sicilians, holding the fortified town on the island. Salicetti's spies obtained information that Capri was not prepared for a siege, for the peaceful possession of the island during long years had made an attack seem improbable. Murat reviewed the garrison of Naples on 2 October. The troops had hardly returned to barracks when a brigade and some batteries of artillery were ordered to prepare to embark, and an embargo was laid on all shipping in the port. Escorted by the frigate *Cerere*, the corvette *Renommée* and twenty-six gunboats, the expedition was crowded on board a fleet of requisitioned transports. General Lamarque and the Neapolitan general, Pignatelli Strongoli, were in command. They landed on the island, and besieged the town on the land side while the flotilla blockaded and bombarded the sea front. On the 16th the garrison surrendered for want of food, just as a relief expedition was ready to start from Sicily. Murat announced his success to Napoleon by a dispatch from his minister, San Gallo, to the French Minister of Foreign Affairs, Champagny.

The Emperor, instead of congratulating him, wrote him a series of scolding letters. He was angry at the dispatch being addressed to Champagny, as if a foreign power were courteously sending news of victory to an ally. 'This is ridiculous,' he wrote; 'Capri having been taken by my troops, I ought to have heard of this event through my Minister of War. You must take care in such matters to do nothing offensive to me and to the French army.' In other words, Murat must consider himself only as a French general commanding in southern Italy.

Then there was sharp criticism of his administrative acts. 'I have seen decrees of yours,' wrote the Emperor, 'which have no sense. You are drifting into reaction. Why recall the exiles and restore property to men who have arms in their hands and are conspiring against me? I declare to you that you must take steps to cancel this decree, for I cannot endure that those who are contriving plots against my troops should be received and protected in your States. The decree as to the fisheries is not more prudent. It will be the means for the English to find out all the sooner what is going on. You are making sacrifices to a false popularity. It is ridiculous to cancel the sequestration of this property and so provide support for those who are in Sicily. You really must have lost your head!'

Another outburst was provoked by the news that, after the reconquest of Capri, Murat, doubtless thinking more of pleasing the Neapolitans than of any devotion to their patron saint, had driven to the cathedral in state in a royal carriage drawn by eight white horses, made a rich offering at the shrine of St. Januarius, bestowed gold medals on the canons, and the Order of the Two Sicilies on the archbishop, and decreed an annual grant of 2600 ducats to the chapter. Napoleon told him he was annoyed at seeing him 'aping' the Neapolitans. Then he found fault with the form of King Joachim's decrees. Murat had on more than one occasion made it clear that he was endeavouring to improve on the methods of his predecessor. Napoleon saw in this a censure on the family. ' I must point out to you,' he wrote, ' that I am extremely hurt at the everlasting declamations with which your edicts are filled against the king, your predecessor, who had all the thorns, while you are gathering the fruits, and to whom you owe eternal gratitude. I am annoyed at seeing that you so little understand what you owe to me and at your lack of courteous consideration.'

Murat certainly was being kept in his place. And Napoleon began directly to interfere with the government of Naples. He ordered the confiscation of the property held by Spaniards, who had refused to accept King Joseph's rule, and directed that the confiscation should be carried out by French agents. He insisted on the entire *Code Napoléon* being adopted in the kingdom. The Neapolitans objected strongly to the introduction of the divorce law, which formed a part of it. Murat and his ministers voiced these objections. Napoleon would not listen to them. ' It is part of the foundation of the Code,' he said, ' and you must not touch it in any way ; it is the law of the State. Rather than have the *Code Napoléon* thus mutilated I would prefer to see Naples under the old King of Sicily.'

He insisted that the goods of the Sicilian *émigrés* must not be restored. If they were he would seize them himself. He pressed for the payment of arrears due to the French garrisons. He forbade any Frenchman to enter Murat's service without his express license. He sent French police agents to Naples to watch the proceedings of the king and court. The wonder is not that Murat was eventually alienated from his overbearing brother-in-law, but that the rupture did not come sooner.

What was the reason of this harsh and impolitic treatment of Murat by Napoleon ? Possibly it was partly due to the growing irritation of the Emperor at discovering that he could no longer act as if his decisions were the decrees of an irresistible destiny. Spain was becoming an open wound in the body of the Empire that was eventually to drain away its strength. And bad news meant fits of ill-humour. There may be something, too, in M. Frédéric Masson's suggestion that the *Cabinet Noir*, which opened and reported on all letters of important personages as they passed through the post office, had revealed to the Emperor the fact that more than one prominent politician regarded Murat as a candidate who might be put forward for the Imperial succession, in preference to any of the Bonaparte brothers, in case the Emperor died without an heir. Murat had no direct part in these intrigues, but he had some knowledge of them, and their very existence might well make the Emperor angrily jealous of this possible Pretender.

There was yet another disturbing influence. Napoleon had not only a great affection for his sister Caroline, but also a high opinion of her intelligence and initiative, and when he offered Murat the crown of Naples he had told him that in his wife he had a woman who could act as the chief of a Council of Regency in his absence. Instead of being flattered at the praise of his wife's political capacity, Murat became nervously anxious to prevent any one supposing that she shared the active work of government with him, or inspired or directed his policy. He was essentially a proud man, with a pride that often took the form of almost puerile vanity, and he was determined that the Emperor's sister should be only the queen consort. No one was to imagine that she was the ruler of Naples in right of her name, and that he had been promoted to be a prince consort because he had the luck to marry into the Emperor's family. Caroline was allowed to figure in the pageantry of State ceremonial, and to take her place as the hostess of his palaces, but she had not the slightest voice in State affairs and was forced to pass long hours with her ladies amusing herself as best she could with music, fancy work, and novels. Rumour said she found other amusements, and the scandal of Naples coupled her name with those of more than one of her husband's officers. Murat was deaf to any such reports and content to have her keep her place in the background of political life. In this period of growing tension between him and the Emperor, Caroline unconsciously became the centre of a French party surrounding the Imperial ambassador, and her correspondence revealed to Napoleon a divergence of views between the king and queen, in which the latter was on his side, while the French ambassador's reports more than hinted that Caroline was being neglected. This helped to increase Napoleon's feeling of disappointment with his vassal King of Naples.

In the spring of 1809 the tension was somewhat relieved by the prospect of war with Austria giving the Emperor something else to think of. For Murat, too, the rumour of war was enough to turn all his thoughts in a new direction. The French ambassador at Naples reported that the king had spoken to him of his anxiety to clear himself of 'any suspicion that might have arisen against him in the mind of his Majesty.' He had expressed his desire to take the field again beside the Emperor, or, if this could not be, to attempt the conquest of Sicily during the war. He had spoken of his absolute devotion, his entire submission to Napoleon, his readiness even to resign his crown if the annexation of Naples to the Empire would advance Napoleon's projects. The ambassador added that the king seemed hurt in his feelings, but he would be at once calmed and consoled by a friendly letter from Napoleon.

With a large part of his army locked up in the Peninsula, and Austria preparing to act in three different theatres of war, the Grand Duchy of Warsaw, north Italy, and the upper Danube valley, Napoleon needed the support of all his friends and could not afford to alienate any of them. He did not recall Murat to his old post at the head of the cavalry of the Grand Army, but he assigned to him a modest part in the defence of Italy. He was to occupy Rome with his army and set free the French army of occupation under General Miollis, which was to march to join the Viceroy Eugene in the north. It was a disappointingly small mission for Murat, but it led him to expect that part of central Italy might be added to his dominions, and rumours of an Anglo-Sicilian invasion of his kingdom afforded another reason for his remaining at Naples.

In April the French armies had won their first victories. By the end of the month the Archduke John in Venetia and the Archduke Charles on the Danube were both in full retreat; on 10 May Napoleon was in Vienna. Thence he wrote to Murat the friendliest of letters. He spoke of the good work done by the cavalry of the Grand Army, and said they regretted the absence of their famous leader. But he could not call him to the Danube. He could serve him better in Italy. An English descent was now, he thought, unlikely. Murat was to send all available troops to Rome, and go there himself to complete the annexation of the Papal States.

He had sent a division to Rome, and was preparing to follow it at the head of another, when, in the last week of May, he was kept at Naples by the appearance of the Anglo-Sicilian expedition of which his brother-in-law had written so carelessly. A force of Sicilian troops was thrown into Calabria to organize an insurrection. General Partounneaux, who commanded there, blew up the fort of Scilla, and retreated northwards before the invaders. An English squadron, escorting a convoy of transports from Palermo, appeared off Naples, and the Sicilians seized the islands of Ischia and Procida. Murat concentrated some thousands of civic guards to reinforce what was left of his army in and near the capital, and prepared the forts for defence. His warlike energy called forth an outburst of enthusiastic loyalty to himself and ardent hostility to the Bourbon king. The defence of Naples became a national movement in which all classes united. But no attack was made on the city. At Palermo it had been anticipated that the mere appearance of the fleet in the Bay of Naples would produce an insurrection against the French king. But it had just the opposite effect, and the enthusiasm of the Neapolitans rose to fever point when Murat's solitary frigate, the *Cerere*, and some of the gunboats went out to exchange a distant fire with the enemy's ships that had stood in to reconnoitre.

MARIE CAROLINE, QUEEN OF NAPLES
FROM AN ENGRAVING BY MARIE ANNE BOURLIER

The desultory fight took place in sight of the city, and while the cannonade echoed along the water Caroline drove out in an open carriage and was saluted by cheering crowds on the Chiaja. The legend arose that as the queen drove along the sea-front promenade she was actually under hostile fire. The return of the *Cerere* uninjured was treated as a naval victory.

The whole of the Anglo-Sicilian expedition was mismanaged. When it was found that a mere demonstration against Naples produced no result the fleet withdrew, after re-embarking the Sicilians who had landed on the islands. Partounneaux was reinforced and drove the Calabrian force back to the Straits, the Sicilians abandoning artillery and baggage in their hurried retreat. The insurgents who had joined them broke up into scattered bands that carried on a brigand warfare for more than a year after in Calabria, Basilicata, and the adjacent districts. The French general, Manhès, was at last put in command of the south and given full powers to deal with the brigandage under martial law. He organized flying columns to hunt down the bands, and mastered the terrorism of the brigands by a more merciless system than their own. In a few months gibbets along the highways and at the crossroads, from which dangled the decaying corpses of captured bandits, were the monuments of his success and a grim warning that with Manhès in command brigandage was a losing game.

The decisive victory of Wagram had enabled Napoleon once more to dictate the terms of peace to Austria. After Aspern and Essling, when fortune seemed for a while to be doubtful, he had for a moment thought of calling Murat to his side, but the King of Naples saw nothing of the war. His troops took an inglorious part in the final spoliation of Pius VII. In his letters to Napoleon he expressed his thorough approval of the Emperor's Roman policy.

On his return to Paris after his victories Napoleon was busy with his plans for the divorce of Josephine, and a second marriage with a daughter of one of the historic reigning houses of Europe. In the autumn he invited the members of his family to meet in Paris to discuss the new situation. Murat arrived in the capital on 30 November (1809), and Caroline four days later.

On 28 January, 1810 the Emperor convoked at the Tuileries a family council of the great dignitaries of the Empire to discuss the question of the second marriage. Three ladies had been named as possible candidates for the vacant place, a Russian grand duchess, a Saxon princess, and the Archduchess Maria Louisa, daughter of the Emperor of Austria. Napoleon had not absolutely decided the question, but the whole bent of his mind was towards the Austrian alliance. Murat found himself at the council in a minority, when he opposed the idea and urged that a Russian marriage would be more politic. There was danger, he said, that a marriage with an Austrian archduchess would revive the memories of the 'Austrian woman,' the queen of Louis XVI. It would alienate the men of the new time without conciliating the adherents of the old regime. He had a personal reason for this opposition, though he only made distant allusions to it. King Ferdinand of the Two Sicilies, now reigning at Palermo under British protection, had for his queen consort the Austrian, Maria Carolina, sister of Marie Antoinette. Murat saw in the proposed Austrian marriage of Napoleon a danger to his own position at Naples, and a probability that there would be no longer any prospect of adding Sicily to his dominions.

But his arguments counted for little. Russia was not anxious to send a grand duchess to the Tuileries. The Saxon alliance would have seemed a small affair after the talk of Imperial princesses accepting the upstart Emperor's hand, so the choice fell on Maria Louisa of Austria. Notwithstanding Murat's opposition to the marriage, Napoleon gave to his wife Caroline the office of arranging all the details for the reception of the archduchess, and it was the French Queen of Naples who met her on her way and welcomed her to France.

In the new arrangements made on the occasion of the marriage, and in view of its giving a direct heir to Napoleon, the 'Kingdom of Italy,' that is to say the northern provinces, had been incorporated with the Empire by annexation, and the Roman States were treated in the same way. Rome was to be the second city of the Empire. The emperors were to be crowned there within ten years of their accession, and the heir of the Empire was to be known as the 'King of Rome.'

These arrangements might have made Murat anxious as to the future of his kingdom had not Napoleon shown a disposition to reassure him by unexpected concessions. After the family council at the Tuileries in November Murat had paid a flying visit to Naples. He had obtained a considerable reduction in the claims of the Imperial treasury on his exchequer, and Napoleon had consented to his organizing a Franco-Neapolitan expedition for the conquest of Sicily. He left Paris on 31 January, 1810 and arrived at Naples on 14 February. He stayed there a week, and on the 21st went to review a division of his troops at Capua. He had stiffened his Neapolitan regiments by incorporating in them numbers of French deserters, to whom he gave special inducements in gratuities and the prospect of speedy promotion. On 10 March he started on his return to France in order to be present at the marriage fêtes on the 20th.

During the stay of the Imperial court at Compiègne after the marriage there was a dangerous moment when Napoleon and Murat were on the verge of a serious quarrel. The Emperor had objected to his soldiers being surreptitiously turned into recruits for Murat's regiments. He insisted on all deserters being sent back to their depots. If this were refused he said he would send one of his own generals to take command in southern Italy. Then Murat must pay for all the French regiments in his kingdom. If they were not paid for it must be because they were not wanted. In that case they would be recalled. But the Emperor told him he could not afford to do without them. How could he make the proposed expedition to Sicily with only his Neapolitans? Murat had to yield on every point.

He quitted Compiègne on 10 April to return to Naples, leaving Caroline in France. She was to use her influence with the Emperor in his favour. It was through her that he asked for and obtained the transfer to his army of a battalion of Corsicans and a regiment of Swiss. 'I will give the king as many officers and non-commissioned officers as he wants,' wrote Napoleon to Caroline, 'but I don't want him to take them without my leave, and to disorganize my regiments, while denying that he does so. One must act in good faith and go straight. I cannot tolerate anything done to injure the service of my army.' But at the same time he warned Murat that French troops must not be put under the command of men who had passed into the Neapolitan army, and there obtained rapid promotion without any service in the field, so that they would now claim higher rank that his war-worn veterans. Another step that was not flattering to Murat was the withdrawal of the French ambassador. He had not been treated with proper respect, said Napoleon, and a mere *chargé d'affaires* would do the work in future, and, after all, Naples was not a foreign country.

On his journey through Italy Murat heard rumours that Queen Maria Carolina at Palermo was in communication with Napoleon through the new Empress, Maria Louisa, and anxious to arrange with him to break off the English alliance. In a letter from Alessandria on 22 April, evidently written to sound the Emperor's views on the subject, Murat said: 'News from Palermo tells of serious misunderstandings between the court and the English, who, since the marriage of your Majesty and the preparations directed against Sicily, believe that Maria Carolina has an understanding with your Majesty with a view to expelling them from Sicily and keeping it for herself. These reports are quite positive on the point.'

The Emperor took no notice of the letter. Murat reached Naples on the 27th, and with some anxiety as to Napoleon's real attitude, pushed on the preparations for the invasion of Sicily. The first step would be to ferry the expedition across the Straits of Messina, and within the first week of his stay in his capital he had an unwelcome reminder that the British were still masters of the sea. On 4 May a warship flying English colours appeared in sight of Naples. She was the *Spartiate* of fifty guns. Murat had last seen her twelve years before when she flew the tricolour as a unit in the fleet that escorted the ' Army of the East ' to Egypt. She was taken by Nelson at the Nile, and had since shared the glories of Trafalgar. Seeing her hove to in the bay just beyond gunshot of his batteries, he sent out his one frigate, the *Cerere*, a brig and seven gunboats to attack her. From the shore he watched the fight. It did not last long. The brig was sunk, and presently the frigate and the gunboats ran back under the shelter of the batteries with their rigging badly cut up and their hulls damaged. They landed fifty dead for burial, and sent 110 wounded officers and men into the hospitals. The *Spartiate*, after a leisurely reconnaissance of the shore defences, sailed away to the south-westward.

Though the incident suggested difficulties in the Straits, Murat left Naples on the 16th to establish his headquarters at Piale near Reggio, in Calabria. He made a leisurely journey south, receiving a public welcome in every town and city he passed through, and escorted by four battalions of his guard, which were to form the nucleus of a reserve division for the expedition. Three other divisions were already concentrated within reach of the Straits. These were :—

1st Division.—General Partounneaux, 8,500 men (French)
2nd Division.—General Lamarque, . 10,000 ,, ,,
3rd Division.—General Cavaignac, . 3,500 ,, (Neapolitans
——— and Corsicans)
22,000 men.

The reserve brought the total up to about 27,000, more than two-thirds of them French troops. On 6 June Murat arrived at Piale, took command, and wrote to Napoleon :—
' Sicily will be conquered and the English beaten, or you will have lost your best friend.'

Meanwhile, the English were quite on the alert. Two of their ships of the line, four frigates, and a number of smaller craft were cruising about the Straits and along the Italian coast, and every day they attacked and destroyed or took some of the crowd of fishing-boats and coasting craft that were creeping along near the shore to join the flotilla of transports at Reggio. While Murat looked forward with light-hearted confidence to the enterprise, the Emperor fully realized the danger of an attempt to cross the Straits while the enemy held the sea. Even if the expedition reached Sicily there was the prospect of its being cut off from its base by a British squadron holding the Straits, and then a marshal of France, his own brother-in-law, might be forced to surrender with 25,000 men, a worse disaster than Dupont's capitulation at Baylen. It might mean the loss of Naples and Italy. What he wanted was a demonstration that would divert to Sicily British reinforcements that might otherwise be sent to Wellington in the Peninsula. Murat's preparations about Reggio were therefore useful to him, but he hesitated to permit him to run any risks. At the end of May he sent Colonel Leclerc of the War Office staff to Calabria to report on the situation, and to warn Murat that he must not leave the mainland unless he was certain of being able to ferry across 15,000 men at the first attempt. He was also directed to have Gaeta prepared for a siege so as to be ready for all eventualities.

Leclerc's arrival as an inspecting officer made Murat very angry. It was an unpleasant reminder of his subordinate position. He wrote to the Emperor that if no risks were to be taken, of course the expedition must be abandoned. Then he complained of being calumniated and thwarted in his projects by enemies in Paris. But next day he changed his tone and wrote hopefully. The expedition must succeed; there was already a panic at Palermo; he needed no covering fleet, he would cross in the night and the fate of Sicily might easily be decided in forty-eight hours.

In the army, among the French officers of higher rank, the rumour had spread that the proposed expedition was only a feint, a mere sham. Murat had a bad quarter of an hour with General Lamarque, when the latter, on being reproached with slackness in preparing for his part in the coming conquest of Sicily, replied :—' Sire, I don't believe in your gasconades.' Then the chief of the police, Maghella, who had succeeded Salicetti, sent Murat a letter that one of his Corsican agents at Palermo had received from Queen Maria Carolina. It showed that the Bourbon queen was really in correspondence with the Empress. She had been lured into using Maghella's agent as her courier. Murat resolved to bring matters to a crisis and used his wife's influence with her brother to obtain from the Emperor permission to make the attempt. On 3 August he issued orders for the crossing of the Straits.

But it had to be again deferred, for the English squadron was unpleasantly vigilant. The Emperor's fête day, 15 August, was then chosen for the enterprise, but the English ships watched the royal camp at Piale all day, and in the evening, when there was a banquet and a display of fireworks, the hostile cruisers made the camp the target of some long ranging shots. Again and again the attempt was put off. By the middle of September all local supplies had been eaten up, and bad weather was threatening. Murat was afraid that he would have to break up his camp and disperse his flotilla. On the morning of 17 September he ordered that the attempt to cross should be made in the following night.

It ended in failure. The plan was that the Neapolitan division under Cavaignac should cross first from the little port of Pentimele, and march on Messina to divert the enemy's attention from the crossing of the main expedition under Murat himself—Partounneaux and Lamarque's French divisions embarked at and near Reggio. At midnight the troops were crowded on board the flotillas. But the English ships appeared, dimly seen in the strait between Reggio and Messina, and Murat waited hour after hour for Cavaignac's demonstration to draw them off. The Neapolitan division, some 3000 men, got across and actually landed. The Corsican regiment struck into the hills on the flank of the Messina road. Cavaignac, with the rest, halted on the road near the shore waiting for some sign that Murat was coming over to support him. At dawn he learned that the main body had never left the Calabrian shore, and found that the Anglo-Sicilians were advancing on him in superior force. Presently the English squadron would cut off his retreat. He hurriedly re-embarked and regained Pentimele, without being able to rally the Corsican battalion to his flag. Surrounded in the hills, the missing battalion surrendered the same day. Eight hundred officers and men were marched as prisoners into Messina, and the standard given by Murat to the regiment was hung up as a trophy in the cathedral.

On the 18th Murat wrote to the Emperor that although some men had been lost he had proved that the Straits could be crossed whenever the Emperor decided to renew the attempt. He promised a fuller report. The same day he endeavoured to disguise his failure by a general order to the army announcing that the expedition was deferred till next year, and that meanwhile the army and flotilla would disperse. The Emperor's present object, he said, had been attained, for it had been proved that, in spite of the enemy's fleet, troops could be sent into Sicily in an improvised flotilla of fishing-boats.

Napoleon was angry at the failure and still more at the lame explanations put forward by his brother-in-law. 'The King of Naples,' he wrote, 'has no right to talk thus about my plans without any authorization from me. My object was to make an expedition against Sicily. Sicily not having been conquered my object has not been attained. I consider it most extraordinary that he speaks of me in this incorrect way. It may have the disadvantage of leading men to suppose that I do not always mean to succeed.' He ordered the troops to remain in position about Reggio till the end of the year so as still to menace Sicily and divert English reinforcements thither. Murat marched them away, and told the Emperor that first, he could not find supplies for them if they remained concentrated, and secondly, that his object had been attained as the English were still sending reinforcements. Napoleon replied that on the contrary all the troops intended for Sicily had been stopped and landed in Portugal as soon as the king's proclamation of 18 September was known. ' If you wanted to go back to Naples,' he said, ' what need was there of declaring the expedition at an end ? But you act without any kind of prudence.'

Thus the abortive enterprise had widened the breach between Napoleon and Murat. When he returned to Naples on 3 October he found Caroline awaiting him there. She had left Paris in the beginning of August. Possibly if she had remained in France she might have used her influence with Napoleon, whose favourite sister she was, to plead her husband's cause and prevent his relations with him being further embittered. For months to come things went from bad to worse. The flight of Louis Bonaparte from Holland, the occupation of that kingdom by French troops, and its annexation to the Empire, made Murat feel that his turn might come next. The Emperor seemed thoroughly hostile. His letters were full of censorious criticism of everything done at Naples, and Murat, though at times he sought for some way of regaining Napoleon's good graces, began to think more and more of organizing the means of asserting his independence. The Emperor complained of the bad quality and alleged misconduct of the Neapolitan corps in Spain. Murat asked him to send them back to Naples, and replace them by taking away some of the French troops he found it so difficult to pay for. The Emperor told him he could not withdraw the French army of occupation. If they went, he said contemptuously, Naples would be at the mercy of 12,000 English from Sicily. Even 40,000 Neapolitans could not stop them. Then there were angry complaints that British goods were being covertly imported into Naples. This was true, though Murat denied it. American ships brought regularly cargoes from the West Indies to his ports and this was how he was able to place a United States merchantman at the disposal of Lucien Bonaparte for his flight from Cività Vecchia.

On 20 March, 1811 the long-hoped-for heir to the Empire, the 'King of Rome,' was born. Murat had at once asked permission to come to Paris to take part in the rejoicings that saluted the great event. He left Naples on 26 March and arrived at Paris on 3 April. He had not waited for the Emperor's permission to come, and he found Napoleon in a bad humour. The first interviews were not pleasant to either of them. But Murat's protestations of devotion to his old leader, and his obviously sincere eagerness to serve him again in the field when Napoleon spoke to him of a possible war with Russia, helped to produce a temporary reconciliation. It was agreed that in case of war Murat should supply a contingent of 30,000 Neapolitans to the Grand Army and himself command its cavalry. On 26 May he left Paris to return to Naples, where he arrived on the 30th.

But again the relations with the Emperor were strained to a dangerous point. There were rumours that Murat was to be deposed like Louis of Holland—rumours too of strange conversations he had held with prominent men in which he spoke of taking a line of his own and showing that he was his own master.

The Emperor had opposed his desire to have embassies at Vienna and St. Petersburg. The French Foreign Office and its envoys were to attend the foreign relations of the vassal State. Murat was thus forced to enter into private and unavowed correspondence with the Czar and the Austrian Emperor when the time came for endeavouring to secure the permanence of his rule. He published an ill-advised order that all Frenchmen in his service should take out papers of naturalization as Neapolitan citizens. The Emperor replied by a decree to the effect that as Naples was part of the Empire all Frenchmen had already full rights of citizenship in the kingdom of Joachim Napoleon. Then the French troops in south Italy were withdrawn from Murat's command and formed into an army of observation under General Grenier, who was to report directly to the Paris War Office.

This made the quarrel public, and numbers of French officers, fearing to be compromised with Napoleon by continuing in the Neapolitan service, asked and obtained leave to quit Murat's army. From this point his policy became more and more Italianist in its tendency. There is not the least reason to suppose that the Gascon King of Naples had any real sympathy with the aspirations of the Italian Liberals, who dreamed of a united and free Italy. But he chafed at his vassaldom; like many more he believed that there were difficult times in store for the Empire, and he looked forward to a crisis when he might exact as the price of his support for Napoleon the recognition of his claim to be the head of the new Italy, provided he could put that claim forward with a strong Neapolitan army at his back and the rest of Italy ready to rally to his standard. His aim was to cease to be a vassal and become an ally—an ally of the Emperor, for whom he still had an intense admiration, and some of the devoted loyalty of earlier years. He was not yet thinking of offering his alliance to the best paymaster.

Henceforth he steadily increased the numbers of his army, which he flattered himself that he would be able to make the nucleus of a future national army of Italy. At the same time he sought to establish friendly relations with the various secret organizations that were then seeking to leaven the people with the new ideas of Liberalism and national unity. In the year of Wagram he had been elected Grand Master of the Masonic organization in the kingdom of Naples, but the order was French, the lodges being established by the officers of the army of occupation in the various garrison centres. Through his minister of police, Maghella, who had ambitious ideas of the part he himself might play in a future Italy, Murat was able to communicate with what might prove a more useful organization, the *vente* of the Carbonari. He was becoming popular with the Neapolitans and Agar's administration was doing real service in promoting the prosperity of the people. He might hope some day, in a great crisis in Italy, to pose as a patriot king.

In September Caroline went to Paris to use her influence with the Emperor in order to promote better relations between him and her husband, and she stayed there most of the winter. Murat wrote to Napoleon protesting that he was still the soldier of Wertingen and Eylau, still devoted to him, but he asked him to make his position at Naples more endurable. It was the growing shadow of the coming war with Russia that partly relieved the tension. At the beginning of 1812 Napoleon asked for a first contingent of 10,000 men to be sent into Germany. Murat raised difficulties: he needed the men for the defence of his kingdom, he could ill afford to pay for the French troops which he did not even command. The Emperor had better take away these. An acrimonious controversy followed. Murat fell ill, and refused to see any one or attend to business. Some said it was a diplomatic illness, others more probably saw in it the result of a nervous breakdown induced by worry and disappointment, like his former attack at Madrid. When he recovered Napoleon would not answer his letters. In April Caroline wrote to him that matters were so serious that he had better come to Paris and plead his cause in person with the Emperor.

He prepared to go, announced his departure, and then suddenly put it off on the pretext that the English were threatening Calabria from Sicily and he must go there. But he remained in Naples. The real reason was that friends had warned him that if he left Naples he might be deposed by a French *coup d'état* in his absence. Then further letters from Paris telling him that his change of plans had made a bad impression gave him a new alarm. On 26 April he saw the Baron de Durant, the French envoy, and told him that he was being calumniated by men in the Emperor's circle who said that he would not

## JOACHIM NAPOLEON, KING OF NALPES

go to Paris because he was busy organizing a party in Italy. He was ready to go at once and discuss his position frankly with Napoleon. Durant wrote that he thought Murat was sincere, because he stated his position frankly. 'He declared that as a Frenchman and a soldier he considered himself the Emperor's subject, but as King of Naples he claimed complete independence.'

Perhaps this was the phrase that suggested to Napoleon the easiest solution for the crisis. War with Russia was now actually in sight. The Emperor was giving his final orders for the concentration of the Grand Army in Poland and eastern Germany. Once he was ready to employ Murat as 'a soldier and a Frenchman,' the King of Naples would become once more the bold leader of his cavalry. In May he wrote to him to come to Paris, but when Murat arrived there he found the Emperor had started for eastern Germany, where he was directed to rejoin him and take command of the largest body of horsemen that had been arrayed under a European banner since the days of chivalry. The march to Moscow was about to begin.

## CHAPTER XIV

### THE CAMPAIGN OF RUSSIA

#### 1812

THE army of many nations that Napoleon concentrated on the Russian frontier, in the early summer of 1812, numbered nearly half a million fighting men. No such force had been till then assembled under a European standard. The cavalry placed under Murat's command formed an army of horsemen exceeding in numbers by many thousands the armies with which Napoleon had conquered in the battles of 1796 and on the decisive day of Marengo.

There were in all 36,000 mounted men, with 132 horse artillery guns. They were organized in four corps, commanded by Generals Nansouty, Montbrun, Grouchy, and Latour-Maubourg. The heavy cuirassier regiments formed a strong element in three of these corps, the 1st 2nd, and 4th being each made up of a division of light cavalry and two divisions of cuirassiers. The 3rd corps (Grouchy) was composed of a division of light cavalry, a division of dragoons, and a division of Polish lancers.

Belliard again acted as Murat's chief of the staff. But it was now a king that commanded the cavalry of the Grand Army, and he went to war in kingly fashion. Besides the military staff a royal household accompanied him. There were equerries, chamberlains, secretaries, pages, and a crowd of servants, footmen and grooms, and a staff of cooks commanded by a famous Paris chef, specially engaged for the campaign. Three tables were to be ready each day, the king's table, a second table for the officers

# THE CAMPAIGN OF RUSSIA

of rank and the higher officials, a third for the minor dignitaries of staff and household. The royal baggage train was a long array of wagons destined to supply abundant booty to the Cossacks when the days of disaster came. It crossed the frontier laden with tents and furniture, plate and china, an elaborate *batterie de cuisine*, a store of choice wines. The chief valet of his Majesty of Naples was in charge of a whole wagon load of uniforms and court costumes, with a supply of scent and pommades for the toilet, for Murat had a strong dash of 'dandyism' in his character. He had invented a new battle uniform even more elaborate than the costume in which he had led the charges at Eylau. It was made up of long boots of bright yellow leather, crimson riding-breeches embroidered with gold; a sky-blue tunic covered with gold lace, over which hung loosely a pelisse of scarlet velvet, with gold embroidery and fur linings. The diamond-hilted sword that he seldom drew, even at the head of a charge, hung in an embroidered crossbelt, and his long curled hair fell on his shoulders from under a three-cornered hat, heavily braided with gold, and decorated with white ostrich feathers and an aigrette fastened with a diamond buckle. His charger was as elaborately adorned as the rider—tiger-skin saddle-cloth, gold bit and stirrups, embroidered holsters from which projected the long butts of a pair of pistols bright with gold and gems.

Sixty horses, selected for him by Belliard, were distributed among the various corps and divisions, under the care of a staff of grooms, so that wherever he went he could find plenty of fresh mounts. For the long marches when he was not in the saddle he had the choice of several carriages.

All this elaborate display, this far-sighted provision for making war in the midst of palatial ease, would have been ridiculous in another man, and would have set men thinking of 'carpet knights' and feather-bed soldiers, but every one knew that the theatrically dressed cavalry commander was also a leader who was ready without a moment's hesitation to ride into the thick of the fiercest mêlée. He had the reputation not only of the reckless courage of action but also of the cool disregard of danger while waiting for his opportunity—inactive under a deadly fire. It was told how more than once, when an aide-de-camp brought him a message and waited near him, he would turn to the officer and say—' You had better ride off, sir, or I shall be getting you killed.' He could leave all the comforts of his palace of tents and his well-served table to sleep by a watch-fire on the steppe after a supper of dry biscuit. The soldier, who had first learned his business as a trooper in the Chasseurs de Champagne, lived on in the King of Naples.

He left Paris on 12 May, after signing a decree appointing Caroline regent of his kingdom, and, travelling by way of Cassel, Berlin and Posen, joined the Emperor at Dantzic. There he succeeded in obtaining from him two concessions he had long been asking for, the return to Naples of the Neapolitan troops employed in Spain, and the withdrawal from his dominions of Grenier's French ' Army of observation.' This would seem to show that Murat and Napoleon were again on good terms, and throws considerable doubt on the stories of violent scenes between them during their stay at Dantzic.

By the middle of June the corps forming the left of the Grand Army were concentrated on the Niemen, and, in the night of the 23rd to the 24th, the crossing of the frontier river began at Kovno. Murat pushed on in advance with the cavalry corps of Nansouty and Montbrun, driving before him the swarms of Cossacks that screened the retirement of the Russian army.

Napoleon hoped to bring the enemy to action near Wilna, but they abandoned the town. Great magazines of supplies had been accumulated there for Barclay de Tolly's army. Eager to secure these before the Russians could remove or destroy them, Napoleon personally directed Montbrun with the 2nd cavalry corps to make a forced march, drive the enemy's rearguard out of Wilna, and seize the magazines. The regular course would have been to send the order to

# THE CAMPAIGN OF RUSSIA

Murat, but the Emperor was in a hurry and disregarded regulation routine.

Montbrun had paraded his men and was preparing to start, when Murat rode up and asked what he was doing. Montbrun explained that, by order of the Emperor, he was marching to seize Wilna. Murat angrily replied that the order ought to have come to him, in any case he would see to the work being done, and Montbrun was to dismiss his men to their lines. The general objected that he had received precise instructions in detail, and feared the anger of Napoleon if he neglected them. 'What is that to him provided the thing is done?' exclaimed Murat, and repeated his orders for Montbrun's corps to remain in camp. Then he paraded Bruyère's light cavalry division, put himself at the head of it, and marched on Wilna. The delay in starting had not been great, but it was sufficient to give the last of the Russian rearguard time to slip away after firing the magazines. As Murat rode into Wilna the smoke and glare of a great conflagration told him he had come too late.

The Emperor was furious when he heard of the failure to surprise the place. He rode up to Montbrun, who was at the head of his corps, reproached him with his disobedience to orders, and told him he thought of sending him away to the line of communications as a man who was good for nothing in the field. Montbrun tried to explain. 'Be silent, sir,' shouted the angry Emperor. 'But, sire——' began the general. 'Silence!' repeated Napoleon. This was hard treatment for the veteran leader of cuirassiers, who had fought his way up from the ranks in the Republican army of the Rhine, and since then led many a charge in Germany, Italy, and Spain. Murat was riding with the Emperor. Montbrun looked at him with a silent appeal for him to speak. But the King of Naples had too much selfish vanity to intervene and take the blame on himself. Napoleon continued his scolding tirade, but Montbrun had now come to the end of his patience. Suddenly he drew his long cuirassier sword, reversed it, caught it by the

P

blade, whirled it on high, and, letting it go, sent it whistling through the air fifty feet away. Then putting spurs to his horse he called out, ' You may all go to the devil ! ' and rode off to his tent.

Napoleon was struck dumb. Pale with rage he turned his horse and rode away in silence, followed by his staff. Every one expected that Montbrun would be arrested and court-martialled. But that same day he was told to resume the command of his corps, and nothing more was heard of the incident. It would seem that after the explosion had taken place, Murat, as he rode away with Napoleon, entered into a frank explanation, and so saved Montbrun by doing, when almost too late, what ought to have been done at once.

Napoleon established his headquarters at Wilna on 29 June. Then came a foretaste of later troubles. Though it was the summer the weather became suddenly cold, and then for three days there was a wild storm with a ceaseless downpour of icy rain. Thousands of horses perished under the stress of bad weather and scanty food, for the roads had become muddy tracks, all transport was stopped, and the only forage available was the green and sodden rye in the fields. The cavalry lost fewer horses than the artillery and transport train, but even before the weather had changed numbers of the cavalry horses showed signs of breaking down.

From Wilna onwards the daily loss in horses was heavy. Murat has been blamed for this by historians of the Russian campaign. It has been said that though none could excel him as a leader on the battlefield, he did not know how to take care of his horses on the march or in camp, or was careless on this all-important matter. He could conduct a campaign, say his critics, on condition of being allowed to use up some hundreds of horses every day. With scores of them at his own disposal, and a fresh one to mount every few hours, he did not realize that the heavily equipped cuirassier or dragoon had only one horse, and that horse could not work all day and all night without suffering for

# THE CAMPAIGN OF RUSSIA 227

it. But the blame of overworking the horses cannot be entirely laid at his door. On 28 June Napoleon had ordered that small patrols, even patrols of fifty men, should not be employed against the enemy, as such detachments were too easily cut off and overwhelmed by a rapid concentration of the ever vigilant Cossacks against them. The cavalry should therefore work in bodies of a thousand or even fifteen hundred men in the service of reconnaissance and screening. Even such masses of horsemen as Murat commanded could not furnish detachments of this strength for prolonged work day after day without serious losses.[1]

The enforced halt at Wilna came to an end when the cold and rain gave place to normal summer conditions. Then in hot, dry weather the march was resumed. Murat commanded the advance guard—Nansouty and Montbrun's cavalry corps and the infantry divisions of Friant, Gudin, and Morand. Grouchy's cavalry corps was with Davoût, and Latour-Maubourg's on the right with King Jerome. Barclay, with the main Russian army, held an entrenched position at the crossing of the Dwina near Drissa, and there was a hope that a decisive action might be fought there, but on the approach of Murat the enemy began to retire up the river towards Witebsk. There was some fighting between the French cavalry and the Russian rearguard and continual skirmishing with the Cossacks. Then, when Barclay reached Witebsk, there seemed again a prospect of forcing on a general engagement, for the Russian leader had halted in the hope that Bagration with the southern army would come up and join him.

This halt led to two days' fighting, which began on the 25 July, about Ostrowno. Murat's cavalry, first into action, bore the brunt of the fighting, and he himself led more than one charge. Once, to rescue a hard-pressed regiment, he dashed at the Russian horsemen with his staff and

[1] It must be admitted that in one respect Murat was a bad 'horse master.' On days of battle he would keep thousands of men sitting inactive on their horses, sometimes for hours, waiting for the moment of action. One seldom hears of cavalry being dismounted to rest their horses while halted. But this was a fault he shared with most cavalry leaders of the time.

personal escort, some sixty sabres at most. It was one of the few occasions when he drew his diamond-hilted sword at the head of a charge. His life was saved by one of his equerries killing a Russian who was on the point of cutting him down. On the 27th he was in contact with the Russians before Witebsk. The enemy was formed up for battle. The columns of the Grand Army were rapidly closing on the vanguard. Murat wanted to attack at once, but Napoleon deferred the action till next day. In the night the enemy disappeared, abandoning Witebsk on the news that Bagration had been beaten and forced away to the eastward by Davoût.

Next day Witebsk was occupied and the cavalry pushed on in pursuit of the Russians. But the Cossack screen covered its line of retreat so well that the pursuit completely missed the track of the main body, and had an exhausting march over dry, sandy ground under a burning sun without ever sighting the Russian columns. Eager as he was, Murat now recognized that his men and horses must have a rest. Of the horses, one-third were completely broken down or temporarily disabled. The light cavalry, continually employed in attempts to close with the evasive Cossacks, had lost one-half of its effective strength through sheer exhaustion of its mounts. Belliard was sent to represent to the Emperor the necessity of a rest, and it was decided to halt for a few days at Witebsk.

Barclay was retiring to Smolensk on the Dneiper, where Bagration was to join him. Napoleon had ordered Davoût and all the troops on the right to converge on his own intended line of advance so that, when Smolensk was attacked, Murat would have all his four corps of cavalry in hand.

In the first days of August the advance was resumed. At Inkowo, on the 8th, Murat, with Nansouty, Montbrun, and Grouchy's cavalry, fought a battle with Barclay's rearguard. It began by the Russians suddenly taking the offensive and surprising Sebantiani's light cavalry division. Murat, attacking in his turn with only some of his cavalry

## THE CAMPAIGN OF RUSSIA 229

in hand, and without waiting for his guns and the infantry to come up, at first ran serious risks and suffered severe losses. He had another and still harder fight with the rearguard at Krasnoi on the 14th. The Russians finally drew off, leaving eight guns and a thousand prisoners in his hands.

On 16 August Murat's cavalry, supported by Ney's infantry corps, were in sight of Smolensk. Grouchy, with his dragoons and horse artillery, drove the enemy's cavalry into the suburbs, but in the fight for the crossing of the Dnieper and the occupation of the city, the work fell chiefly on the infantry corps. The Russians held on just long enough to clear out some of their magazines and fire the rest. When Napoleon entered Smolensk on the morning of 19 August the city was wrapped in a fog of smoke from half a dozen huge conflagrations. Barclay and Bagration, covered by swarms of Cossack light horsemen, were retiring by the Moscow road.

Murat was sent after them with Montbrun and Nansouty's cavalry, supported by Davoût with five divisions of infantry. Davoût and Murat had never been friends, and old dissensions helped to accentuate the divergent views they took of the situation. Murat reported to the Emperor that the enemy were thoroughly demoralized and that a little pressure would turn their retreat into a rout. Davoût sent back a more accurate judgment on the position. He wrote that the Russians showed no sign of disorganization or indiscipline, and were making their retreat in good order, with a probability that they would presently halt and offer battle.

At Dorogbuz, some fifty miles east of Smolensk, they showed such a determined front that it looked as if they meant to make a stand in earnest. Napoleon hurried up with the Imperial Guard, but when he arrived the enemy were again retiring. The Emperor, who had thought at first of wintering at Smolensk, now found himself committed to the pursuit. The whole of the Grand Army moved eastward in three huge columns. In advance of them

Murat and Davoût hung on the Russian rear, no better friends than before, for daily incidents showed the growing tension between them. Murat was all eagerness to fight. Davoût, who did not share his anticipations of easy victory, was anxious not to be involved suddenly in an action with superior numbers, which might well be the result of giving the enemy an opening for a counter-attack. Once there was an open quarrel. Murat had flung himself on the Russian rearguard with a single regiment of Polish lancers and had been roughly handled and repulsed. He ordered one of Davoût's batteries to come into action in support of the renewed attack. The battery commander replied that he could only take orders from the marshal to whose corps he belonged. Davoût supported his subordinate when Murat complained to the Emperor, and said the King of Naples was too ready to risk weak and unjustifiable attacks. Murat retorted that Davoût was ready to leave him in the lurch. The Emperor begged them both to try to work together more amicably.

For a fortnight the Russian army steadily retired, and the Grand Army followed them up through a desolate country where the enemy had consumed or destroyed all supplies, and where the only thing the invaders could take to help themselves was the abundance of wood for the bivouac fires supplied by the endless belts and patches of stunted forest. 'Each morning,' writes General Morand, 'we saw the Cossacks stretched out in an immense line across our front, while their nimble skirmisher patrols defied us by almost riding into our ranks. We would form up and march to attack the Cossack line, but as we neared it they would disappear in the distance, and the horizon would show us nothing but firs and birch trees. But an hour later, when we halted to feed our horses, they would come on again, and the long black line would develop and close in once more. These manœuvres would go on all day, and the finest and bravest of cavalry was gradually exhausted and worn out.'

At Gzazt, which the Emperor reached on 31 August, the

## THE CAMPAIGN OF RUSSIA

advance was stopped for three days by a break in the weather and a steady downpour of rain that turned the roads of the steppe into impassable sloughs. The horses of the cavalry, artillery and transport began to drop in scores. Berthier, Ney, and even the impetuous Murat proposed to Napoleon to abandon for that season the idea of reaching Moscow. But on 4 September, when the bad weather changed to bright sunshine, Napoleon ordered Murat and Davoût to press on and gain touch of the enemy. That afternoon at Gridnewa, and next day at Koletkoi, Murat charged the Cossacks and broke through their moving screen of horsemen, but on each occasion they showed a disposition to fight that suggested a change of plans on the Russian side. On the afternoon of the 5th Murat was able to report that the Russian army was halted on the fortified position of Borodino, its right flank resting on the river Moskowa. The long-desired battle was at last to be fought. Prepared as they were to continue the retreat, which was wearing out the strength of the invaders, the Russian leaders had had to yield to the clamour of those who were indignant at the thought of abandoning the holy city of Moscow without striking a blow in its defence. Barclay had insisted, nevertheless, that a continued retreat was the best policy, but Kutusoff, who had lost the battle of Austerlitz, had superseded him in the supreme command.

On the 6th, while Murat cleared away the enemy's horsemen from the front of the position, and enabled Napoleon thoroughly to reconnoitre it, the Grand Army closed up and formed for the fight. On 7 September came the great struggle which the French call the battle of the Moskowa, the Russians Borodino.

Both victors and vanquished rightly remember it with pride, for never was there a more recklessly brave and persevering attack, and more dogged and persistent defence. It was the last victory in Napoleon's unbroken career of conquest, a Pyrrhic victory that was the herald of disaster. Kutusoff had in line 121,000 men, 15,000 of them raw militia. Napoleon had 130,000. The Russian line bristled with 640 guns, many of them mounted in redoubts and earthwork batteries. Napoleon brought 587 guns into action. Of his army not more than half were Frenchmen; the rest were Germans, Italians, Switzers, Poles, Dutchmen—western Europe in arms against the Muscovite. But in his anxiety to keep something intact amid the fierce destruction of the fight some 20,000 of his splendid Guardsmen never fired a shot, an error he would not have made in the earlier days of his conquering career. The fight lasted fifteen hours, from early morning till darkness covered the slow retirement of the Russians. They left 37,500 killed and wounded on the field, and 5000 prisoners in the hands of the French, a loss of more than a third of their fighting strength. But when they abandoned the field they took with them some 7000 French prisoners, and the victory had cost Napoleon 24,000 killed and wounded. It was a costly success, and the Russians, though defeated, were not discouraged. It was still an army that tramped back to Moscow, ready and even eager to fight again.

Of the tens of thousands who shared the dangers and glories of the day none had displayed more reckless courage and untiring energy than the soldier King of Naples. Under close fire, or in the thick of cavalry mêlées, his brilliant battle-costume made him a marked man, but he seemed invulnerable, escaping ball and bullet, bayonet and sword, as if by a miracle. In the first stage of the fight, while the artillery was preparing the way for the infantry attack on the redoubts, the cavalry was in the second line. Napoleon received a report that Davoût was mortally wounded, and ordered Murat to take command of his infantry. Davoût had been rolled over by a cannon-shot killing his horse, and had been so bruised and shaken that he became for a while a mere spectator of the battle on the French right. Murat galloped to the marshal's position just in time to see Razout's infantry division recoiling in disorder from the earthworks on the enemy's left. He rallied them by the mere magic

THE RETREAT FROM MOSCOW
FROM THE PAINTING BY MEISSONIER IN THE LOUVRE, PARIS

of his presence, and the sight of his imperturbable courage. Then dismounting, sword in hand, he placed himself at their head, ordered the charge to be sounded, and with the rush of bayonets behind him, dashed into the earthworks and cleared them, after a hand-to-hand fight, in which he took part like the youngest soldier. Mounting again he called up another division, sent for Nansouty's cuirassiers and horse artillery, and launched a fierce attack of horse, foot, and guns against the exposed flank of the Russian line. Then, as he gained ground, he flung Latour-Maubourg's cavalry on the enemy's flank and rear. The sight of long trains of transport retiring eastward made him think that the enemy was giving way everywhere. Ney, who was now supporting him, joined him in an earnest message, sent by General Belliard to Napoleon asking him to intervene with the Imperial Guard. But the Emperor hesitated to employ his last reserve.

Murat had, meanwhile, massed the rest of his cavalry on the right. Montbrun, riding up at the head of his cuirassiers, was mortally wounded by a cannon-shot, and Caulaincourt replaced him. Poniatowski appeared with a bristling forest of Polish lances. There was a succession of cavalry mêlées as the Russians threw all their mounted men into action to restore the fight. The Russian cuirassiers charged in vain on to the bayonets of Friant's infantry, only to be driven back with terrible loss. 'Soldiers of Friant, you are heroes!' shouted Murat, riding up to one of the squares as the broken cavalry retired.

Then the battle raged round the great redoubt in the enemy's centre. Murat helped to decide the fight for its possession by sending Caulaincourt and Grouchy's cuirassiers to attack the rear of the defence. Grouchy was badly wounded, but several squadrons of his steel-clad horsemen penetrated into the redoubt by its open rear. On the right, when night fell, the Russians still held out with some three hundred guns in action. In the darkness they began their retreat towards Moscow.

At dawn, on the 8th, Murat was again in the saddle, following up the retiring enemy with his sadly thinned squadrons. He would have pressed the pursuit hotly, for he believed that the Russians were badly beaten and demoralized, but he was restrained by the Emperor's orders. Napoleon had better judged the position of affairs, and knew there was still plenty of fight left in the enemy. He had, therefore, ordered Murat to move slowly, so that the infantry could be at hand to support him at once if the Russians again turned and offered battle. At Mojaisk, on the 8th, there was a sharp fight with the enemy's rearguard, mostly composed of cavalry under Miloradovitch. Then, for a week, the two armies moved slowly eastwards. It was not till the afternoon of the 14th that Murat, riding up to the crest of a long swell of the steppe, saw the gilded and painted domes of Moscow and the turrets of the Kremlin, with the Russian cavalry—Cossacks and regulars —forming a strong screen in the plain between him and the city.

It was here that a flag of truce arrived from Miloradovitch with a proposal which Napoleon ordered Murat to accept. The Russians declared that they were anxious to avoid a fight in the streets of Moscow, and would therefore allow the French to occupy it without opposition, provided the Emperor would agree that his cavalry should, for the next two days, follow up the retreat of the Russian rearguard without pressing it or attacking. That Napoleon accepted such a truce shows how thoroughly exhausted the Grand Army must have been, and how anxious he was to enter Moscow without another Borodino.

Far from wishing to spare the city, the Russians had prepared its destruction. They were setting a trap for the invader and anxious for time to complete the evacuation of the place, remove the host of fugitives that was to accompany their army, and put the last touches to their arrangements for the coming conflagration. On the 15th the Russian cavalry had retired to the east of the city, and Murat, with no suspicion of what was coming, rode proudly into Moscow. He made his entry at the head

## THE CAMPAIGN OF RUSSIA 235

of a regiment of Polish hussars. Then came a battery of artillery, Caulaincourt's cuirassiers and light cavalry, and Dufour's division of infantry.

Few witnessed the triumphal entry. The streets were empty, most of the houses deserted. Murat went out with a French escort to the east of the city and came upon a line of Cossack outposts. Taking advantage of the truce he rode up to them. The French and Russian officers talked together. The Cossacks gathered round Murat, who evoked their admiration by riding along their line at a headlong gallop, acknowledging their cheers with a wave of his hand. They told him they wished he could be their *hetman*. He showed a boyish pride in their applause, and gave his watch and some of the watches of his staff to those who were most prominent in their expressions of admiration.

There is no need to tell again the story of the burning of Moscow. The cavalry camped outside the city were not disturbed by its destruction. They sent parties to help in fighting the fire, and others came in without orders to assist in the wholesale plundering that went on for days, and encumbered the baggage-trains of the army with miscellaneous booty, destined to become sooner or later the prey of the Cossacks. Murat himself was with Napoleon when the approach of the flames forced the Emperor to abandon the Kremlin. For some days Napoleon expected that his occupation of Moscow would enable him to impose his own terms on Russia, and he was misled in this direction by half-hearted overtures for peace. All touch with the Russian army had been lost for a while, and the reconnaissances of the cavalry, never pushed far enough, gave the impression that the enemy had drawn off to the south-eastward. Even the appearance of Cossack raiders to the south and southwest of the city conveyed no warning either to Murat or to Napoleon. It was supposed that these were wandering bands of plunderers with nothing behind them. There must have been something like a paralysis of energy and initiative in the French army or surely something serious would have been done to ' clear up the situation.'

It was becoming very perilous. Kutusoff, after evacuating Moscow on 15 September, had marched eastwards for two days along the banks of the Moskowa river, then, finding that there was no pursuit, he had turned and, marching under cover of the screen of Cossacks that continually watched the enemy and effectually concealed his movement, he had worked round well to the south of Moscow. By the first of October he had massed his army about Tarutino, forty-five miles from the city and to the south-west of it, so that he threatened the French line of retreat. The presence of the Russian main army in this direction was not suspected, even when it was discovered that all the country south of the city was infested with strong bodies of Cossack cavalry.

By the second week of October it was evident that the Russians had no intention of making peace, and the first falls of snow warned Napoleon that the retreat could no longer be delayed. To winter at Moscow, in the heart of a hostile country, would have meant starvation. The first movements of the retreat began on the 15th.

Murat and Bessières had already been sent out to the south of Moscow to keep the enemy's raiders in check, and clear the country. Murat had under his orders the cavalry of Nansouty, Sebastiani, and Latour-Maubourg, and Poniatowski's Polish corps. There were daily skirmishes and the Russians everywhere gave way, but it was discovered that they had the support of formidable forces in their rear, which indicated the presence of Kutusoff's army. Murat had had to leave his chief of the staff ill at Moscow, and his letters to Belliard show that the columns in the field were short of supplies and suffering severe privations. In one letter to him Murat says that he is tired of running from barn to barn and is half dead with hunger. In another he begs him to have a convoy of flour sent out as soon as possible, for his force has none left. At dawn, on 18 October, he was surprised at Winkowo and narrowly escaped destruction. He was asleep when Platoff's Cossacks

# THE CAMPAIGN OF RUSSIA 237

drove in his outposts. Half-dressed, he mounted and led more than one charge, but the most he could do was to drive the enemy from their position on his line of retreat, and withdraw, leaving thirty-six guns and some seven hundred prisoners in the hands of the Russians.

The retirement from Moscow had already begun. In the weary march through the devastated and now storm-swept and snow-covered country the cavalry lost hundreds of horses daily. At the battle of Malojaroslawetz, on 23 October, there were still nearly ten thousand mounted men in the reserve, the corps cavalry and the cavalry of the Guard. When Smolensk was reached on 9 November, there were only four thousand four hundred, and of these twelve hundred, united under the command of Latour-Maubourg, were all that was left of the cavalry reserve. After the passage of the Beresina, on 26 November, only eighteen hundred were left, and Latour-Maubourg's command had dwindled to one hundred, of whom eighty were Saxon cuirassiers.

During the retreat Murat was continually beside Napoleon, travelling with him in his sledge or carriage. There is a legend that a 'Sacred Cohort' was formed of cavalry officers, under the command of Grouchy, to act as the Emperor's bodyguard. But his escort was to the last supplied by a detachment of the cavalry of the Guard. In the latter stages of the retreat the chief use of the cavalry was to supply horse-flesh for the camp-kettles. Few of the unfortunate horses were fit even to carry their riders, far less to charge. Murat's rôle as a cavalry general had for the moment disappeared.

From Molodetchno, on 3 December, he wrote to his daughter :—' You will see by the date of this letter that I am two hundred leagues nearer you, but how far away I still am from you! It is a long time since I last wrote. We are continually on the march. I am very thin and very tired, but nevertheless I am well, but I am very unhappy at being so far from my dear family. When shall I see you all again, my dear ones ? '

It was at Molodetchno, in the midst of the wreck of his army, that the Emperor received the news of Malet's conspiracy at Paris, and realized that, after his disastrous failure, his throne itself was in danger. He quickly made up his mind that he must at once return to France, leaving to one of his marshals the difficult task of concentrating the remnants of the Grand Army on the frontiers of Germany, and preparing to make head against a Russian invasion in the coming year, which might well herald a national uprising of the German people.

Next day, as his carriage was dragged slowly along the snowy road in the midst of the columns of ragged, starving men, and while, from time to time, distant firing told that the Cossacks were hanging close upon his track, the Emperor told Murat that he was to take command, and discussed with him the dangers and possibilities of the situation. On the 5th, at Smorgoni, Napoleon held a council of war of the marshals. Murat, Berthier, Ney, Davoût, Lefèbvre, Mortier, and Bessières were present. He told them of his intended return to Paris, and formally appointed the King of Naples to his new command. Then he bade them good-bye and drove away in his sledge, taking with him Caulaincourt, Duroc, Lobau, and Lefèbvre-Desnouettes.

## CHAPTER XV

MURAT LEAVES THE ARMY—RETURN TO NAPLES—
QUARREL WITH NAPOLEON—OVERTURES TO THE
ALLIES—GOES TO DRESDEN

### 1812-1813

THE orders which Napoleon gave to Murat before parting from him at Smorgoni were thus summed up :—

'Rally the army at Wilna; hold that city and take up winter quarters there, with the Austrians on the Niemen covering Breszc, Grodno, and Warsaw, the Grand Army about Wilna and Kovno. In case the enemy's army continues its advance, and it is not considered possible to hold on east of the Niemen, the right will cover Warsaw, and if possible, Grodno, with the rest of the army in line behind the Niemen, holding Kovno as a *tête de pont*.'

There were magazines of supplies and ammunition accumulated at Wilna and Kovno. Napoleon's orders seemed simple enough on paper, but the task he had left to Murat was a burden for a giant. It was easy to write that the Grand Army was to spend the winter holding Wilna, or in any case the line of the Niemen, but the Grand Army was no longer an effective fighting force. Seven weeks of misery had reduced it to a wreck, a dispirited, disorganized crowd, wasted with hunger and disease, losing hundreds daily as it was hustled back through the driving snow, and hundreds more each night in the frozen, often fireless, bivouacs. The Prussians on the left and the Austrians on the right had not ventured so far, had suffered comparatively little, and had preserved their organization, but in the face of disaster these were doubtful allies. At any moment they might range themselves on the side of the advancing enemy.

And Murat was no giant. At the best of times he could not have grappled with the problems of a vast campaign, and now he was broken in spirit and worn out with fatigue and cold. Worst of all he had ceased to believe in Napoleon's star or in the possibility of final success. The Emperor, when he parted with him, had no idea of his state of mind. One of his last acts had been to prove his friendship for him by conferring on young Achille Murat the principality of Ponte Corvo, forfeited by Bernadotte after his defection from Napoleon's cause. He thought he could rely on his old companion-in-arms, the husband of his favourite sister. But Murat was now beginning to think again of how best he could keep his kingdom amid the coming downfall of the Imperial system. He was anxious to be back at Naples again, and fighting for his own hand. The Grand Army he regarded as beyond saving.

He reached Wilna on 8 December. The Emperor's trusted friend, Maret, Duke of Bassano, met him there, gave him an account of the supplies collected in the place, and spoke of arrangements for spending the winter there. 'No, no,' replied Murat, 'I don't mean to get myself caught in this hole.' Berthier, who asked for orders for the army, was curtly dismissed. 'You know better than me what ought to be done. Give the orders yourself,' said Murat. There is no doubt that Berthier, as chief of the staff, ought to have taken the responsibility of at once setting to work to distribute the clothes, rations, and cartridges in the magazines, but little was done, and when the place was hurriedly evacuated, on the approach of the Russians, most of these supplies fell into their hands. They occupied Wilna on 10 December.

During the retirement from Wilna on Kovno a great part of what remained of the military train, including the treasure of the army, was abandoned because the exhausted teams could no longer drag the wagons over the icy ground.

Ney, with his corps reduced to 1500 men, covered the movement. But it was found impossible to make a stand even at Kovno. On the 13th Murat recrossed the Niemen and ordered the army to concentrate about Gumbinnen, on the line of the river. On the evening of the 15th he established his own headquarters at Wirballen, and next day wrote to the Emperor that everything was going from bad to worse; that he could do no good and intended to hand over the command to Eugène, 'who had more experience of administration,' and that he thought he himself would be more useful at Paris or Naples. He would leave the army if he did not hear to the contrary from the Emperor in a fortnight. On the same day Berthier sent Napoleon a dispatch in cipher in which he said :—

'The King of Naples is the first of men for executing the orders given by a Commander-in-chief on the battlefield. The King of Naples is in every way the most incapable of acting as Commander-in-chief himself. He ought to be at once superseded. The viceroy (Eugène) is full of energy and health, and the Duke of Elchingen (Ney) and Marshal Gouvion St. Cyr have his entire confidence.'

Berthier had seen that Murat was helplessly despairing of the situation. Murat himself confirmed the secret message of the chief of the staff by writing the very next day to Napoleon that he could not remain with the army. He had done enough, he said, to show his devotion to the Emperor, and he would return to the front when there was again a chance of fighting, but now it was a matter of administration and reorganization and he could not stay when the interests of his kingdom and his subjects called him back to Naples.

On the 18th he held a council of war of the corps commanders at Gumbinnen, and the state of nervous anxiety and irritation in which he was, led to a painful scene. He insisted that the line of the Niemen was now untenable, and he intended to withdraw his headquarters to Königsberg. To those who urged that an effort must be made to carry out the Emperor's plan of holding the line of the frontier river, he replied with an outburst of despairing anger against him. 'What could they do to save a madman?' he asked. 'His cause was hopeless; there was not a prince in Europe who would now trust his word or his treaties. As for himself he was sorry he had rejected advances made to him by the English. Only for that he would still be as safe on his throne as the Emperor of Austria or the King of Prussia.' Davoût broke in with an indignant protest. 'They are princes,' he said, 'by the grace of God, long possession, and the traditional loyalty of their people, but as for you, you are only king by the grace of Napoleon and at the cost of French blood. You can only be king while you stand by Napoleon and France. It is black ingratitude that is blinding you.' 'I am as much King of Naples as Francis is Emperor of Austria, and I can do as I please,' answered Murat, but the looks of the marshals told him that he had gone too far, and he returned to the discussion of military details. Berthier, with perhaps an excess of caution, did not report Murat's outburst to Napoleon, but he wrote to him: 'The King of Naples is very unsettled in his ideas and I insist more than ever on the statement in my cipher dispatch.'

Murat was indeed unsettled. On 21 December he had approved of the secret armistice between Schwarzenberg and Miloradovitch, by which it was agreed that the Austrians were simply to manœuvre against the Russian left without fighting, as if at peace manœuvres, the result being that Schwarzenberg gradually evacuated the Grand Duchy of Warsaw. About the same time Murat sent to Vienna on a confidential mission two of his Neapolitan staff-officers, Prince Cariati and the Duke Caraffa de Noja, both of whom had connections in the Austrian capital by marriage. They were to find out if an arrangement with Austria was possible for the maintenance of Murat at Naples in case of a disaster to the French Empire.

The line of the Niemen was abandoned to the Russians, who were now free to enter East Prussia. On 19 December Murat established his headquarters at Königsberg. There for a moment he seemed to recover something of his old spirit, and wrote to Belliard a letter that was in strange contradiction with his own dispatches to the Emperor. ' Every one,' he said, ' is asking for permission to leave the army. I am indignant at this state of demoralization. If this state of things continues one cannot foresee where the mischief will stop. Speak to the generals of the cavalry ; talk of their glory ; remind them of the days of Wertingen, Prenzlau, Lubeck, Eylau, and the Moskowa. Is the cavalry to retire any further before miserable Cossacks that it once drove before it, with drums beating, for three hundred leagues ? ' But the ink of the letter to Belliard was hardly dry when once more he wrote to Napoleon that he thought he could now return to Naples without detriment to the army, as it was about to take up its winter quarters in East Prussia.

The first reinforcements were arriving from France, half-drilled conscripts, many of them mere boys. Macdonald, with a mixed force of Polish, Westphalian, and Bavarian troops, had evacuated Courland and, occupying Tilsit, regained touch with the centre of the Grand Army. Murat issued orders for a counter-attack on the Russians and thought for a moment of regaining the line of the Niemen, but, on 26 December, came the news that Yorck and the Prussians had declared for the enemy. Murat wrote to Macdonald that ' the treason of Yorck ' altered everything. There must be a general retreat on Elbing, Dantzic, and the line of the Oder.

Murat arrived at Elbing on 2 January. Leaving a large garrison under Rapp at Dantzic, he directed the main body of the Grand Army, now numbering only some 20,000 effective men, on Posen. Kutusoff had crossed the Niemen with 40,000 men. He, too, had suffered during the march from Moscow, and he had left 70,000 behind him in two months and abandoned 400 guns on the way.

At Posen, on 15 January, Murat, who had now lost all confidence in the Emperor's cause, announced to Berthier that he must leave the army. He gave as his reason that he was ill. There is no doubt that he was anything but well, but he exaggerated on this point. He told them he was going to rest for a while as King Jerome's guest at Cassel. Berthier tried to dissuade him, but all he could obtain was that he should remain two days longer at Posen to give time for Eugène to arrive and take over the command. That same day Murat wrote to Napoleon :—

'SIRE. Although I have already written to your Majesty that I could not retain the command of the Grand Army, nevertheless I would not have taken the step of leaving it, only that the state of illness to which I am reduced during the last five or six days makes it absolutely impossible for me to occupy myself with business. In this state of things I find myself compelled to write the two letters of which I herewith send copies to your Majesty. I flatter myself that you will do justice to my sentiments towards you to the extent of believing in the sorrow I feel at ceasing for the moment to serve you, but I hope that a stay of some months in the favourable climate of Naples will enable me in the spring to return and resume my old command.'

And he added in a postscript :—

' I have fever and the beginning of a marked attack of jaundice.'

The letters enclosed were addressed to Berthier as chief of the staff and to Eugène as his successor in the command. After an interview with the latter he left Posen on 17 January, accompanied by his aide-de-camp, General Rosetti. Instead of paying a visit to Cassel he travelled right through to Naples. ' Not bad for a sick man ! ' wrote Eugène.

Napoleon was very angry at what he described as Murat's desertion of the army. To Eugène he wrote : ' To me the conduct of the King of Naples seems utterly irregular, and such that I was almost inclined to have him arrested as an example to others. He is a brave man on the battlefield, but he is lacking in consistency and moral sense.' The Emperor further showed his feeling by publishing an implied censure on Murat in the following announcement in the *Moniteur* : ' The King of Naples, being indisposed, has had to give up the command of the army, which he has handed over to the Viceroy. The latter is more accustomed

## RETURN TO NAPLES

to administrative work on a large scale, and has the entire confidence of the army.'

Murat arrived, on the last day of January, at the castle of San Leucio near Caserta, where he found the queen and her children waiting to welcome him. Caroline thought his departure from the army a mistake, and on the 15th she had written to persuade him to remain with it, but he was on his way home before the letter reached him. As regent during his absence she had shown a tact and energy worthy of a sister of Napoleon. Her position had been rendered difficult by a provision in the decree of regency stipulating that all matters of importance should be referred to Murat himself, and her husband had sent to her for publication orders imposing new taxes, a somewhat shabby attempt to evade his share of the unpopularity they might cause by letting it be supposed they were levied only by a proclamation of the queen regent. Caroline, however, had prudently suspended all questions of new taxation till the return of the king, and, on the other hand, she had taken it upon herself to act on more than one important matter without the long delay that would have resulted from a correspondence with a distant headquarters in Russia. Murat was not quite satisfied with the display of independence, and he was troubled by rumours that had reached him as to Caroline's private conduct in his absence. This, added to her dissatisfaction with his abrupt departure from the army, made the relations between the king and queen anything but cordial for a while.

On the day he reached Caserta Murat wrote to Napoleon announcing his arrival and saying that he was still very unwell, and was only sorry that his state of health made it impossible for him to serve his Majesty actively for a while. He no longer spoke of fever and jaundice, but attributed his illness to fatigue and exposure and the after effects of two minor wounds received in action in Russia, a lance wound in the thigh, and the blow of a spent bullet that had caused a severe contusion and a tumour in his side. Those who saw him on his arrival reported that he looked worn and haggard. Anxiety and mental worry had told on him even more than the exposure and fatigues of the disastrous campaign.

Napoleon did not answer this letter. But it was hardly dispatched when a letter from the Emperor reached him, dated 26 January, 1813. Napoleon wrote in anger :—

'I don't want to talk to you of the displeasure I feel at your course of conduct since my departure from the army, for that is the result of your weakness of character. However, I have thought it right to give my opinion of it frankly to your wife, the Queen of Naples. You are a good soldier on the field of battle, but elsewhere you have neither energy nor character. I presume you are not one of those who think the lion is dead. If you count on this you make a mistake. Since my departure from Wilna you have done me all the harm you could. The title of king has turned your head. If you want to keep that title you must conduct yourself differently from what you have so far done. The opportunity for reinstating yourself in my good opinion will not be long before it presents itself.'

The letter to Caroline, to which Napoleon alludes, had arrived two days before, but she had hesitated to show it to Murat. It was a brief note :—

'Your husband, the King of Naples, deserted the army on the 16th. He is a brave man on the battlefield, but he is weaker than a woman or a monk when he is not in sight of the enemy. He has no moral courage. I leave it to you to express to him all the displeasure I have felt at his conduct in this matter.'

Napoleon's letters and the hardly veiled censure in the *Moniteur* made Murat angrily suspicious. He thought that Berthier had probably spoken on a hint from the Emperor, when at parting he had said that he knew Murat was too good a Frenchman not to be ready to sacrifice his crown, if need be, for the sake of Napoleon. He suspected that the return of the Bourbon king and his Austrian queen to Naples might be part of a bargain made without consulting him. When he re-entered his capital on 4 February the acclamations of the crowd made him flatter himself that he

## QUARREL WITH NAPOLEON 247

was a popular king, who could rule even without Napoleon's gracious consent. He was now really ill. For some days he saw no one. On the 9th he met his council of ministers for the first time. On the 11th, for the first time, he rode out.

Till the end of the month he was waiting impatiently for a reply from Napoleon to letters which Caroline had written to him. No answer came. Through his wife he had offered to send a small reinforcement of cavalry to the Imperial army. No notice was taken of the offer. On 26 February there were signs that he might soon need all his troops in Naples. Two British frigates suddenly appeared off the island of Ponza, and landed a battalion from Sicily. The garrison of Ponza, after a brief show of resistance, surrendered the fortress.

On 10 March Durant, the French ambassador at Naples, reported to Paris that he did not like the attitude of the king. Murat was reserved and suspicious. He had gone so far as to say that he thought the Austrians would be wise if they stood neutral and acted as mediators in the quarrel between the Allies and Napoleon, and the ambassador thought the King of Naples was inclined to the same policy.

Durant had judged rightly. Murat was already in secret unofficial communication with Metternich, through Prince Cariati at Vienna. Presently Metternich refused to pledge himself to anything definite, or even seriously discuss the situation with Murat's envoy, unless he could show that he was provided with full powers. Accordingly, on 20 April, Cariati was named Neapolitan ambassador to the court of Vienna. It was Murat's first definite step towards defection from Napoleon.

Caroline had told Durant that the Emperor's angry silence was alarming her husband, and the ambassador urged him to write some reassuring message to his brother-in-law. Durant considered that otherwise Murat would take a line of his own in the hope of securing his crown. He was already increasing his army, and had started on a journey through the southern provinces in order to try to call forth the personal loyalty of the people.

Before setting out on this journey from Naples on 12 April, Murat had written to Napoleon telling him he was at last sending off two squadrons to join the Imperial army. He referred to the censure in the *Moniteur* and protested that he had not deserved it. During the Russian campaign he had risked his life like a common soldier. When he bade farewell to the Emperor at Smorgoni he had promised to remain with the army so long as he could be useful, and he declared that he had kept his word and only left Posen when, broken in health, he could no longer usefully command. He asked his brother-in-law to tell him frankly what he wished him to do. He protested his devotion to him. He would like to be beside him, but he thought he would be more useful if he stayed in Italy and organized the defence of the peninsula.

He was travelling about Apulia, Basilicata and Calabria till the end of the month. Everywhere he met with a loyal reception. One incident of his progress is worth noting. He spent a few hours at the little town of Pizzo, on the west coast of Calabria. He talked a while with the aged parish priest, Canon Masdea, and gave him alms for his church and for the poor. The priest and the soldier king were to meet again some two years later under very different circumstances.

On 29 April he was back at Naples. There he heard that Napoleon had left Paris to join the army in Germany without taking any notice of his letter. This ended all his hesitations. He set himself to find among the opponents of Napoleon allies who would buy his defection from the Emperor by guaranteeing him his throne.

Cariati's mission to Vienna had opened the way for an arrangement with the Austrians, and while Murat was away in the south his minister of police, the Duke of Campochiaro, had prepared an opening for negotiations with the English. On the pretext of discussing with Colonel Coffin, the commandant of the garrison of Ponza, trade questions arising

## OVERTURES TO THE ALLIES

out of the blockade system, Campochiaro had sent one of his agents, a certain Cerculi, to the island. Cerculi, after the formal business was ended, told the colonel that there was a quarrel between Napoleon and Murat, and that the latter would be glad to know if any arrangement could be made to conciliate his own interests and those of England in order to save his crown. There is no proof that Murat had authorized this communication. It was Campochiaro's own act, arising out of his shrewd judgment of the situation. Colonel Coffin said he could not himself do anything, but promised to refer the suggestion to his chief, Lord William Bentinck, who represented England in Sicily.

On 7 May Bentinck authorized Coffin to enter into unofficial negotiations with Campochiaro. He told him to find out precisely what Murat wanted, and suggested that to prove he meant business the King of Naples should, at an early date, hand over the fortress of Gaeta to the Anglo-Sicilians. Writing on 16 May Bentinck further proposed as a possible basis of agreement that Murat should declare for the Allies against Napoleon, and march northward with his army. But on the conclusion of the war he was to retain Naples only until another kingdom was found for him elsewhere. Bentinck meant that whatever happened the kingdom of the Two Sicilies was to be restored to the Bourbons.

On 29 May Cerculi came again to Ponza to discuss the proposed bargain with Coffin. Even now Murat did not appear in the negotiation. He had left Naples again and gone to spend the month of May with Caroline at Portici. He was anxiously watching the course of events in Germany. For a while it seemed as if Napoleon would hold his own. He had won the battle of Lutzen, occupied Dresden, and then beaten the Allies at Bautzen. In the last week of May there was an armistice. Russia and Prussia were negotiating with the Emperor. Austria, till now neutral, but with her armies on a war footing, was anxious for peace. But if the armistice came to nothing she was ready to throw her sword into the scale on the side of the Allies.

No wonder Murat was hesitating. Durant wrote to the Emperor that the King of Naples was 'on the edge of an abyss,' and urged that Napoleon should appeal to his old comradeship and at the eleventh hour secure his loyalty.

Cerculi returned to Naples with the news that Bentinck himself was coming to Ponza on his way to Spain, and wished to meet a duly authorized representative of Murat. At this stage of the proceedings the king must have been aware of what was in progress, for Felice Nicolas, the keeper of the archives at the Foreign Office in Naples, who was sent to Ponza on 1 June, was given full powers to treat and precise instructions as to what Murat wished. Nicolas met Bentinck on 2 June. The Englishman put forward the proposals he had sent from Palermo. Nicolas replied that his master could not hand over Gaeta and would not renounce his rights to Naples even for a compensation elsewhere. But if England would guarantee his crown he was ready to march northwards with 40,000 men. Bentinck pointed out that at a later stage of the war England might not be so anxious to accept Murat's help. It would be useful now. It might count for very little soon. If his terms were accepted he would sign a convention at once, and he was sure his Government would ratify it. Murat might not have such an offer again. Nicolas said his instructions would not allow him to go further, and the conference ended, but, before sailing from Ponza, Bentinck left with Coffin a draft convention on the lines he had laid down, and authorized the colonel to sign it if Murat would accept the offer.

While Nicolas was at Ponza, Durant had been asked by Queen Caroline to request the Emperor, in her name, to send a friendly letter to his brother-in-law. Before Durant's dispatch could reach Dresden there arrived at Naples an angry letter from Napoleon addressed to the Duke of San Gallo, the Neapolitan Minister of Foreign Affairs, demanding the instant recall of Prince Cariati from Vienna. For three days San Gallo hesitated to show the letter to the king. When at last Murat read it there was a furious

## OVERTURES TO THE ALLIES

outburst. He was on the point of revolt. But more prudent counsels prevailed. On 11 June San Gallo wrote to the Emperor that Cariati, though he would remain at Vienna, would be directed to act in concert with the French ambassador there.

Events now moved rapidly. Though Murat was not aware of what was happening, the English Government was in close consultation with Metternich as to his proposals, and, influenced by the Austrian, was disposed to go far beyond Bentinck's offer. It seemed now likely that the war would be renewed, with Austria added to the Coalition. The help of the Neapolitan army would be enough to paralyse the action of Eugène and the French in northern Italy. Metternich thought it was worth buying at Murat's own price. The London cabinet was coming round to the view that he might be allowed to rule at Naples, and a compensation could be found elsewhere for the Bourbons of Sicily. But by the time this was arranged and Cariati was informed of the joint views of Austria and England, Murat had changed his mind. The change came not a day too soon.

In the middle of June Napoleon had directed his war minister, Clarke, Duc de Feltre, to write to Murat that Austria was about to join the Coalition, and he must therefore ask him to send a division of the Neapolitan army to Bologna by 15 July. On 18 June Durant informed the Duke of San Gallo that if the division did not march from Naples by 10 July he would have to leave the city and break off diplomatic relations with the king's Government. The same day Murat replied that if Austria joined the Coalition he would himself march northward with 25,000 or 30,000 men. But he would not hand them over to Eugène or have them divided among the French garrisons and corps. He would keep them under his own command. This would, of course, preserve his eventual liberty of action.

At this critical moment the *Moniteur* published a statement that Ponza had been betrayed to the English. Murat sent an indignant denial. The garrison, he said, though surprised, had made a brave defence and only yielded to superior force. Then the *Moniteur* published a paragraph from a London paper announcing that one more of the marshals was about to desert Napoleon, that trade had been reopened between Sicily and Naples, and that King Joachim's Government was in friendly negotiation with Austria and England. The publication of the news was no doubt intended by Napoleon as a warning to Murat. Its effect was to make him for the moment more bitterly hostile than ever, and Caroline now for the first time seemed to share his views. So far in his reports to Vienna, the Austrian ambassador at Naples, the Count Von Mier, had spoken only of the king's desire for an understanding with Austria. But on 29 June he wrote to Metternich : ' *Their Majesties* are awaiting impatiently a reply to Cariati's proposals, in order to know what course they are to take in case of war between France and Austria. The king is always disposed to support our interests.'

To Mier, Murat had said that he was tired of being insulted in the *Moniteur* and was half inclined to send Durant his passports. To Durant he denied the alleged negotiations, and San Gallo explained that at Ponza there had been question only of commercial matters. In the first days of July Murat was still waiting impatiently for news from Cariati. He would have to make a decision soon for the 10th was the day when Durant would leave Naples if he did not obey the order to send a division northwards. On the 3rd Caroline wrote to Napoleon appealing to him to adopt a more friendly attitude towards her husband. Next day Murat followed this up with another letter to Napoleon in which he defined his policy. He was under no obligation, he said, to supply further contingents to the Imperial army. Enough of Neapolitan blood had already been shed all over Europe. He would keep his army for the defence of Italy, and, after the injurious way in which he had been compared with Eugène in the *Moniteur*, he would not send any of his Neapolitans to serve under the Viceroy. But he was ready to march northwards with 25,000 men,

# OVERTURES TO THE ALLIES

keeping them under his own orders, and as he would have to leave most of his artillery in the south and wanted arms for new levies, he would ask for cannon and muskets to be supplied from the French arsenals. He also asked for the Neapolitan troops in Spain to be sent back to him. If this were done he would answer for the defence of Italy. Then he went on :—

'I know your Majesty believes that you have cause of complaint against me, and perhaps I have sometimes expressed too strongly the sorrow I was made to feel at the injustice to which I saw myself subjected, but the remembrance of all you have done for me, the attachment that I have vowed to you, the feelings I must have for France, have always filled my mind, and my most ardent wish has always been to take my place again beside you as your lieutenant, as a French soldier, and as king of a nation which I have tried to inspire with the military spirit with which you have animated France. Resume, Sire, the confidence that was founded upon twenty years of tried fidelity. The oldest of your lieutenants, your sister, your nephews, ask for your affection, and ask it in the name of your dearest interests. For it is not well that Europe should believe that your Majesty can cast away a friend such as I am, and yet this is the report our common enemies are trying to spread. Remember, Sire, that I consider my honour involved in myself commanding the Neapolitan troops which fight for you, and that I can end the noble career through which I have lived, under your auspices, by losing my throne and my life, but not by sacrificing my honour. Write to me, Sire, that you accept my offer, and on the battlefield your enemies shall see that I am worthy of you, worthy of myself.'

While waiting for a reply he wrote to inform Clarke and Berthier of his proposal to the Emperor, and asked for arms to be sent to Naples, and for the return of the Neapolitan troops serving in Catalonia and in the fortresses of northern Italy. He persuaded Durant to defer his departure from Naples on the ground that he was daily expecting a reply to his offers from Dresden. On 26 July a letter arrived. It was addressed by Napoleon, not to Murat but to Caroline. The Emperor told his sister that her husband was refusing to send the reinforcements required from him to the army of Italy because he was in treasonable correspondence with Prussians, Austrians, and English—with all the enemies of France. If this was not true let him come to Dresden and clear himself of the accusations made against him. It was an unpleasant answer to his eloquent appeals. All day Murat and Caroline were together discussing the difficult situation. They saw no one. Next day the king met the Council of Ministers.

Without telling them all that had occurred, he informed them that he had been summoned to Dresden. They all opposed his departure. Most of them were more or less openly committed to the policy of revolt. He surprised them by replying that he must go to Napoleon. Perhaps, if he could have seen the letters from Cariati and Metternich that were already on the way from Vienna, he would have decided differently.

On 30 July Caroline wrote a letter to Napoleon intended to prepare the way for her husband's arrival at Dresden. She said that he had been pained at the Emperor not writing to him and sending her a letter full of accusations against her husband. It is not easy to believe that Caroline had been left in complete ignorance of the negotiations with the Allies, but in her letter to her brother she boldly denied them. Murat, she said, was furious at the idea that the Emperor could think him capable of such conduct. His enemies had been trying to make a breach between two faithful friends. Her husband was not such a fool as to fall into the clumsy traps laid for him by the Allies. His presence at Dresden would prove how false such stories were, for he could not live without loving and serving his Emperor.

Murat wrote more briefly. He protested his loyalty. If the war was renewed the Emperor's enemies would soon see that they could not count upon him. 'Sire,' he said, 'do not doubt about my heart, it is worth more than my head,' and he described himself as Napoleon's 'most affectionate brother.'

## GOES TO DRESDEN

After placing the regency once more in Caroline's hands, he left Naples on 2 August. He knew Napoleon's affection for young people, so he took with him letters from his sons and daughters congratulating their uncle on his coming fête day, the 15th. On the 3rd, as he drove across the Campagna, he met a courier travelling post-haste for Naples with Cariati's long-expected dispatches. He took them and tore them open, but they told him nothing. They were all in cipher, and the key was in San Gallo's hands at Naples. He sealed them up and handed them back to the messenger. Could he have read them he might have turned back, for they contained Metternich's offer to guarantee him the crown of Naples if he would declare for the Allies. Austria had decided to join the Coalition.

## CHAPTER XVI

THE LEIPZIG CAMPAIGN—MURAT ABANDONS THE FALLING EMPIRE—TREATY WITH AUSTRIA—HESITATING PART IN THE ITALIAN CAMPAIGN

### 1813-1814

LATE on the evening of 3 August, Murat reached Rome. He had an interview with the French military governor, General Miollis. He told him that if there was peace he would be back in a fortnight. If there was war, he would stay with the Emperor. In that case the Anglo-Sicilians would probably raid his kingdom, but he had left 30,000 men to defend it. Travelling by way of Roveredo and through the Tyrol, by Innsbruck and Botzen, he reached Dresden on the 14th. He had passed through Austrian territory on the eve of the declaration of war, from Vienna.

Perhaps it was fortunate for him that he came at a moment when for Napoleon all other considerations were dwarfed by the necessity of at once facing the armies of the Coalition on the battle-ground he had himself chosen in Saxony. The Emperor had gathered more than half a million men to meet the forces of Germany, Austria, and Russia, acting from widely separated bases against his own central position. It was largely an improvised force. The ranks of the infantry were filled with beardless boys hurried up from France, by anticipating the conscription of coming years. The cavalry made a formidable show on the muster-rolls of the Grand Army, some 40,000 horse-

## THE LEIPZIG CAMPAIGN 257

men organized in five corps.[1] But they were no longer the splendid squadrons of the great days of the Grand Army. These had been destroyed amid the snows of the Russian steppes. Infantry could be improvised, but not cavalry. Tens of thousands of trained horses could not be provided by signing a decree. In this autumn campaign of 1813 the cavalry were 'the weakest part of Napoleon's organization. They were, as a whole, mounted on horses not broken, but broken down.'[2] In such an emergency it was something to be able to give them a chief whose name was an inspiration, and who had so often shown the magnetic faculty of imparting his own headlong courage to thousands of horsemen in the crisis of a fight.

So, instead of the stormy interview he expected, Murat found himself welcomed by his Imperial brother-in-law. It was no time for recriminations on his past conduct. He was given the opportunity of wiping out all memory of it by new services in the field. The day after he reached Dresden, he rode beside Napoleon at the review that celebrated his fête day, and an order to the Grand Army gave the King of Naples his old position of commander-in-chief of the cavalry.

Some of the historians of the campaign view his conduct in the field in the light of the shifting policy he had adopted, and see in his mistakes and failures deliberate acts of treachery. But their theory fails to explain the fact that more than once he rendered brilliant and whole-hearted service to the Emperor, even in those dark days when,

[1] Colonel Maude (*The Leipzig Campaign*, p. 148) thus tabulates the organization and numbers of the cavalry:—

|  |  |  | Squadrons. | Guns. | Men. |
|---|---|---|---|---|---|
| 1st Cavalry Corps.—Latour Maubourg, | . | 78 | 36 | 16,537 |
| 2nd ,, ,, Sebastiani, | . | . | 52 | 18 | 10,304 |
| 3rd ,, ,, Arighi, | . | . | 27 | 24 | 6,000 |
| 4th ,, ,, Kellerman, | . | . | 24 | 12 | 3,923 |
| 5th ,, ,, L'Héritier, | . | . | 20 | 6 | 4,000 |
|  |  |  | 201 | 96 | 40,764 |

Besides the cavalry of the Guard and the army corps.

[2] Maude, *The Leipzig Campaign*, p. 150.

R

after a first flash of victory, defeat seemed all but inevitable. There is no need to blacken Murat's memory with the accusation of having consciously played the traitor while he rode at the head of his squadrons, and of representing him as having deliberately chosen to incur defeat, or held back from reaping the fruits of success.

It is true that his whole conduct was inconsistent. His action as a king and a politician was in flagrant contradiction to his action as a soldier and a general While he commanded the French cavalry his agent, Cariati, was still either at Vienna or actually in the field with the headquarter staff of one or other of the allied armies, and, during the campaign, Murat received from him reports on further offers made by Austria and England. Von Mier, the Austrian ambassador, was still at Naples, and the regent, Queen Caroline, was finding one pretext after another for refusing to send a single soldier to reinforce the army of Italy, notwithstanding pressing requests from Durant, the French ambassador, and Eugène, who was commanding against the Austrians in northern Italy. But, though he was thus keeping in reserve the possibility of an arrangement with Austria, and holding his army of Naples back, to be used, perhaps, to decide the fate of Italy at a later period, his own ardent nature made it all but impossible for him to play a half-hearted part on the actual field of battle. With his squadrons behind him, and before him even the very Austrians who might soon be his allies, he felt the battle ardour in his blood, and for the moment was a fighting leader and nothing more, ready to charge with all the old furious energy of Aboukir, Wertingen, Eylau, and Borodino.

For a man of solid character, accustomed to act on calm reason and conscience, not on the impulses and feelings of the moment, the position would have been impossible. But Murat was now like one of the old *condottieri*, enjoying fighting for its own sake, without disregarding the solid gains it might bring him, and, at the same time, quite prepared to fight on the other side as soon as it was clear that

## THE LEIPZIG CAMPAIGN 259

there lay the more brilliant prospects for the future. He was no champion of lost causes, and he knew more of horsemanship than of chivalry.

In the first great encounter of the autumn campaign, the battle of Dresden (26 and 27 August), Murat did splendid service. On the first day darkness had left the battle undecided. In the night Napoleon planned a counterstroke. Before sunrise Murat was marching to turn the Austrian left with Latour-Maubourg's cavalry, reinforced by a division under Pajol (sixty-eight squadrons and thirty guns), and supported by Victor's infantry corps and Teste's division (forty-four battalions and seventy-six guns). In all he commanded some forty-five thousand men. He marched through a deluge of rain. The infantry were sent to attack the Austrian left wing in front, while the cavalry moved round to charge them in flank and rear. The enemy formed squares to meet the cavalry charges, but it would seem that during the rain-storm the Austrians had not taken care of their paper-covered cartridges. When the squares were attacked only a few straggling shots could be fired from them. Most of the ammunition was soaked and useless. Under these conditions square after square was broken. The Austrian cavalry, coming to the rescue of the infantry, was charged by the French cuirassiers and routed. The fight had begun at ten o'clock; by two the whole Austrian left was thoroughly broken up. Murat had taken thirty guns and twelve thousand prisoners, and more than four thousand of the enemy had been killed and wounded. He had opened the campaign by scoring an exceptionally complete and brilliant success.

Following up the retiring enemy with his cavalry and Victor's infantry, he next day collected some six thousand more prisoners and captured a quantity of baggage and ammunition wagons. But the effect of Napoleon's victory of Dresden was sadly marred by the destruction of Vandamme's corps, overwhelmed in its attempt to cut off the retreat of the Allies, and by the news that Blücher had beaten Macdonald on the Katzbach.

During September Murat was generally at the Emperor's headquarters, and left the actual leadership of the cavalry to his lieutenants. The defeat of Ney at Dennewitz, coming after the failures of Macdonald and Vandamme, made him take a gloomy view of the outlook. On 19 September he wrote to Campochiaro: 'Everything is going badly. The army is longing for peace. The Emperor alone stands out against the general feeling.' In this state of discouragement he was further depressed by a dispute with Napoleon. Durant had reported from Naples that it was impossible to persuade Murat's Government to reinforce the army of Italy, and there were disquieting reports of Cariati's activity at Vienna. Napoleon had an angry scene with his brother-in-law, and told him he must at once send the Austrian ambassador away from Naples and recall Cariati from Vienna. The only result was that Cariati left Vienna to join the Austrian headquarters in the field. On the eve of Leipzig he was able to send a Neapolitan staff officer to Murat with the news that Austria was still prepared to guarantee him his throne as the price of his defection from Napoleon.

In the first days of October, under the pressure of the Allies, Napoleon abandoned Dresden and the line of the Elbe and retired on Leipzig. While the Emperor engaged Blücher and Bernadotte, Murat was to delay the advance of the Russians, and was given command of the corps of Victor, Poniatowski, and Lauriston, and the cavalry of Pajol and Kellerman. On 10 October he turned upon the Russians and stormed the town of Borna, inflicting a loss of 4000 men on the enemy. Forced to retire before Schwarzenberg's Austrians he fought, on the 14th, the battle of Liebertwolkwitz, famous for the hardest cavalry fighting of the campaign. Murat had under his personal command three French and two Polish cavalry divisions, eighteen regiments in all, opposed to twenty-two Austrian, Prussian, and Cossack regiments. He held his own, and during the fight led charge after charge against the enemy's cavalry and artillery. Once he was cut off, and nearly

# THE LEIPZIG CAMPAIGN 261

taken prisoner. '*Rends-toi, roi!*' shouted a Prussian officer, threatening him with his sword point. Murat's orderly ran the Prussian through, and a party of French horsemen came to the rescue. A thousand prisoners taken during the day proved that Murat had won a solid success.

Two days later the Grand Army was concentrated round Leipzig, and the greatest battle of the nineteenth century began. Four corps of cavalry were present on the field on the 16th. Murat kept in reserve, under his personal command, Latour-Maubourg's corps and one of Pajol's cuirassier divisions. They were not in action till late in the day, when the Emperor ordered a great cavalry attack in two columns.

General Letort charged on the right with the 4th and part of the 5th corps, and the dragoons of the Guard, under Bessières, and Murat with the reserve on the left. Murat scattered the Russian cavalry of Pahlen, broke a square of infantry, rode over two batteries of artillery, and actually charged a screen of light cavalry that was protecting the rising ground where the Czar was watching the fight. The French onset was only checked by the rush of horsemen plunging into a stretch of marshy ground, where the Russian artillery opened on them at short range, and the tired horses could no longer struggle forward. Prince Cariati was riding beside the Russian Emperor, and the story goes that, as Alexander saw the storm of cavalry bursting through the Russian ranks with a leader well to the front, all flashing with gold and colour, he recognized that it was Murat, and turning to Cariati, said, 'Our ally is rather overdoing his part in concealing the game he is playing.'

On the 17th there was a pause in the fighting. The French drew closer in upon Leipzig and took up their positions for the final two days' struggle. All day Murat was with Napoleon and Berthier, riding over the new positions and helping in the preparations for the decisive engagement. The night before he had actually received, by a roundabout way, one more reassuring message from Cariati. During the final struggle round Leipzig the cavalry had few opportunities. Murat commanded the centre of the line of defence. He directed one successful charge of Latour-Maubourg's cuirassiers against the Russian cavalry. It was during this stage of the fight that the Saxon cuirassiers attached to Latour-Maubourg's corps though they did not, like so many of their comrades, desert to the enemy, refused to draw swords and charge beside the French.

On the 19th Murat accompanied the Emperor in the hurried retreat from Leipzig. He went with him as far as Erfurt, which was reached on the 24th. He had made up his mind that Napoleon's cause was hopeless, and had decided to accept at the eleventh hour the offer made to him by Metternich through Cariati. If he delayed longer his defection might not be worth buying.

At Erfurt he told the Emperor that letters from Naples showed that his presence there was essential. He argued that he could be more useful in Italy than with the retreating army. He would march with the Neapolitan army to the help of Eugène, who must be now in serious difficulties in the north. Napoleon was at first reluctant to agree to his departure. Speaking of the interview to Von Mier, Murat said : ' I showed such a firm determination that I wrung his consent from him, and then I lost no time. I hurried away for fear he should withdraw it. Our farewell was not particularly cordial. He showed some ill-humour and reproached me with always leaving him when things were difficult.' They were never to meet again.

After his hurried departure from Erfurt, Murat travelled by way of Basel and the Simplon to Milan. On the way he sent a cipher dispatch to Cariati telling him that, as soon as he reached Naples, he would raise his army to 80,000 men and declare for the Allies, but he now raised the price of his desertion. Sicily, he argued, was historically part of his kingdom. If the Bourbons were to retain the island he ought to have compensation elsewhere, and he suggested that it might be provided by adding part of the Papal States to Naples.

At Basel he met Louis Bonaparte, the ex-King of Holland. Louis was writing long memoirs to Napoleon urging that he should restore him to his kingdom. Murat told him bluntly that he would have a better chance of regaining his throne if he threw in his lot with the Coalition, as he himself intended to do.

After leaving his carriage half-buried in the snows of the Simplon, and riding forward on horseback, he reached Milan on 31 October. The Milanese had not forgotten his residence among them in the days of the Cisalpine Republic. His fame as a cavalry leader made them see in him a heroic figure, and those who were hoping for a united Italy regarded the soldier King of Naples as a possible rallying point for the movement. He was received with acclamations in the streets of the Lombard capital.

This was perhaps what suggested to him that he might make himself master of Italy without an open rupture with the Emperor. So from Milan he wrote a kind of ultimatum to Napoleon. It was practically a request to be given the command of all Italy:—

'I am about to arrange to march at the head of 30,000 men, but I must know your intentions in a positive way. I beg your Majesty to let me know them without delay. It is no longer the time for temporizing or eluding a reply. I have the greatest desire to support you, but I must know how I am to do this. If I march I must have the command of the Roman States, and in case of a junction with the Viceroy's forces, who is to command? I beg your Majesty to reply at once. Meanwhile I shall put everything to work to mobilize my army. I shall be all my life, Sire, the best and most attached of your friends.'

Murat was now fully embarked in a course of thoroughly unscrupulous double-dealing. The wonder is that Napoleon had not already given up all belief in his protestations of devotion. But though, since the parting at Erfurt, he had received damaging reports of his brother-in-law's overtures to the Allies, he still hesitated to abandon all hope of his support in Italy.

At Milan Murat saw some of the chiefs of the Italianist party, and met his former aide-de-camp, De la Vauguyon. The talk was of an independent kingdom of Italy, extending from the Alps to Calabria. Vauguyon was directed to travel by Bologna to Rome, interviewing on his way the known sympathizers with this patriotic dream, amongst others, General Pino, who commanded a division of the army of Italy.

From Milan Murat travelled to Florence, where he saw Elisa Bonaparte; then to Rome, where he interviewed Miollis. He reached Naples on the evening of 4 November.

There could be no answer yet to the letter he had written to Napoleon from Milan. But he was not so anxious now for a favourable reply, for he found that Caroline had also made up her mind that the Emperor's cause was hopeless, and had been preparing everything for the Austrian alliance. She had kept Von Mier at Naples, even after San Gallo had given him his passports, and she told him how well pleased she was with the 'generous proposals' of the Emperor Francis. On 28 October, while Murat was still on his way to Milan, she had told the Austrian envoy that she considered the time was come to accept them, and she had authorized him to go to Germany by way of Trieste to close up the bargain before it was too late. He was preparing to start when Murat arrived. She then wrote to him, telling him the king was sending proposals to Austria, and asking him to let it appear the offer came spontaneously from her husband. At the same time she promised that she would persuade Murat to accept whatever conditions were offered. So Von Mier remained at Naples to discuss the situation with the king.

On 6 November Murat issued a general order to his army in which he spoke of a coming march to the north, but added that the troops would not be employed outside of Italy. This left the question open on which side they would be used. On the same day his official journal, the

## MURAT ABANDONS FALLING EMPIRE

*Moniteur des Deux Siciles*, published a note stating that he had come back to Naples, by the Emperor's permission, to spend some time with his family, but would return to the front when his services were required. This *communiqué* made Von Mier anxious, but in an interview, which began on the evening of the 8th and lasted far into the night, Murat reassured him as to his intentions, and authorized him to go at once to Germany and lay before Metternich the conditions on which he was ready to co-operate with the Austrians. Von Mier thought the claim for compensation for renouncing all rights to Sicily, which Murat had never possessed, was an exaggeration, but he made no objection. He wrote to Metternich that he thought it was better to say nothing that would prevent the king from fully committing himself. Details could be discussed later. While Von Mier was on his way to Vienna, Murat sent an employé of his Foreign Office to Palermo to try to arrange for a truce with England and the reopening of trade between Naples and Sicily.

It was soon after this that Fouché arrived in Naples. Driven by the Austrians from his governorship of the Illyrian provinces of the Empire, he had gone to Bologna, where he had talked with the local leaders of the Italianist party of the independence of Italy and of the help that Murat might give them if he placed himself at the head of a national movement. He was already preparing to find a place for himself in the new state of affairs that he anticipated would result from the downfall of Napoleon. He was about to return to France, when the Emperor, who had no suspicion of his contemplated treason, directed him to proceed to Rome and Naples, and report to him on the situation in central and southern Italy.

Playing his double game, he wrote to Murat announcing his coming, and at the same time urged him to march his army up to Bologna as soon as possible. 'We both owe our fortune to the Emperor,' he wrote. 'It depends on him and on the integrity of his power.' When he arrived at Naples he found that Murat had just heard from

Napoleon. One of his conditions had been granted. The Neapolitan army was to form an independent command, and not to take orders from Eugène. The Emperor flattered himself that this would be enough to secure the loyalty of his vassal. Durant had no such illusions. He wrote to Napoleon that Campochiaro and San Gallo were negotiating with Austria and England, and Murat was dreaming of making himself the chief of a united Italy. Perhaps it was the memory of his recent services in the field that made Napoleon write that if the King of Naples would march northwards with his army all would yet be well, and Italy would be saved for the Empire.

The army was already moving. On 21 November the 1st division, under General Carascosa, left Naples. On 2 December it arrived at Rome, where Miollis was directed to put the French supply magazines at Carascosa's disposal. The Royal Guard followed the 1st division to Rome. In the first week of December the 2nd division, under General d'Ambrosio, marched by the Adriatic coast roads to Ancona. But the secretary of the Austrian embassy at Naples, whom Von Mier had left there to represent him, was told by San Gallo to inform General Hiller, who commanded the Austrian armies in the north, that the advance of the Neapolitans into central Italy must not be considered as a hostile movement against Austria.

The news of the movement was hailed by the Italianists in the north as the first step towards a national rising. At Bologna five battalions of volunteers were enrolled to join the Neapolitans. Carascosa met General Pino at Ferrara and was assured by him that, the day that Murat proclaimed the unity of Italy, the Italian regiments in Eugène's service would come over to his flag.

But he was still halting between two ways. Fouché was with him at Naples, from 1 to 19 December, and discussed very frankly with him the possibilities that would be opened out either by fidelity to the Empire or by throwing in his lot with the Allies. He was a master of the art of fishing in troubled waters, and it would seem that the practical conclusion to which he tried to lead his pupil was that, with dexterous management, he might keep his army in hand as a trump card to be played at the critical moment, in order to secure a good bargain for himself with whichever side proved the victor.

Murat was already working for this end. He was not anxious to fight against his old comrades. His idea apparently was that he could confine the operations of his army to a demonstration about Bologna, and satisfy his projected agreement with the Austrians by occupying as much territory as possible without actual fighting, leaving it to their generals to meet Eugène. He hoped that thus, before the end of the campaign, which was expected to come soon, he would hold Italy from Calabria to the south bank of the Po, and would have called forth such a manifestation of Italian feeling in his own favour that, when the map of Europe was rearranged, he would be allowed to retain not only Naples but part of central Italy.

It was no doubt part of the result of his talks with Fouché that when, a little later, he wrote to Paris that it would be a good plan to divide Italy into two kingdoms, north and south, of which he would hold the latter, Fouché sent a similar proposal from Rome to the Emperor.

The Austrians saw that Murat was hesitating, and were not satisfied with a mere march of his troops into central Italy, to be followed by a benevolent neutrality during their further operations against Eugène. In the beginning of November Hiller had driven the Viceroy from the line of the Brenta, and Eugène had withdrawn his headquarters to Verona. At the same time another Austrian corps, under Nugent, had been transported across the Adriatic from Trieste, and had landed at the mouth of the Po to occupy Ferrara and Bologna. If Murat meant to act it was time for his troops to join Nugent.

Metternich sent to Naples General Von Neipperg, the Austrian soldier diplomatist, who was afterwards the second husband of Maria Louisa, when she was Grand Duchess of Parma. Neipperg informed the King of Naples that if he persisted in standing neutral the negotiations with Austria must come to an end; but on the contrary, if he would act at once with the Coalition, Metternich was ready to guarantee him his crown and a moderate addition of territory in central Italy. He would also secure the consent of England to this arrangement. This last was an important point, for the negotiations with England had hung fire. Castlereagh and the majority of the Cabinet in London were ready to grant anything that Metternich thought necessary, but Bentinck, as the fast friend of the Neapolitan Bourbons, was moving every influence he could command to prevent the concession being made, and was urging that Naples should be restored to its old masters, and Murat forced to content himself with some minor compensation, such as the principality of the Ionian Islands.

Neipperg had arrived at Naples at the end of December. When he found Murat still hesitating he told him that further delays would mean the withdrawal of Metternich's offer. Austria would then regard him as an enemy, and there would be an end of his kingdom. In the first days of January, 1814, Von Mier returned from Vienna to Naples and advised Murat and Caroline to sign the treaty of which he brought a draft from his master. The allied armies had entered France, the last stage of the struggle with Napoleon had begun, and even a day's delay in accepting the offer of Metternich might make Murat's alliance not worth bargaining for.

On 11 January San Gallo, on behalf of Murat, and Von Mier, as the plenipotentiary of the Emperor Francis, signed the Treaty of Naples. By this treaty it is agreed that Murat shall place at the disposal of the Allies an army corps of 30,000 men, and he is not to make peace with France except with the consent of Austria. The Austrian Emperor guarantees to Murat the kingdom of Naples, and agrees that if he takes the field with his army he shall command also the Austrian troops acting with it. In his absence an Austrian general is to command the united forces. Secret articles annexed to the treaty set forth that Murat renounces all claims to Sicily, and that the Austrian Emperor will use his good offices to secure from the ' King of Sicily ' a similar renunciation of all claims to Naples, and will also assist in a friendly arrangement between Murat and the British Government, and secure for him a cession of further territory in central Italy at the peace.

Bentinck no sooner heard of the signature of the treaty than he urged his Government to oppose its ratification. Italy under Murat's influence would be, he wrote, a continual menace to the peace of the world, and with the thorough-going hatred of Napoleon and all his lieutenants that characterized patriotic Britons in that time of stress and strife, he added that ' it was lamentable to see such advantages given to a man whose whole life had been a crime, who had been the active accomplice of Bonaparte for years, and who now deserted his benefactor through his own ambition and under the pressure of necessity.' But a few days later he received a note from Castlereagh directing him to arrange at once for a suspension of hostilities between Sicily and Naples, reserving the rights of the royal family (the Bourbons) for future discussion.

The Italian generals in the north, Pino, Pepe, and the rest who shared their hopes that Murat would put himself at the head of a national movement, were disappointed at the slow progress of events ending in their hoped-for champion becoming a subordinate agent of Austria. The first effect of Murat's defection on the northern campaign was that Eugène abandoned the line of the Adige and retired to the Mincio. He had hoped to the last that the Neapolitans would make a diversion in his favour on the enemy's flank. Now he knew that Murat's generals were marching to join Nugent at Bologna as his allies. Miollis, with the small French garrison at Rome, was blockaded in the castle of Sant' Angelo. Barbou, who commanded at Ancona, held out in the citadel till 15 February, when he was forced by famine to surrender to the Neapolitans.

Murat thus became for the moment master of central Italy.

But he gave no active co-operation to the Austrian armies in the field. He was so doubtful about his position that he meant to remain at Naples till the treaty, signed by Von Mier, had been ratified by the Austrian Emperor and accepted by other members of the Coalition. It was Caroline who overcame his hesitation and hurried him away to Bologna. As regent in his absence she showed no lack of energy in the execution of the still unratified treaty. She seized the principalities of Benevento and Ponte Corvo, put an embargo on French shipping, and expelled all French officials from the kingdom. Von Mier reported that her conduct was 'admirable.'

Her husband, who had now his headquarters at Bologna, was seriously alarmed at the delay in the ratification of the treaty, and still more when he was informed that, as the result of English opposition, it might be necessary to leave the decision as to his kingdom to the Congress that would assemble after the close of the war to rearrange the map of Europe. Another disquieting fact was the proclamation to the Italian people, issued by the Austrian commander in the north, in which it was announced that the French usurpers were to be expelled from the peninsula and the former dynasties restored. Murat wrote pressing letters to the Austrian Emperor. But this was not all. He entered into correspondence with his old rival Eugène, and sent some strangely worded letters to Napoleon himself. Possibly the successes won by the Emperor in the opening stages of the campaign of 1814 made him wonder if he had wrongly judged the probable result of the war. He was preparing to change sides again in case Austria played him false.

During February frequent communications had passed between the headquarters of Murat and Eugène. In the last week of that month Murat, who had just written to the Emperor Francis protesting his devotion to the allied cause and begging for a prompt ratification of the treaty,

## TREATY WITH AUSTRIA

sent to Eugène a proposal for a joint action of the French army and the Neapolitans, with the understanding that, if the Austrians could be driven out, the peninsula was to be divided between the two leaders. Eugène sent the letter on to Napoleon on 1 March, with a covering letter, in which he spoke of the proposal as a piece of madness. But he was at the same time able to tell the Emperor that Murat undertook not to act against the French army till he had a reply to his communication. On the same day Murat wrote a strange letter to Napoleon :—

'SIRE. Your Majesty is in danger. France is menaced even in its capital, and I cannot die for you, and your Majesty's most affectionate friend is in appearance your enemy. Sire, say only one word, and I am ready to sacrifice my family, my subjects. I shall ruin myself, but I will have served you and proved that I have always been your best friend. I ask nothing else for the moment, only let the Viceroy inform you what has been my conduct. The tears that fill my eyes prevent me from saying more. I am here alone in the midst of strangers. I must hide even my tears from them. This letter makes you, Sire, the master of my fate. My life is in your hands. It is as though I had sworn to die for you. If you could see me and know what I have suffered during these two months, you would pity me. Love me always. Never was I more worthy of your affection. Your friend till death,
'JOACHIM NAPOLEON'

This almost suggests that, under the strain of anxiety, its writer's mind was breaking down. Next day, 2 March, he found himself face to face with a French line of battle, when Grenier's division attacked the Neapolitan and Austrian outpost line before Parma. The action had hardly begun when Murat ordered the Neapolitans to retire, and their withdrawal forced the Austrians also to give way. Grenier took some sixty of Murat's men prisoners in the pursuit, but next day Eugène sent them back to his lines. With the liberated prisoners the Viceroy sent Murat a letter urging him to lose no time in declaring for France. No doubt he hoped to force his hand by compromising him with his Austrian allies.

Napoleon had already asked his brother Joseph to use his influence with Murat to win him back before he had actually fought a battle against his old comrades, and Faipoult, formerly Joseph's minister of finance at Naples, was on his way to Italy, as his envoy to Murat. On 12 March, Napoleon received Murat's letter of 1 March, and the proposals for the partition of Italy forwarded by Eugène. He wrote to the Viceroy :—

'I send you a copy of a very extraordinary letter that I have had from the King of Naples. Whilst they are assassinating me—me and France—such sentiments are inconceivable. I have also received the letter you wrote me with the project for a treaty sent to you by the king. You regard this idea as a folly. Nevertheless send an agent to this extraordinary traitor and make a treaty with him *in your own name*. Don't touch Piedmont and Naples, but divide the rest of Italy into two kingdoms. Let the treaty be a secret till the Austrians are turned out, but let the king, within twenty-four hours after signing it, declare himself and fall upon the Austrians. You can do what you like on these lines. In the present situation nothing should be spared to unite the efforts of the Neapolitans to our own. Later on we can do as we please, for after such ingratitude, and in such circumstances, *nothing is binding.*'

In other words, Eugène was to fool Murat to the top of his bent, try to induce him to turn suddenly upon his new allies, and this on the strength of a secret treaty which the Emperor had not signed, and held himself free to disavow. But before this intrigue was ready for action, and before Faipoult had reached Murat's headquarters, there came a letter from the Emperor Francis, dated from his headquarters at Troyes in France, promising that the Treaty of Naples should be ratified, with some slight modifications, pledging his word for the security of Murat's throne, and promising to obtain the support of the other allied sovereigns for his claim to Naples. Russia and Prussia had already agreed to it. Murat suddenly threw over all his ideas of an agreement with Eugène. He wrote

JOACHIM MURAT, KING OF NAPLES
FROM A LITHOGRAPH BY SCHUBERT

to Metternich that Austria could now count upon him to co-operate in restoring a lasting peace to Europe, for he was 'the irreconcilable enemy of Napoleon's system of universal domination, which had cost France so much blood and treasure, and brought so many awful calamities on Europe.'

Whether he sent any warning of his change of plans to Eugène, we do not know. If he did, the warning came too late, for, on 6 March, Murat broke the informal truce by suddenly attacking, with 10,000 Austrians and Neapolitans, the town of Rubiera, held by only 3000 men of the army of Italy, under General Severoli. Severoli was wounded and handed the command over to General Rambourg, who fell back to Reggio Emilia, where he made such a vigorous stand that Murat agreed to let him withdraw unmolested and join the main body under Grenier. Eugène had not yet heard of this fighting when on the 7th he wrote to Murat, proposing that a line should be marked out across which neither should advance without giving four days' notice. Next day, having received reports of the actions at Rubiera and Reggio, he informed Murat that for the present he could hold no further communication with him.

Now that he seemed to have chosen a definite course, a new incident revived Murat's anxieties. On 9 March Bentinck landed at Leghorn with an Anglo-Sicilian force, proclaimed that he had come to restore the Grand Duke of Tuscany, and demanded that the Neapolitans should withdraw from all the territory of the old duchy. It was only the intervention of the Austrian general, Bellegarde, that averted an actual conflict between Murat's army and these new allies of Austria. Bentinck's repeated assertion that nothing was really settled about Naples, and that his Government would maintain all the rights of the Bourbons, made Murat fear that after all he was not secure for the future. The result was that he reopened communications with Eugène. The secret truce was renewed. On various pretexts, messages passed between

s

the Neapolitan and the French headquarters. Eugène informed Murat of Faipoult's mission, and also let him know that he was ready to arrange the proposed treaty for the partition of Italy. General Zucchi on the part of Eugène, and General Carascosa on that of Murat, met to discuss details of this new secret bargain, but Murat, through his envoy, raised claims that delayed an agreement. Faipoult, under an assumed name, reached Murat's headquarters, and reported that the king was inclined to break with Austria. Looking for a pretext for such a revolt, Murat found it in the fact that, instead of speaking of the independence of Italy, the Allies in their proclamations spoke only of restoring the old dynasties. But his inaction was by this time making his Austrian employers discontented. 'If the king will not do us any service, he will drive us into taking up the interests of Sicily,' wrote Metternich to Von Mier. Von Mier was trying to put an end to a difficult situation by persuading Murat to give the command of his troops to the Austrian, Bellegarde, and himself return to Naples.

On 1 April, Pope Pius VII arrived at Bologna. The Austrians spoke of his early return to Rome and the reconstitution of the Papal States. This would be an obstacle to Murat's hope of increased territory in central Italy. By this time, however, news had arrived of the allied advance on Paris, and Murat hastened to assure Von Mier and Bellegarde that he would co-operate actively with an Austrian advance against Eugène. Then came the tidings that the Allies had entered Paris on 31 March, and that all hope of further resistance in France was at an end. The result was the convention, between Eugène and the Austrians, that put an end also to the war in northern Italy.

Murat had disappointed everyone—the Italians, because he had done nothing for the cherished dream of an independent Italy, and sought only his own interests; the Austrians, because they declared he had only hampered

## THE CAMPAIGN IN ITALY 275

their operations, and done nothing to fulfil his promises. On 2 May he returned to Naples, amid the acclamations of the people. But he was disappointed at the inglorious campaign in which he had taken so strange a part, and was very anxious about the future.

## CHAPTER XVII

MURAT RAISES THE STANDARD AGAINST AUSTRIA—DEFEAT AND DISASTER—MURAT A FUGITIVE DURING THE HUNDRED DAYS—THE TRAGEDY OF PIZZO

### 1814-1815

EVEN before the Congress of Vienna set its official seal on the new state of things, the old Italy, of the days before the Revolution, was partly reconstituted. The Republics of Genoa and Venice had disappeared, but the King of Sardinia was back at Turin; the grand duke at Florence; and an Austrian commandant at Milan. The Pope had been brought back to Rome in triumph. But the Bourbons were still in Sicily, and Murat was still at Naples, with a division of his troops temporarily holding Ancona.

He relied on the pledged word of the Emperor Francis to maintain his throne, even though he well knew that he had not fulfilled his own part of the compact. England he knew was hostile to him. Anxious to obtain whatever support he could, he approached Pius VII and offered to hand back at once to him Ancona and the Marches, and recognize the old feudal rights of the Holy See over the Neapolitan kingdom, if the Pope would crown him, and so give a new sanction to his claims. But Pius VII refused to intervene in the question.

The loyalty of the Emperor Francis to his engagements finally obtained for him the recognition of his right to Naples. He received no increase of territory and had to evacuate Ancona. But he was content to be in possession of his kingdom again, though he felt that he held it by a doubtful tenure. The Bourbons of Sicily had not given up the hope of yet expelling him from Naples, and organized a political brigandage in Calabria, by sending across the Straits of Messina disbanded soldiers of their Neapolitan regiments, with arms in their hands. At the same time, there were continual disputes and growing friction over the regulation of trade between Naples and Sicily. The Austrian politicians regarded Murat as a dangerous element in the Italian situation, and again and again, in the conference at Vienna, it was suggested that it would be better for the peace of Europe if the old kingdom of the Two Sicilies were restored under its former rulers, and this French adventurer persuaded to accept some minor principality elsewhere.

Murat felt that sooner or later he would have to defend his throne. During the remaining months of 1814 he devoted all his energies to increasing his army, and reopened communications with the Italian leaders throughout the peninsula. They were now dreaming that perhaps Napoleon himself would make his island Empire of Elba the starting-point of a movement for unity and independence. For them the Corsican was still an Italian. Murat cherished the hope that, if he could raise the standard of the new movement, Italy would fly to arms, and, notwithstanding his treason, his old chief would, at the critical moment, bring to his aid the magic of his name and the power of his genius. He could not imagine Napoleon looking on quietly from Elba while the tricolour was flying in triumph from the Alps to the southern sea.

At the beginning of 1815 he flattered himself that he had again won the confidence of the 'patriots' in central and northern Italy. He counted especially on the Italian generals of the various armies in the peninsula who had fought under Napoleon or under his own command. He expected that, when the critical moment came, they would bring over to his standard considerable bodies of their troops. But his plans were not yet complete, nor had anything occurred to alarm him as to the immediate security of his throne, when, in the first week of March, the startling news arrived that Napoleon had escaped from Elba and landed in France, and was boldly marching on Paris.

While the result of the daring enterprise was still doubtful, Murat was prudently reserved. He informed the British consul at Naples that he had written to the British Government to assure them that he would not in any way change his policy of peace. He sent the same message to Palermo. But he had already tried to establish a network of secret relations in Sicily, and he strangely suggested that if any of the Neapolitan regiments in the pay of the Bourbons would prefer to serve on the mainland, perhaps the Sicilian and British authorities might be persuaded to transfer them to his army—an absurdly impossible proposal at such a time.

But when the news of Napoleon's victorious advance reached Naples, he sent one of his aides-de-camp to offer his services to Napoleon, and, without waiting for the Emperor's reply, without the least knowledge of what his views and plans were, he embarked in a wild attempt to conquer all Italy.

If Napoleon, starting with a few hundred grenadiers, was marching in triumph from the Mediterranean shore to the Tuileries, why could not he with 40,000 men set Italy in a flame of patriotic enthusiasm, and march from Naples to Milan, gathering strength as he advanced, and finally, at the head of Italy in arms, drive the Austrians over the Alps? His realm would be no longer a vassal kingdom of Naples, but the 'Kingdom of Italy' in the widest sense of the word, and henceforth he would deal with Napoleon as an equal. His victories, his offer of the support of millions of Italians, would wipe away the memory of 1814.

These were the dreams with which, on 15 March, 1815, he declared war against Austria, and, proclaiming himself the liberator of Italy, called upon all her people to rally to the standard of unity and independence.

He thought he was helping Napoleon. He could not have done him a worse service. At the outset of his adventure the Emperor had cherished the hope that he might be able to persuade the Powers to consider the expulsion of the Bourbons from France as a purely internal question, and, failing this, that he might at least prevent all Europe from uniting against him in a new coalition. He knew that there were serious dissensions in the Vienna Congress, that the quarrels of the Allies had once, at least, threatened an open rupture among them. Above all he trusted that, through the influence of his wife and her father, the Emperor Francis, Austria might be held back. He declared that the restored Empire would mean peace; that he no longer dreamed of conquests; that he would respect the conditions of the Treaty of Paris. From Lyons, on 10 March, he had written to his brother Joseph, then in Switzerland, telling him to assure the Russian and Austrian ministers, accredited to the Swiss Government, that he had no idea of winning back the provinces taken from France by the treaties of 1814, and that he intended to devote himself entirely to the peaceful development of the country. He wrote in the same sense to Maria Louisa, asking her to secure her father's influence on his behalf. He wrote also to Lucien at Rome, telling him to influence diplomatic opinion there in his favour and assure the Pope that he had no idea of disturbing Italy.

Then came Murat's sudden proclamation of war against Austria, his summons to Italy to rise against the foreigner. It seemed to be a practical demonstration that the reappearance of Napoleon in France was the signal for rekindling the flame of war in Europe. The news shattered Napoleon's hopes of peace with the Allies. It is true that they had already determined to act in concert against him, but Murat's conduct seemed to be their justification. After the complete failure of his rash enterprise Murat pretended that he had been encouraged by Napoleon to raise Italy against the Austrians. The only possible pretext for this plea was a letter he received from Joseph, which he might have supposed to be inspired by the Emperor. But it could not have determined his course of action, for he did not receive it until his armies were already on the march northward.[1]

He once more entrusted the regency to Caroline and left 10,000 men in the garrisons of the kingdom. The forces available for the field operations amounted to 40,000 men with 56 guns. But the rapid expansion of his army had not improved its quality. The ranks were full of half-drilled recruits, and the officers included many who had had no long training, no useful experience of war. He left Naples on 17 March and began his adventurous march, dividing his army into two columns. As in 1814 the first was to advance by Rome into Tuscany, the second by Ancona towards Bologna.

Pius VII, refusing to be reassured by Murat's friendly messages, fled from Rome to Genoa on the approach of the Neapolitans. At first Murat met with no opposition, but, though he was received with acclamations, few recruits joined him, and there was no sign of a great popular movement in his favour. The people were more alarmed at the renewed outbreak of war than enthusiastic for Italianist ideals.

Until the beginning of April there were only some insignificant skirmishes. The Austrian detachments retired before the Neapolitan advance, and Murat reunited his two

---

[1] 'It was a letter dated 16 March, 1815, and written by Joseph on the eve of his departure from Prangins for France. Like Joseph's former letter to Napoleon at Fontainebleau urging him to resistance in 1814, when he had already abdicated and all was over for the time, Joseph's letter to Murat is an incomprehensible document, for it was written in direct opposition to Napoleon's appeal to him to do all he could to persuade the Powers that the restored Empire meant peace, not war; and it was more especially opposed to Napoleon's policy of trying to win the friendship, or at least the neutrality, of Austria. One can only suppose that on this, as on the other occasion, Joseph had for the moment lost his head. He called on Murat to "support by his armies and his policy the generous movement of the French people, and to give pacific assurances to Austria, at the same time marching forward to the Alps but not passing them." But what use were "pacific assurances" if he was to march his armies into provinces held by the Austrian troops, and proclaim the liberation of Italy from the control of the Viennese Government?' (*Napoleon's Brothers*, pp. 423-24).

columns at Bologna. Jerome Bonaparte, on his way from Trieste to join the Emperor in France, was beside him as he rode in triumph into the city amid the clang of bells and the cheers of the people.

Here he received disquieting news from Caroline. Bentinck was preparing an Anglo-Sicilian expedition against Naples, and the British cruisers were threatening the coasts of the kingdom. To a note informing Bentinck that the Government of Naples wished to maintain peace with England, the British agent had bluntly replied that his Government intended to co-operate with Austria in dethroning Murat. But he had enough to occupy him at Bologna. The Austrian generals, Neipperg and Bianchi, were approaching; Neipperg with 16,000 men from the northward through the Romagna, Bianchi with 30,000 from the north-westward.

Murat had no tactical imagination except on the battlefield. As he had once said, he made his plans in sight of the enemy. If he had had a fragment of Napoleon's genius, or even the habit of applying to a fairly simple situation the elementary maxims of the art of war, he could easily have interposed between the two small Austrian armies and beaten them in detail. Possibly he did not trust his half-trained troops sufficiently to make the attempt. Perhaps he was waiting for the expected national rising that never came. The first serious engagement took place at Carpi, in the Modenese territory. Bianchi drove the Neapolitans out of the town, but they made a good stand on the banks of the Panaro. Murat thought at first that he was victorious, but, on the forcing of the line at the bridge of Occhobiello, the defence collapsed. There was a general retreat on Bologna and the two Austrian corps joined hands.

At first there was an idea of standing on the defensive about Bologna. But reinforcements were known to be on the march to join the enemy, there were no signs of the hoped-for insurrectionary movement in the north, and Murat reluctantly decided to retreat towards his kingdom. A successful rearguard action against Neipperg, on the banks of the Ronco, revived his hopes for a moment. Then came the surprise of General Napolitani's brigade at Casenatico, and a last glimmer of success in the rearguard action of Macerata as Murat drew off by the coast road through the March of Ancona. After this there came a succession of defeats, ending in the disastrous battle of Tolentino on 3 May.

The position of the Neapolitan army was now hopeless. Murat made a hurried retirement across the frontiers of his kingdom, fighting, almost daily, rearguard actions and seeing his forces dwindling rapidly by continual desertions. At Capua he had hardly twelve thousand men left, and these were wearied, dispirited and demoralized. News reached him that an Anglo-Sicilian army was preparing to cross the Straits and march on Naples from the southward. It was impossible to continue the struggle.

He handed over the command to General Carascosa, told his Minister of Foreign Affairs, San Gallo, to enter into negotiations for an armistice, and himself rode on to Naples with a few companions. He entered his capital for the last time at five in the afternoon of 18 May, escorted by four Polish lancers.

In the streets the people cheered him as if he were a victor. But at the palace Caroline, who had tried to dissuade him from his desperate venture, received him with chilling coldness in this hour of failure. 'Madame,' he said, in bitter disappointment, 'do not be surprised at seeing me alive. I have done all I could to meet death.' A number of nobles and officers came to greet him, and were astonished at the calmness that he showed in the midst of disaster.

Next morning there was disappointing news from San Gallo. Bianchi, the Austrian commander, had refused to hear of armistice or negotiations. He declared that he was now master of the kingdom of Naples, and would not recognize King Joachim. All that he would agree to would be a military convention with General Carascosa, from the advantages of which 'Marshal Murat' must be excluded.

An English squadron lay in sight of Naples, and Caroline

had averted a threatened bombardment of the capital only by surrendering the few armed vessels that flew the Neapolitan flag. Gaeta still held out. Murat announced his intention of going there and sharing the fate of its garrison. But would Gaeta venture to resist the Austrians ? and even if it did, a capitulation must come sooner or later. His friends persuaded him that his best course would be to try to reach France.

On 19 May he spent his last day, in his palace at Naples, preparing for his flight. It could not be long delayed, for there were already signs of a revolutionary movement among the fickle people, and rumours of a hostile landing from the British squadron. It was decided that, to prevent his departure being at once discovered, Caroline should for the present remain at Naples, and rejoin him later in France. It was thought that she could always count on a safe conduct and free passage even from the Allies.

After nightfall, with his diamonds and some 300,000 francs in banknotes, and some gold sewn into his clothes and belt, he dressed in civilian costume and rode out of Naples. He was accompanied and immediately followed by his two nephews, the Bonnafous, his aide-de-camp, Colonel de Beauffremont, the Polish colonel, Malchewsky, the Duke di Roccaromana, the Marchese Giulano, his secretary, De Coussy, and his valet, Leblanc. At the coast village of Miniscola the fugitives hired and embarked in two fishing-boats and put to sea in the darkness.

One of the boats was captured by an English cruiser, with half the party, but Murat escaped in the other to Ischia. Before sunrise he had landed on the island and found a hiding-place in the house of a French merchant who lived there.

Next morning, by lucky chance, he learned that a small coasting craft, the *Santa Caterina*, had come into the port, and that General Manhès, with his wife and some friends, was in hiding on board of her. He joined them with his party, and, after more than one narrow escape of capture, the *Santa Caterina* anchored on 25 May in the port of Cannes.

From Cannes, where for the present he observed a strict incognito, Murat wrote to Fouché to know if the Emperor would receive him, and told him he was anxious only to offer his sword to France. Napoleon was angry at his treason of 1814 and his recent disastrous escapade. He told Fouché to inform him that for the present he did not wish to see him and had no intention of employing him with his army. Fouché, in sending this reply, advised Murat to be patient, and hope for better things when the Emperor had won new successes and felt his throne secure.

Cannes was not then the cosmopolitan city of pleasure of to-day. There was only the old town, with its harbour crowded with the masts and long lateen yards of coasting craft, and the fort, held by a garrison of veterans, some of whom must have recognized the restless man, with wrinkles in his face and grey hairs among the black, who walked on the jetty or smoked over the newspapers in a second-rate café. He was spending an anxious time during these first three weeks of June, almost alone, and without any news of his wife and children or of what was happening at Naples. How he must have chafed at his enforced idleness when the newspapers told that the Emperor had crossed the northern frontier. Men who had been his subordinates in earlier campaigns were now marshals of France, in command of veterans he had once led to victory. One Sunday evening —it was 18 June—Cannes was wild with excitement. News had come that the Emperor had proved himself ònce more the man of Marengo and Austerlitz and routed the Prussians and the English. It was the news of Ligny. He would soon be in Brussels. But that same night the routed army of France was streaming in confused flight across the frontier, and the Emperor was himself a fugitive. It was the evening of Waterloo.

Would things have been different if Murat had been there to lead the fierce onset on the ' rocky squares '? Probably it would have made little difference. Berthier's absence was a heavier loss to Napoleon than that of his great cavalry leader.

## A FUGITIVE

Murat's position was now one of serious peril. The 'White Terror' had broken out in France. Partisans of Napoleon were being hunted down and arrested. Some, like Brune at Avignon, were murdered by Royalist mobs. Fearing that he was known to too many at Cannes to be safe there, Murat went away to Plaisance, near Toulon, where he was joined by De Beauffremont and three of his Neapolitan officers. Thence, through an old employé of his Government, Macirone, who had gone to Paris, he asked the new Government to protect him till his fate was decided by the allied sovereigns. At the same time Macirone was to communicate with their representatives in his master's interest.

While waiting for a reply from Macirone he became alarmed about his safety, and arranged, through Colonel Bonnafous and the Duke di Roccaromana, to get away from Toulon on board a Swedish ship. Nearly all that was left of his fortune, some 200,000 francs, was sent on board, but at the last moment he missed his friends at the appointed rendezvous, and the ship sailed without him. He had still his diamonds and a few hundred francs, but he was in momentary fear of arrest, and to try to sell the jewels might have betrayed his identity. He left Toulon and wandered aimlessly for two days and nights in the country, along the coast to the eastward. He was in such a state of nervous panic that he avoided villages and houses, and lived on fruit he gathered furtively on his way, and slept at night under the stars in the corner of a field. At last he ventured to ask for a meal at a lonely farm, and found the proprietor was a veteran soldier of the Empire, to whom he revealed himself, and who not only promised to hide him, but also helped him to find some friends. Three of them were old officers of the navy, Captain Oletta and Lieutenants Donnadieu and Langlade. The fourth was Blancard, a retired army officer who had served in Spain. These new friends became devoted to him, and it was decided to take refuge in Corsica, where a marshal of the Empire could hope to be welcomed by Napoleon's countrymen. Some of the diamonds were sold, a small coasting ship was hired, and, on the night between the twenty-second and twenty-third of August, the party embarked and put to sea.

They encountered a fierce gale, and were in danger of foundering when they met the post-packet plying between Toulon and Bastia, and on her way to the latter port. Murat and his friends ran the risk of asking to be taken on board, and the captain of the packet agreed to receive them without suspecting who the chief of the party was. On board the packet Murat found a certain Galvani who had been in his service at Naples. Bastia was reached on the 25th, and Murat, still keeping his incognito, put up at a small inn.

The new arrivals were soon suspected. The three naval officers were arrested, and Murat, escaping with difficulty from the town, found a new hiding-place at the village of Vescovato, where he was protected by a retired Corsican officer, General Franceschetti. The general's father-in-law, Ceccaldi, the *maire* of Vescovato, was a Royalist, but he assured Murat he would not betray or molest him. But a report reached Bastia of his presence there, and ten gendarmes were sent to arrest him. On their arrival the tocsin was rung, the villagers assembled, many of them with guns, all with long knives in their hands, and the gendarmes made a hurried retreat. After this, the house of the general was guarded day and night by the people. Murat thus realized that he could find supporters in Corsica, and began to dream of another enterprise to be carried out with their aid.

He had heard that a handful of French troops, left in Elba when Napoleon embarked for France, still kept the Imperial flag flying. He thought of crossing over to the island with a levy of Corsicans, and making it the base of operations for a raid on his old kingdom, where he flattered himself the people would welcome him. But an envoy sent to Elba brought back news that the

# A FUGITIVE 287

French garrison had just capitulated. Another Corsican went to Naples and saw General Filangeri, who assured him that any enterprise against the new Government was doomed to fail, and begged the messenger to return and persuade Murat not to engage in such a desperate attempt.

When his envoy returned to Corsica on 12 October, Murat was no longer in the island. After the riot at Vescovato he had been left in peace for some weeks. Of the officers in command in the island, some were unwilling to molest him. Others feared that an attempt to arrest him would provoke a dangerous insurrection. Murat's mind had become fixed upon the idea that, if he could land in Calabria, even with a handful of men, he could raise an insurrection against the Bourbons and regain his kingdom, perhaps revolutionize all Italy. Franceschetti and other friends, who had joined him at Vescovato, tried to dissuade him from this piece of rashness, but at the same time declared that if he persisted they would accompany him. There is no doubt that there was a personal magic in the man that made it easy for him to attach others to his cause, even in such desperate circumstances. In the third week of September he enrolled a number of partisans at Vescovato, and marched on Ajaccio at their head. In all the villages on the way he was welcomed enthusiastically, and armed recruits joined him at every halt. He had 400 men with him when he occupied Ajaccio.

There he printed a proclamation to the Neapolitan people, and a decree establishing a new Liberal constitution. He seized the shipping in the port and prepared to embark for Calabria, promising his Corsican followers glory and wealth in his reconquered kingdom. While he was completing his preparations, Macirone arrived from Paris. He had looked for Murat at Vescovato, and then came on to find him at Ajaccio. He brought with him a safe-conduct for him from the Allies and a letter from Metternich, offering him, on the part of the

Emperor of Austria, a place of residence in his dominions. Metternich's note ran thus:—

'Monsieur Macirone is authorized by these presents to inform King Murat (*sic*) that His Majesty the Emperor of Austria will grant him an asylum in his States under the following conditions:—

'1. The King will take another title. The Queen, having already taken that of the Countess "of Lipona," this title is suggested for the King.[1]

'2. The King will be free to choose as his place of residence some city in Bohemia, Moravia, or upper Austria.

'3. The King will pledge his word to his Imperial and Royal Majesty that he will not leave the Austrian States without his Majesty's express consent, and that he will live as a private individual of rank, in submission to the laws in force in the Austrian States.'

Macirone also brought back the 200,000 francs that had been sent on board the Swedish ship on Murat's first attempt to escape from Toulon. He was able to inform Murat that, after his departure from Naples, Caroline had gone on board the English warship *Tremendous* with her children and the Comte de Mosbourg, and was now living at Trieste under the name of the Comtesse de Lipona. Murat had had no letters from her. He did not know that she had taken refuge on board the British ship when Naples was on the verge of insurrection, and that she had been conveyed to Trieste against her will, though she protested that she wished to rejoin her husband. He thought that Caroline had willingly abandoned him and sought safety among his enemies. To Manhès, who had rejoined him at Ajaccio, he exclaimed, 'I endured everything—the loss of my fortune, the loss of my kingdom, and what a kingdom! But to find myself abandoned by the mother of my children, who prefers to give herself up to my enemies rather than come back to me—no—I cannot stand up against such a blow. What a misfortune is mine! I shall never see wife or children again.'

[1] 'Lipona' is an anagram of 'Napoli' (Naples).

# A FUGITIVE 289

To the dismay of his friends, he refused to hear of Metternich's offer. In his agitated frame of mind, he thought only of facing any danger at the head of his Corsican partisans rather than disappearing into the obscurity of some inland town, where he would live under the surveillance of the Austrian police.

Some writers on Murat's last tragic enterprise have put forward the theory that the Bourbon King of Naples lured his enemy to destruction by sending to Ajaccio traitorous agents, who invited him to land in Calabria, and encouraged him with delusive promises of local support. The facts are all the other way. He sent to Corsica a trusted agent named Carabelli, whose mission was not only to watch and report on Murat's movements, but also to do all he could to dissuade him from any attempt to land in Italy, and urge him to proceed to Trieste and rejoin his family there.

But he would listen to no arguments against what was now his fixed purpose. On the night between the twenty-eighth and twenty-ninth of September he embarked his expedition, on board of five small ships and a felucca, in the bay of Ajaccio. In all he took only some 250 men with him. Next day the little squadron passed through the Strait of Bonifacio, and anchored under the lee of the desert island of Tavolara. Murat landed and reviewed his men, and on re-embarking gave to some forty of them uniforms he had had made at Ajaccio. The squadron then headed for the Neapolitan coast. On 5 October, Vesuvius was in sight, a blue cone among the clouds on the horizon.

Next day the squadron was off Paola in Calabria Citeriore, where Murat thought of attempting a landing, but a sudden gale drove the ships out to sea, and next morning the felucca was missing. On the 7th the town of Lucido was in sight. One of the officers, Major Ottaviani, was sent ashore to reconnoitre, but did not return. He had been arrested by the custom-house officers. The same day two of the ships deserted the squadron. Murat had lost nearly half

T

his small party already. When he proposed to land at Amantea, he found that his officers had lost heart. It would be useless, they said, to attempt anything with such a handful of men. Murat then spoke of giving up the enterprise, and said he would go on to Trieste.

Then he parted company with the remaining two ships, and sailed along the coast alone till he was off Pizzo. There Barbara, a Maltese, who was the captain of the ship, told him the weather was likely to be bad, and it would be better to go into Pizzo and there try to find a larger ship for the long voyage to Trieste. He assured Murat that there would be no difficulty in making the exchange.

It would seem that when the ship headed for Pizzo Murat had no other idea than to secure there better means for continuing his voyage. But before the anchor was let go he had changed his mind, and was once more dreaming of repeating Napoleon's exploit of the landing from Elba and of calling Calabria to arms at the head of the few men who were still ready to risk anything for him.

He put on a colonel's uniform, with a three-cornered hat adorned with the Neapolitan cockade surrounded by a circle of diamonds. As soon as the ship anchored he landed at the head of twenty-six of his Corsicans, having told Captain Barbara to get the ship that had brought him under way, and be ready to run in and take him off if the enterprise miscarried.

There was no garrison at Pizzo. There were only a few customs officers and police, and the old castle was the place of residence of a Spaniard named Alcala, the local agent of the Duke de Infantado. The duke had large estates in Calabria. They had been confiscated by Napoleon's orders during King Joachim's reign because their owner refused to accept the rule of Joseph Bonaparte in Spain. They had been restored by the Bourbon king. It was a market day in Pizzo, and the town was crowded with peasants from the surrounding country.

Murat marched into the market-place surrounded by his escort, who shouted, ' *Viva il nostro re Giaochimo !* ' ' Long

# THE TRAGEDY OF PIZZO

live our king, Joachim!' But there was no response. After a few moments of astonished perplexity the people gathered in hostile crowds, and with sticks, stones, and knives made a fierce attack on the handful of adventurers. One of the Corsicans was killed. Every one of them was more or less injured. A woman—doubtless a mother of brigands, whose sons had been among the victims of Manhès—struck Murat in the face, yelling out, 'You talk of liberty and you had four of my sons shot!'

Driven from the market-place, the party fought their way to the seashore, only to find that Barbara had taken alarm and was running out to sea, heedless of their signals. Then they tried to escape into the country, but were broken up and made prisoners in twos and threes. Murat, with his clothes torn and bleeding from a cut in the forehead, was marched back a prisoner with the captured Corsicans. They were all huddled together in one of the lower rooms of the Castello.

Here the Spaniard, Alcala, came to their assistance. He persuaded the gendarmes who had taken charge of them to give them more roomy quarters, and himself brought a doctor to attend to their wounds, provided Murat and others who needed it with a change of sound clothes, and had a meal served to them with some good wine. Murat thanked him for his courtesy, which was continued during the few days of his imprisonment.

General Nunziante, the commandant of Calabria, promptly arrived with a detachment of troops. Murat was brought before him and questioned. He denied that he had come to Pizzo to attempt an insurrection. He declared that he was on his way to Trieste to avail himself of the Emperor of Austria's offer, and that he had been driven into Pizzo by bad weather and want of supplies, and had come there only to obtain provisions and the means of continuing his journey. He declared further that it was against his wishes that his escort had raised the cry of 'Long live our king, Joachim!'

On 13 October a court-martial was assembled at the

Castello to try him on the charge of exciting to civil war and appearing in arms against the King of the Two Sicilies. The court was composed in part of officers who owed him their promotion. Murat refused to plead before them or to make any defence. On one accusation only, which was not brought against him, but which he thought was in the minds of the Bourbons who now sought his death, he spoke strongly. 'I had nothing to do,' he protested, 'with the tragedy of the Duke d'Enghien, which King Ferdinand wishes to avenge on me. I call God, before whom I am about to appear, to witness that I speak the truth.' We may believe that he spoke in good faith.

There were two sittings, at ten in the morning and at four in the afternoon, when the evidence of various witnesses was taken. At the second sitting the court unanimously found the prisoner guilty, and sentenced him to be shot in the courtyard of the castle within an hour.

When he heard the sentence, which was read to him in the room used as his prison, he asked to be allowed to write a last letter to his family. This was what he wrote :—

'MY DEAR CAROLINE,—My last hour is come. In a few minutes I shall have ceased to live; in a few minutes you will no longer have a husband. Never forget me; my life has not been stained with any injustice. Adieu my Achille, adieu my Letitia, adieu my Lucien, adieu my Louise; show the world that you are worthy of me. I leave you without a kingdom and without resources, in the midst of my many enemies; show yourselves superior to misfortune, think of what you are and what you have been, and God will bless you. Do not speak ill of my memory. I declare that my greatest sorrow in the last moments of my life is to die far from my children.'

He enclosed a lock of his hair in the letter and handed it to one of the Neapolitan officers. While he had been writing it the curé of Pizzo, Canon Masdea, a venerable man of seventy years, had entered the room. Murat rose and greeted the priest, who asked him if he remembered meeting him and giving him an alms for the poor and money for the repairs of his church when he visited Pizzo two years before? Murat replied that he remembered the incident. 'Sire,' said Canon Masdea, 'I have come to ask you for a far more important favour.' Murat asked what could he do in his actual position, and the priest then said he wished him to confess.

Murat refused, but in a way that showed Masdea he was thinking that what was asked for was an admission that he had been justly sentenced to death. 'Sire,' said the priest, 'I am not speaking of a judicial confession, but of a sacramental confession to reconcile you with God, before whom you are going to appear at the end of the next quarter of an hour.' 'Ah, yes. I am ready, but how can it be done in so short a time?' asked the prisoner.

At this moment the officer who was to command the firing-party intervened, and said there was no time to spare. Five minutes of the quarter were gone already. Masdea turned to him and said that the quarter of an hour must not even begin till he had given his penitent absolution, that no power on earth would prevent him from doing his duty, and that if he were interfered with he would appeal to God against such treatment. The officer was evidently impressed and retired.

Turning to Murat Masdea continued, 'I am here for your sake. Do not fear anything.' The prisoner offered him a chair and sat down beside him, but he had hardly begun his confession when he fell on his knees.

It is unlikely that he had observed any religious practices for years. The armies of the Empire had neither chaplains nor church parades. But face to face with death he had returned to long-neglected observances, and, in the light of stern reality before him, felt the reality of his early beliefs. It is easy to cast doubt on a death-bed repentance. But a man placed as Murat was had no motive for playing a part. Those who share the faith of the good priest of Pizzo will see in the soldier king's act of penitence a grace given, perhaps, in reward for such charitable acts as that of which Masdea had reminded him. Even those who hold other forms of Christian belief may recognize in Murat's humble acknowledgment of his misdeeds an act at least as honourable to him as the intrepidity with which he met his doom.

As he rose from his knees after receiving absolution, resignation was added to his habitual courage. 'Now let us go,' he said, 'and God's will be done!' Masdea asked him to state in writing that he meant to die as a Christian. Murat hesitated. A vague suspicion of some use that might be made of the paper by his political enemies flashed across his mind. 'Do you mean to dishonour me after my death?' Masdea replied that on the contrary he wished to have evidence to confound those who would misrepresent him. Murat took up the pen with which he had written his last letter, and wrote on a piece of paper, '*Je meurs en bon chrétien,*' signed it, and handed it to the priest saying, for the second time, 'Let us go, and God's will be done!'

Outside in the narrow courtyard of the castle the firing-party was mustering, twelve men, commanded by a sergeant. Presently the officer who was to carry out the execution entered and bade Murat follow him. He said farewell to Masdea and walked out with a firm step.

He faced the firing-party, refusing either to have his eyes bandaged or to turn his back to them. 'Soldiers,' he said, 'do your duty. Fire at the heart, but spare the face.' He stood unflinching and smiling while the musket-barrels were levelled, and as the volley rang out he fell on his face without even a groan. Six bullets had struck him in the chest, and one in the right cheek. The same evening his body was placed in a plain coffin and buried in the common grave of the churchyard of Pizzo.[1]

. . . . . .

[1] A horrible story was circulated some years later to the effect that Murat's head was cut off and sent to Naples that Ferdinand and his court might gloat over the destruction of their enemy. M. de Sassenay (*Les Derniers Mois du Roi Murat*) examines all the evidence and rejects it as a fiction. He points out that all contemporary writers, even those most hostile to the Bourbons, say nothing of it. It is a malicious invention of a later time.

## THE TRAGEDY OF PIZZO

So ended a career that is one of the romances of history. In the noblest sense of the word Murat was no hero. But he had the courage both of action and of endurance in a high degree. His last act is enough to prove this, even without the record of his exploits on fifty battlefields. His reckless daring, his faculty of inspiring it in others, his rapid grasp of the possibilities of the moment amid the danger and confusion of the fight, and his swift decision and unhesitating action, made him a great cavalry leader. But he was not a great general in the sense of being fitted to plan and conduct the co-ordinated movements of armies in a campaign, and even as a cavalry leader this lack of strategic insight led him into errors.

As King of Naples he was a popular ruler, and the people he governed were the better for his rule. As a man his faults lie on the surface. His character was marred by almost puerile vanity; he was led into weak following of the easier of two courses by his self-seeking ambition; and he again and again showed a want of balanced judgment and a liability to be dominated by the impulse of the moment. The best side of his character was the kindly part of his nature. In days when men had been steeled against pity by war and revolution there was no cruelty in Murat.

Strange as it may seem, this thorough soldier, whose orders on the battlefield often meant swift death to hundreds and prolonged suffering to hundreds more, shrank with horror from the idea of killing a fellow man. Agar tells how more than once he said to him at Naples, 'What gives me the most heartfelt satisfaction when I think of my military career is, that I have never seen a man fall killed by my hand. Doubtless it is possible that in firing a pistol-shot at enemies who attacked me, or whom I was pursuing, I may have wounded some one, even mortally; but if so I knew nothing of it. If a man had ever fallen dead before me by my act, the picture of it would always be before me, and would pursue me to the grave.' This was why, as he led his most famous charges, the diamond-hilted sabre remained in its scabbard. He had the same horror of military executions. Caroline used to tell how, after a mutiny at Leghorn, when a court-martial had condemned the three ringleaders to death, he was so impressed by the men's regret for their misconduct and filled with such pity for their fate, that he carried out a sham execution at sunset, arranged that the condemned men should fall before a volley of blank cartridge, and had them covered up for a while, and removed in the dark to a place where they were given disguise and shipped away from the port.

All who knew him well told of his affection for his wife and children. Napoleon joked at his cavalry general's being unable to read a letter from Caroline without tears starting to his eyes. His thoughts continually went back to the old home at La Bastide. He was not content with mere expressions of affection for his aged mother and his brothers and sisters. He took care that they should share his prosperity. André became his almoner for the poor of the district. As King of Naples he wrote to him to take care that the venerable curé of La Bastide, then broken in health, should want for nothing; arranged for the repair of his church and presbytery, and rejoiced the old priest by sending him a gift of altar plate that is still treasured in the village church.

It was doubtless this gentle, kindly side of his character that won him so many friends, even in the days of his adversity, when there was only danger and loss in espousing his fallen cause. Those who had known him best, like Agar, Count of Mosbourg, his lifelong friend, were as devoted to him after his tragic end, and refused to believe any evil of him. There must have been good in the man who could inspire such devotion.

Agar, in the hope that some day his remains might be removed from their nameless grave at Pizzo and consigned to a fitting monument, wrote an epitaph which sums up his career, noting the dates of his birth and death; enumerating his titles and dignities; reciting the names of the countries that were the scenes of his military exploits; and ending with the record that "he knew how to die":—

JOACHIM-NAPOLÉON MURAT

NÉ À LA BASTIDE-FORTUNIÈRE, DÉPARTEMENT DU LOT

LE 25 MARS 1767

MORT AU PIZZO, LE 13 OCTOBRE 1815

IL FUT SOLDAT

MARÉCHAL DE L'EMPIRE FRANÇAIS

PRINCE ET GRAND AMIRAL DE FRANCE

GRAND DUC DE BERG

ROI DE NAPLES

BEAU-FRÈRE DE L'EMPEREUR NAPOLÉON

SA GLOIRE MILITAIRE IMMORTALISA

EN ITALIE ET EN EGYPTE, SON NOM DE MURAT

EN AUTRICHE, EN PRUSSE, EN POLOGNE

SON TITRE DE GRAND-DUC DE BERG

EN RUSSIE ET EN SAXE

SON TITRE DE ROI DE NAPLES

IL SUT VAINCRE, IL SUT RÉGNER

IL SUT MOURIR.

# APPENDIX

## NOTE ON SOME SOURCES AND AUTHORITIES FOR THE LIFE OF JOACHIM MURAT

THE story of Joachim Murat is so closely linked with that of Napoleon that the standard authorities for the history of the latter and his correspondence are also sources for the life-story of Murat.

The earlier biographies of Murat by Coletta (Paris, 1821) and Gallois (Paris, 1828), and even Helfert's work (Vienna, 1878), have, in many important points, been rendered obsolete by the publication of documents not available at the time these works were written.

The best modern biography is the work of MM. Jules Chavanon and Georges St. Yves, *Joachim Murat*, 1767-1815 (Paris, 1905). It is especially valuable for the use it makes of the mass of MS. materials in the French archives, and the list of sources in print and manuscript prefixed to each chapter supplies a very complete bibliography of the subject up to the date of publication. Documents published since 1905 by the Murat family have since cleared up important points, and suggest revision of the view taken by MM. Chavanon and St. Yves of Murat's relations to Bonaparte during the later stages of the campaign of Italy.

Lumbroso's *Correspondance de Joachim Murat* is a selection of his letters. A complete collection is in process of publication from the family archives. The three volumes that have appeared bring the series up to August 1805. The documents are illustrated with valuable notes by the editor, M. Paul le Breton, librarian of the Bibliothèque National. (*Lettres et Documents pour servir à l'Histoire de Joachim Murat.* Publiés par S. A. le Prince Murat. Avec une Introduction et des Notes par Paul le Breton. Paris,

# APPENDIX 299

1908-1910. Vol. i., 1767-1801. Vol. ii., 1801-1803. Vol. iii., 1803-1804. Vol. iv. 1805-1806.)

General Thoumas's *Les Grands Cavaliers du Premier Empire*, 1ère Série (Paris, 1890), includes a brilliant sketch of Murat's military career, and incidental light is thrown upon it in some of the other biographies included in the series, notably that of Montbrun.

The memoirs of General Belliard, Murat's chief of the staff in his most famous cavalry campaigns, were published in 1842-43 (*Belliard Mémoires*, écrits par lui-même et mis en ordre par Vinet l'un de ses aides-de-camp). A very full and competent work on Belliard's life, based on these memoirs and other sources, was published last year: *Le Lieutenant-Général Comte Belliard, Chef d'état-major de Murat*. Par le Général Derrécagaix.

M. Frédéric Masson, in his *Napoléon et sa Famille* (nine volumes, bringing the history up to 1814), deals largely with Murat's career, but the writer's standpoint and his desire to explain everything on the theory that Napoleon was an incomparable genius whose plans were frustrated by the incompetence and the perversity of his relatives, makes him bitterly hostile to Murat. His attitude towards him and Caroline is that of a counsel for the prosecution. But his untiring industry has collected a mass of interesting details.

Light from a very hostile source is thrown on Murat's dispute with Landrieux, in M. Léonce Grasilien's *Mémoires de l'Adjudant-Général Jean Landrieux* (Paris, 1893).

Murat's part in the affair of the Duke d'Enghien is discussed by most of the writers on the subject. Henri Welschinger's *Duc d'Enghien* is a special study of the affair. Mosbourg's defence of his friend is reproduced in the third volume of the *Lettres et Documents* with remarks by Prince Murat, and is discussed in the introduction to Count Murat's work on Murat in Spain.

Murat's brief reign as Grand Duke of Berg has been studied by a German historian, Rudolf Göcke, *Das Grossherzogthum Berg unter Joachim Murat Napoleon und Ludwig Napoleon* (Cologne, 1877). Another episode in his career is elaborately dealt with in Comte Murat's work on his Spanish mission: *Murat, Lieutenant de l'Empereur en Espagne, 1808. D'après sa Correspondance inédite et des Documents originaux.* Par le Comte Murat (Paris, 1897). The introduction contains interesting documents and details on his previous career. M. H. Weil's work, *Le Prince Eugène et Murat*, throws great light upon the period of Murat's revolt from Napoleon. For the story of his flight in 1815 and his tragic end, among other sources there are his agent Macirone's narrative, *Faits intéressants relatifs à la Chute et à la Mort de Joachim Murat*, and the Marquis de Sassenay's elaborate study, *Les Derniers Mois de Murat*.

Other sources on various points are the lives of Napoleon's sisters, the military memoirs of the time (especially Marbot), and the detailed histories of the various campaigns in which Murat took a prominent part. The mass of this incidental material is so great that I make no claim to have collected all the detail available. But I hope I have neglected nothing of importance.

# INDEX

ABOUKIR, battle of, 48.
Agar, Count of Mosbourg, 105, 143, 144, 145, 155, 198, 201, 202, 296.
Alcala, 291.
Ambrosio (Neapolitan general), 266.
Auersperg, Count, 131, 132.
Auffenberg (Austrian general), 122.
Augereau, 155, 160, 162, 163.
Austerlitz, battle of, 135.

BAGRATION (Russian general), 133, 134, 168, 229.
Barclay de Tolly (Russian general), 227, 229, 231.
Barras, 19, 28, 29, 38, 52, 53.
Bastide and Bastide Murat. *See* La Bastide.
Bastit family, neighbours of the Murats, 8, 12.
—— François, 13, 70.
—— Mion, Murat's love affair with, 8, 12, 13.
Bathori, the sword of, 157.
Beaumont (French cavalry general), 121, 126, 140, 141, 147, 150.
Becker (French cavalry general), 147.
Bellegarde (Austrian general), 273, 274.
Belliard, General (Murat's chief of the staff), 116, 146, 222, 223, 228, 233, 236, 243.
Benningsen (Russian general), 154, 158, 159, 162, 163, 165, 166, 168.
Bentinck, Lord William, 249, 250, 251, 268, 269, 273.
Bernadotte, 70, 73, 117, 128, 152, 153, 159, 240, 262.
Berthier, Alexandre, 35, 37, 38, 52, 63, 64, 66, 87, 106, 107, 109, 166, 231, 240, 241, 242, 243, 244, 253, 261.
—— César, 69, 106, 107.
Bertrand, 114, 131.
Bessières, 8, 50, 56, 134, 163.
Blücher, 141, 142, 150, 152, 153, 259, 260.
Bonaparte, Caroline, wife of Joachim Murat, 32, 54, 55, 67, 73, 75, 78, 83, 88, 93, 95, 99, 102, 110, 111, 112, 113, 139, 144, 169, 170, 171, 172, 206, 209, 210, 212, 217, 220, 224, 245, 246, 247, 249, 252, 253, 254, 255, 258, 264, 268, 270, 282, 283, 288, 292, 296.
Bonaparte, Jerome, King of Westphalia, 154, 155, 156, 169, 227, 244.
—— Joseph (King of Naples, and later of Spain), 33, 57, 70, 91, 123, 138, 169, 194, 196, 197, 198, 200, 201, 279, 280.
—— Josephine (Empress), 23, 27, 33, 34, 55, 75, 209.
—— Louis (King of Holland), 91, 138, 169, 172, 263.
—— Lucien (Prince of Canino), 53, 91, 279.
—— Napoleon, 19, 21; campaign of Italy, 22; Egyptian expedition, 39; *coup d'état* of Brumaire, 52; campaign of Marengo, 59; attempted assassination, 75; President of Italian Republic, 92; affair of the Duc d'Enghien, 105; coming of the Empire, 109; projects against England, 113; campaign of Ulm and Austerlitz, 119; campaign of Jena, 146; enters Berlin, 150; Polish campaign, 158; Eylau, 159; Tilsit, 169; Spanish policy, 175; gives Naples to Murat, 174; Russian campaign, 222; Leipzig campaign, 256; the Hundred Days, 278.
Borodino, battle of, 231.
Brueys, Admiral, 39, 44.
Brune, 73, 74, 75, 76, 86, 285.
Buxhowden (Russian general), 154, 158.

CADOUDAL, GEORGE, 108.
Cahors, 1, 3, 101.
Campochiaro, Duke of, 248, 249, 260, 266.
Camprédon, General, 203.
Carascosa (Neapolitan general), 266, 282.
Cariati, Prince (Murat's envoy to Vienna), 242, 247, 248, 250, 251, 252, 254, 255, 260, 261, 262.

Castlereagh, 268.
Cavaignac, General, 203, 213, 215, 216.
Charles, Archduke, 208.
Charles IV of Spain, 173, 180, 185, 186, 187.
Clarke, Duc de Feltre, 251, 253.
Coffin, Colonel, 248, 249, 250.
Consalvi, Cardinal, 80, 88, 93.

DAMPIERRE, General, 13, 14.
Davoût, 117, 120, 135, 148, 154, 155, 159, 168, 228, 229, 230, 231, 232, 242.
Desaix, 41.
Duhesme, General, 174, 178.
Dumouriez, General, 10, 13, 14.
Dupont, General, 174, 182, 214.
Durant, Baron de (French ambassador at Naples), 220, 247, 250, 252, 253, 260, 266.
Duroc, 52.
D'Urre de Molans, General (Murat's patron), 9, 10, 13, 17.

ENGHIEN, DUC D', 104 etc., 292.
Espagne (French cavalry general), 147, 166, 167.
Eugène, 200, 209, 241, 244, 251, 258, 262, 263, 266, 267, 269, 270, 271, 273, 274.
Eylau, battle of, 162.

FAIPOULT, 24, 272, 274.
Ferdinand, Prince of the Asturias, afterwards Ferdinand VII of Spain, 174, 180, 181, 185, 186, 187, 190, 194.
Fesch, Cardinal, 73, 103.
Fouché, 107, 266, 267, 283.

GODOY, 144, 169, 173, 177, 178, 179, 185.
Grouchy (French cavalry general), 147, 150, 162, 163, 222, 227, 228, 233, 237.

HAUTPOUL, D', (French cavalry general), 121, 124, 129, 133, 147, 148, 150, 161, 162, 163.
Hohenlohe, Prince, 150 etc.
Hohenzollern, Prince Charles of, 96, 171.

JENA, battle of, 148.
Jourdan, 203.
Junot, 46, 170, 173.

KIENMAYER (Austrian general), 129, 130, 132.

Kléber, 45, 47, 48.
Klein (French cavalry general), 121, 126, 127, 147, 148, 150, 160, 161, 162.
Kutusoff (Russian general), 128 etc., 134, 231, 236, 243.

LA BASTIDE (birthplace of Murat), 2, 101.
Lamarque, General, 203, 213, 215.
Landrieux, Jean, 15, 16, 17, 18.
Lannes, 45, 48, 51, 52, 54, 55, 57, 117, 120, 122, 124, 129, 131, 133, 134, 135, 150, 151, 155, 168, 199.
Lanusse, General, 43, 48.
Lasalle (French cavalry general), 147, 150, 151, 152, 166, 167.
Latour-Maubourg (French cavalry general, 222, 227, 233, 236, 237, 257, 259, 261, 262.
Leclerc, General (first husband of Pauline Bonaparte), 33, 53, 92, 97.
—— Colonel, 214.
Lefèbvre, 165, 166.
Lowe, Sir Hudson, 203.

MACDONALD, 73, 74, 243, 259.
Macirone, 285, 286.
Mack (Austrian general), 119 etc.
Maghella, 215, 219.
Manhès, General, 203, 209, 283, 288.
Marengo, battle of, 64.
Maret, Duc de Bassano, 240.
Maria Carolina, Bourbon Queen of the Two Sicilies, 212, 215.
Maria Louisa, Empress, 210, 267, 279.
Marmont, 51, 52, 117.
Masdea, Canon, 248, 292, 293, 294.
Masséna, 29, 59, 60, 62.
Melzi, Vice-President of the Cisalpine and Italian Republics, 88, 92, 96 etc.
Menou, General, 89.
Metternich, 251, 254, 255, 268.
Mier, Count Von (Austrian envoy to Naples), 252, 258, 264, 265, 268, 270, 274.
Milhaud (French cavalry general), 127, 129, 147, 162.
Miloradovitch (Russian general), 234, 242.
Miollis, General, 77, 200, 207, 256, 269.
Moncey, 174, 175, 179, 182.
Montbrun (French cavalry general), 222, 225, 226, 227, 229, 233.
Monthyon, de, General, 185.
Moreau, 53, 59, 61, 73.
Mortier, 130, 174.

## INDEX                                                    303

Murat, Achille (eldest son of Joachim Murat), 78, 83, 88, 92, 94, 140, 240.
—— André (elder brother of Joachim Murat), 3, 12, 14, 21, 34, 67, 71, 94, 112, 137, 296.
—— Antoinette (niece of Joachim), 11, 95, 171, 198.
—— Clotilde Jeanne (niece of Joachim), 95.
—— Jean Adrien (nephew of Joachim), 11, 39, 44, 68.
—— Jeanne, *née* Loubières (mother of Joachim), 2, 56, 67, 70, 84, 95, 102, 137.
Murat, Joachim, birth and parentage, 2; education at Cahors and the Toulouse seminary, 3; leaves the seminary to enlist in the Chasseurs à Cheval de Champagne, 4; promotion to non-commissioned rank and long leave at La Bastide, 4; sent to Paris for the Fête of the Federation with the local delegates of the National Guard, 5; recalled to his regiment in garrison at Schlestadt, 6; sent to Montmedy after the king's attempted flight, 7; appointed to serve in the Constitutional Guard, 8; resigns and rejoins his regiment, 8; promoted to lieutenant, 9; mission to Paris, 9, 10; serves on the northern frontier as aide-de-camp to General d'Urre de Molans, 11; again in Paris, 11; return to the army, 13; promoted captain, 14; attached as *chef d'escadron* to Landrieux's Hussars on their reorganization, 15; first war services, 16; quarrel with Landrieux, 17; imprisoned after Thermidor, 18; liberated, and rejoins his regiment at Paris, 19; services to Bonaparte on the day of Vendémiaire, 19, 20; promoted to colonel, 20; *chef de brigade*, 21; aide-de-camp to Bonaparte in the campaign of Italy (1796), 22 etc.; sent to Paris with dispatches and promoted *Général de Brigade*, 23; services in second stage of the campaign, 23 etc.; taken prisoner at Brescia and escapes, 25; exploits at Rivoli, 30, 31; meets Caroline Bonaparte at Mombello during the peace negotiations, 32; expedition to the Val Tellina, 34; shares Napoleon's 'triumph' at Rastatt, 35, 36; Roman expedition, 37; attached to the Egyptian expedition, 38; Governor of Kelioub, 42; campaign against Ibrahim Bey, 42, 43; Syrian expedition, 45; battle of Aboukir, 48;

Murat wounded, 49; promoted to General of Division, 50; returns to France with Bonaparte, 51; prominent part in the *coup d'état* of Brumaire, 53; message to Caroline, 54; courtship and marriage, 55-57; sent to Dijon to command cavalry of the 'Army of Reserve,' 59; services in Marengo campaign, 60-66; command of training camp at Beauvais, 68; command of 'Army of Observation' at Dijon, 71; move to Milan, 74; command in central Italy, 77; negotiations with Pius VII and Cardinal Consalvi, 80; Commander-in-chief of the Army of Italy, 86 etc; buys property in France—the Hôtel Thélusson, 90; religious marriage ceremony, 92; proclamation of Italian Republic, 92; visits to Rome and Naples, 94; troubles with Vice-President Melzi at Milan, 96 etc.; elected to the Corps Législatif, 103; Military Governor of Paris, 103; his part in the affair of the Duc d'Enghien, 104 etc.; Marshal of France and Grand Admiral of the Empire, 109; his fortune, 111; command of the cavalry of the Armée d'Angleterre, 113; reconnaissance of south Germany, 114; command of Cavalry Reserve of the Grand Army, 115; Lieutenant-General of the Emperor during the preparations for the Ulm campaign, 116; campaign of Ulm, 118; battle of Wertingen, 122; operations round Ulm, 124; pursuit of the Archduke Ferdinand and General Werneck, 127; pursuit of Kutusoff, 129; occupies Vienna, 130; seizes the Danube bridge by a trick, 131; battle of Austerlitz, 135; the Grand Duchy of Berg, 139; campaign of Jena, 146; the pursuit after Jena, 149; occupies Warsaw, 156; Polish ambitions, 157; campaign of Eylau, 159; campaign of Friedland, 166; Tilsit, 169; sent to Spain as Lieutenant-General of the Emperor, 175; enters Madrid, 181; suppresses rising of 2 May, 191; accepts crown of Naples, 195; rule at Naples, 198; friction with Napoleon, 204; Sicilian expedition, 215; commands the cavalry in the Russian campaign of 1812, 222; Borodino, 231; enters Moscow, 234; the retreat, 237; given command of the Grand Army on Napoleon leaving it, 238; fails as its commander and returns to Naples, 244; negotiations with the Allies, 248; the Leipzig campaign, 256; renewed negotiations with the Allies, 264; marches Neapolitan army into central Italy, 266; intrigues and hesitating conduct during the campaign, 270; doubtful position at Naples after 1814, 276; raises the standard against Austria, 279; failure of campaign, 281; return to Naples, 282; flight, 283; adventures during and after the Hundred Days, 284; in Corsica, 286; embarks for Calabria, 287; landing at Pizzo, 290; capture and imprisonment, 291; trial and execution, 292.

Murat, Lucien Napoleon (second son of Joachim), 100.
—— Marie (eldest daughter of Joachim), 94.
—— Pierre (father of Joachim), 2, 39, 44, 50, 56.
—— Pierre (brother of Joachim), 7, 9, 11.
—— Pierre Gaëtan (nephew of Joachim), 94, 95.

NANSOUTY (French cavalry general), 133, 147, 148, 222, 227, 229, 233.
Neipperg, Von (Austrian general and diplomatist), 267, 280.
Nelson, 39, 44.
Ney, 117, 120, 124, 125, 126, 149, 154, 159, 166, 231, 241, 260.
Nicolas, Felice, 250.
Nugent (Austrian general), 267, 269.
Nunziante (Neapolitan general), 291.

ORANGE-NASSAU, Prince of, 149.
Oudinot, 123, 127, 131, 132, 135.

PARTOUNNEAUX, General, 208, 213, 215.

Pérignon, Marshal de, 203.
Pignatelli Strongoli (Neapolitan general), 203.
Pino (Italian general), 266, 269.
Pius VII, 80, 88, 94, 173, 200, 209, 274, 276, 279, 280.
Platoff, 236.
Poniatowski, Prince, 157, 233, 236, 260.
Pyramids, battle of the, 41.

RAPP, General, 243.

SANTERRE (General of the National Guard), 10.
Savary, 106, 107, 109.
Sahuc (French cavalry general), 147.
St. Cyr, Gouvion, 100, 241.
San Gallo, Marquis de, 198, 204, 250, 251, 252, 255, 264, 266, 268, 282.
Schwarzenberg, Prince, 242, 260.
Sebastiani, 236, 257.
Sidney Smith, Admiral, 45, 48.
Soult, 117, 120, 129, 133, 134, 152, 153, 160, 162, 166, 168.
Suchet, 135.

TALLEYRAND family, patrons of the Murats, 3.
Talleyrand, 5, 141, 142.

ULM, campaign of, 126.
Urre de Molans. *See* D'Urre de Molans.

VANDAMME, 121, 259.
Vauguyon, Le, 200, 264.
Victor, 152, 259, 260.

WALTHER (French cavalry general), 121, 133.
Weimar, Grand Duke of, 150, 152.
Wertingen, battle of, 122.

ZUCCHI (Italian general), 274.

www.ingramcontent.com/pod-product-compliance
Lightning Source LLC
Chambersburg PA
CBHW070836160426
43192CB00012B/2205